Simon Hughes played county cricket for Middlesex and Durham between 1980 and 1993, winning four County Championship titles and five one-day trophies. After retiring at 33, he became a writer and broadcaster, winning the William Hill Sports Book of the Year with *A Lot of Hard Yakka*, his classic account of the county game. Well known as The Analyst on TV, his insight and innovative ways of presenting the game have won a string of awards. The father of three budding cricketers, he lives just a Chris Gayle straight drive from Lord's.

Who Wants to be a Batsman?

The Analyst Unveils the Secrets of Batting

Simon Hughes

**SIMON &
SCHUSTER**

London · New York · Sydney · Toronto · New Delhi

A CBS COMPANY

First published in Great Britain by Simon & Schuster UK Ltd, 2015
This paperback edition published by Simon & Schuster UK Ltd, 2016
A CBS COMPANY

1 3 5 7 9 10 8 6 4 2

Simon & Schuster UK Ltd
1st Floor
222 Gray's Inn Road
London WC1X 8HB

www.simonandschuster.co.uk

Simon & Schuster Australia, Sydney
Simon & Schuster India, New Delhi

The author and publishers have made all reasonable efforts to contact
copyright-holders for permission, and apologise for any omissions or errors in
the form of credits given. Corrections may be made to future printings.

All photographs in the plate section copyright Getty Images, except page 1 (top)
copyright Winston Bynorth, and page 8 (bottom) courtesy of the author.

A CIP catalogue record for this book
is available from the British Library.

ISBN: 978-1-4711-3561-3
Ebook ISBN: 978-1-4711-3562-0

Typeset and designed in the UK by M Rules
Printed and bound by CPI Group (UK) Ltd, Croydon, CR0 4YY

Simon & Schuster UK Ltd are committed to sourcing paper
that is made from wood grown in sustainable forests and support the Forest
Stewardship Council, the leading international forest certification organisation.
Our books displaying the FSC logo are printed on FSC certified paper.

To Dad – for his eternal enthusiasm
To Mum – for improving my vocabulary

And to all Mums and Dads for encouraging
their sons and daughters to play the game.

CONTENTS

CHAPTER 1

Dicing With Death

I haven't scored any hundreds, but I've given away a few. And I've seen a few more. This story is about the players like Richards and Tendulkar and Pietersen and de Villiers and Sangakkara who made those hundreds. How are they able to consistently crack 90mph deliveries to the boundary, deliveries that many of us can barely see? What makes them so good? How do they control their emotions when the pressure is intense out there in the middle? And, for us normal mortals, what is it like to be walking to the wicket to face a 6ft 6in ogre, fearing the worst? This is about the triumph and torment and trials and tribulations of the men who try, and sometimes succeed, and often fail, to make runs for a living.

Watching the brilliant Brendon McCullum slaying a fearsome fast bowler, Dale Steyn, in the 2015 World Cup semi-final, hooking him into the crowd and driving him spectacularly over the sightscreen, demonstrates the power and exhilaration of batting. Seeing the taut features and stuttering footwork of the once-prolific Jonathan Trott, dismissed for another single-figure score, is a reminder that batting can be a fraught and precarious business.

Batsmen have the best, and worst, of times. They have the most fragile existence of anyone in sport. They are out on their own being preyed upon. They have half a second to react to the ball. They are walking the tightrope between success and failure. One minuscule error and they're toast. *Terminé*. Caput. McCullum was bowled for nought in the first over of the World Cup final. And then they have to slope off in front of everyone, keeping their heartache to themselves. It's like watching a man walking to his grave.

And yet when they stay in and their feet are moving beautifully and the ball is pinging off their bat and the bowlers are at their mercy and they reach the promised land, they feel a huge surge of pleasure and a rush of blood to the head that only one other activity in life can offer. And you can't do that in public. Well, not legally anyway.

Whether you're able, or whether you're not, in cricket, everybody *has* to bat. There's no choice. You can't say, at the sight of a large marauding fast bowler armed with a ball as hard as rock and a menacing stare, 'Sorry skip, I don't fancy it today.' You've got to go out there and face the (chin) music. It's dicey and dangerous and, reflecting on the freakish death of the unfortunate Phillip Hughes, occasionally deadly.

I wasn't a good batsman, but in a 15-year professional career I batted more than 300 times and encountered many of the problems that a good batsman has to handle: ferocious pace, late swing, devious spin, a tricky pitch, a dodgy umpire, a sledging bowler, bright light, bad light, self-doubt, over-confidence, a blow to the head, opening the innings, 10 to win off nine, or holding out for a draw with everyone round the bat.

I didn't overcome too many of these predicaments, but I understood the mistakes I made and I tried to correct them. I mostly failed. But I've worked out, over the course of 30 years of playing and then analysing every ball in slow motion from 28 different angles, and talking to the great and the almost great, what batting entails. I'm fascinated in unravelling this complex art and the characters it reveals.

Anyone who's vaguely interested in cricket has dreamt at least once of playing a match-winning innings for their country. Is it an attainable dream? Can you make someone into a top batsman? What ingredients would they need? Think of two batsmen who indisputably were great – Geoff Boycott and Graham Gooch – and you realise that the answer is not a simple one. You couldn't imagine two men with such contrasting personalities. The proud, indefatigable, call-a-spade-a-spade Yorkshireman who repelled hard-working bowlers with almost sadistic glee, keeping his own score like a king counting out his money. And the self-effacing, laconic chap from Leytonstone with a falsetto laugh which betrayed a murderous intent. He's like the Michael Caine character in *Get Carter*.

I'm interested in finding out if the best batsmen all have certain characteristics in common. How do they overcome the mental and physical hurdles? Why do some of them have such odd routines? How do they hit a bouncer travelling at 90mph? Have the requirements of batting changed as the game enters a more explosive era? And ultimately, why would anyone want to be stuck out there on their own with just a bit of wood for protection against 11 ruthless hunters knowing that one false move will be your last? Is it a job for which only masochists should apply?

I was driving back down the M1 from Trent Bridge in the summer of 2011. It was 11pm. My mobile rang. It was not a number I recognised.

'Is that Simon Hughes?' It was an Australian voice.

'Yes,' I replied, a little circumspectly. 'Who's this?'

'It's Shane Watson,' said the voice. 'Australian opening batsman.'

'Really?' I said, imagining it was probably one of Michael Vaughan's mates winding me up. 'Where are you?' (I thought it was a good way of checking if it actually was him.)

'Melbourne,' he said. 'I wonder if we could have a chat.'

My heart sank. The only time current players called me was to complain about something I'd written or misquoted. Or, occasionally, to write a not-very-humorous piece for their benefit brochure. With Watson, who I had met properly only once at a charity evening I was compering – at which I semi-humiliated him by getting him to chew on a wichetty grub – it could only be a complaint.

'Why, what have I done?' I said defensively.

'Well, you've written about my failure to convert fifties into hundreds,' he said.

Oh here we go, I thought, another precious international player tearing me off a strip for daring to question their ability when I had an iota of their talent. 'How many Tests have YOU played?' and all that. I was bracing myself for a lecture while trying to negotiate the contraflow near Newport

Pagnell. I was praying for the mobile signal to die. Sod's law it never does when you want it to.

'Well, I've only written about that a bit, and that was ages ago, in the Ashes,' I said, 'but I didn't say that made you a *bad* player. I mean, you made more runs than any other Aussie in that series.' Ugh, I was crawling to him now.

'Look, it's OK,' he said, 'I'm not pissed off. I wanted to ask your advice.'

'My advice?!' Images of me being knocked over for not many by a succession of West Indian fast bowlers and South African fast bowlers and English fast bowlers, and spinners, and medium pacers, and in fact just about anyone who could turn their arm over, flashed through my mind. The sound of Geoff Boycott lambasting a second-rate spinner on commentary, saying, 'You could 'ave 'it that lollipop, Simon, and you couldn't bat!' was ringing in my ears.

'My advice . . .?'

'Yes,' he went on. 'I know you analyse the game carefully and write a lot about batting and I want to pick your brain and see if I can learn anything. I have to do SOMETHING. I can't keep making nice fifties and then getting out. It's driving me nuts. I thought you'd be the man to talk to about trying to improve.'

'Really?' I said, trying to conceal the incredulity in my voice. 'You're serious?'

'Deadly serious,' he said. 'Of course, I understand if you feel uncomfortable about helping an Aussie . . .'

Well I did, but there's divided loyalty everywhere these days, isn't there? Swedes and Italians have helped the English foot-ballers, Zimbabweans and Australians have worked with the

English cricketers, the Welsh and Irish rugby teams are coached by Kiwis. So I thought, what the hell. I'll probably just confuse him more anyway, to England's potential benefit.

We talked for so long that I got all the way back to London, and I was sitting in my car outside my house at about half past midnight when we finally terminated the call. And in the course of our conversation we talked about everything to do with batting. I told him everything I'd gleaned from watching and interviewing leading players. We discussed preparation, visualisation, concentration and distraction. We talked about the inherent loneliness of being a batsman and of the importance of working in pairs and the value of strong body language in concealing from the opponent what you are really thinking. We talked about expectation and inspiration and desperation and the rarefied air of total domination. I don't know if any of it helped, but it got him thinking.

It got me thinking, too. Watson began life as a fast bowler who batted at No.8. I wondered if you could *make* someone a good batsman from modest beginnings, or are they born with the talent? If you were seeking to create the ideal player in a laboratory, Frankenstein-style, what raw materials would you need?

A bit of common sense, to start with. Boycott and I were watching the Pakistani Shahid Afridi smacking a few boundaries with typical abandon against England in a one-day international. Predictably, with the match almost won, Afridi had a big wahoo and was bowled.

'What was Afridi thinking?' I said on commentary.

'It's hard to think, Simon, when you've got nothing between your ears,' Boycott retorted.

So, despite Afridi's brilliant hitting ability, you wouldn't want his head. Joe Root's would be more suitable. He seems a more balanced sort of chap. But should your ideal batsman be tall or short, strong or nimble, left-handed or right-handed (or both?!)? Do you need 20/20 vision and amazing reflexes? Or is concentration more important than co-ordination? Is it better being a brash show-off or a selfish loner? Given the importance of a batsman maintaining a look of innocence when they get a faint nick to the keeper, should you be the kind of character who never admits it when they fart?

And once you've established the basics, how do you get better? Is there one practice technique that works above all others? Can you train yourself to handle genuine fast bowling? Can you learn how to read mystery spin? Why do you lose confidence and where can you find it again? How can someone bat for ten hours and not get tired, or bored? Is all the effort and trauma really worth it? Ultimately is making a hundred better than sex?

If you've ever wanted to be a batsman or wondered what it's like to be alone in the middle being hunted down by 11 heartless assassins or are intrigued by this mysterious, painful-sounding world of flying hooks and square cuts and rip-snorters and vicious leg breaks, then this book is for you. It will make you realise that being a batsman is a sporting version of the *Hunger Games*.

CHAPTER 2

Don't Annoy the Coach

'Go on, my son!'

I always wanted to be a batsman. The inspiration was my Uncle Tony. He grew up idolising Denis Compton – England's first modern celebrity cricketer – primarily for his ability to waltz in to the Lord's dressing room the morning after a big night out (still wearing his dinner jacket) and, having been roused from a nap, grab a colleague's bat, stride out and make a scintillating hundred. 'If you can play you can use the leg of a chair,' Compton was fond of saying.

Unable to effectively combine claret-quaffing with run-making, Uncle Tony chose me to atone for his wasted sporting talent. He bought me a Ben Warsop bat and a copy of *Wisden* for my eighth birthday. I kept the *Wisden* by my bed. I liked the Cricket Records section. Two statistics stood out: Garfield Sobers' 365 not out – the highest score in Test cricket – and Hanif Mohammed's 499 for Karachi v

Bahawalpur (he was run out trying to be the first man to make 500).

When I saw England's Colin Cowdrey on TV score a century in his 100th Test, in 1968, my mind was made up. Cowdrey made batting look so easy. A portly figure, he glided about the crease stroking the ball effortlessly into gaps. He was like an overweight Ian Bell. (Apparently he sometimes didn't walk if he nicked it either.) I loved his elegance and style and the nonchalant way he raised his bat to acknowledge the crowd's applause.

I tried to emulate the feats of these celebrated batsmen in the back garden, throwing a tennis ball against the wall and hitting the rebound, just as the great Don Bradman did (only he hit a golf ball with a stump, which is just a *tiny* bit harder). I was either Cowdrey driving an Australian fast bowler on the up, or Ted Dexter hooking Wes Hall, or Geoff Boycott going up on his toes to steer a single past gully. I had an exceptionally bouncy tennis ball to replicate a quick wicket in Brisbane, and a scuffed, bald one to recreate a dry turner in Lahore. Helped by the fact that the wicket was a milk crate and there was only one fielder – my sister Bettany's pram at short midwicket – I made umpteen fifties and raised my bat to Jasper, the cat, dozing on the kitchen window sill.

Dexter was a friend of the family and I liked his majestic batting and his Aston Martin parked outside. I visualised myself as him taking guard at No.3 for England against Australia at Lord's, surveying the field, noting an inviting gap at extra cover and exquisitely driving my third ball towards the Tavern boundary to the impressed Hampshire burr of John Arlott on BBC radio: 'Young Hughes made that look as simple as blowing the head off a dandelion . . .' It would have been an assured beginning, if not quite as memorable as David Gower's first-ball pull to the square-leg fence against Pakistan, or as outrageous as Jason Roy's second-ball reverse sweep for four on his England debut in September 2014. OK, it was a T20 match, but it still took balls to do that.

I imagined stroking a few offside boundaries and unfurling an immaculate straight drive, dabbing a single or two and pulling the Australian off-spinner resoundingly over mid-wicket to lead the players off for lunch, 46 not out, to rousing applause, the members in the pavilion seats standing in appre-ciation, the clapping rising to an echoing climax in the Long Room as I passed the approved glances of Sir Donald Bradman, W.G.Grace and Lord Harris looking down from their portraits on the wall, and winked at Uncle Tony down-ing a bucks fizz in the Long Room bar.

And so the dream went on.

I set out to make it reality. Most nights of summer I was up the road at my local club, Ealing, facing the off-spin of my Sri Lankan friend Dilip in the nets, or driving the ball against the fence if Mac, the cantankerous old groundsman, couldn't be bothered to put the nets up, or fending off Dilip's tennis-ball bouncers in a nearby car park if Mac shouted at us to 'get off the fucking grass – I've just mown that!'

My father was invaluable. He mowed a strip on the lawn exactly 22 yards long and trained as a cricket coach and took over a small indoor cricket school behind a pub and bowled to me till his shoulder ached and his voice was hoarse from saying 'Play *straight*!' He umpired my colts matches and always shook his head dismissively when I was hit on the pad and said, 'NOT out, son!' Even when he was standing at square leg.

He was a keen carpenter and he built a portable wicket out of old broom handles and a chute to feed the ball out of, and a table-tennis table 'to sharpen your reflexes'. He planed and repaired and oiled old practice bats and stuck down the rubber grips with bright green gaffer tape.

My bowling got me plenty of wickets, but I took my batting more seriously. Batting was quite easy against kids who couldn't get the ball down the other end with any speed. Batsmen were the lords and masters. They got congratulations and free kit and man of the match awards. Bowlers just got blisters.

I watched the top batsmen closely on TV – Boycott and Gavaskar and Greg Chappell and Gordon Greenidge. I noticed that most of them were shortish in stature like me. I tried to copy Gavaskar's wristy clip off his pads and Chappell's statuesque driving and Greenidge's astonishing flick-pull and Boycott's incessant chewing. A large photo of Boycott's trademark square drive adorned my bedroom wall. And it's true: his 1970s bat was barely thicker than a stick of rhubarb.

I read books on batting, lingering on every word of Tony Greig's enticingly titled *Cricket*. Well, OK, I looked at the pictures anyway. There is a wonderful image of the left-handed Sobers launching a ball over the sightscreen, front leg cleared out of the way, bat wrapped against his backside, the finish like a full-blooded golf swing (see plate section). It could have been Chris Gayle, minus the helmet and thigh pad and ludicrous gold chain. I've seen thinner bike-locks.

I went to Test matches and one-day finals at Lord's and saw

Sobers make 150, and Dennis Amiss 188, and Bob Woolmer 120, and Keith Fletcher 178. I dutifully filled in the scorecards and stuck them in my scrapbook. We spent the summer holidays in Kent, and my father took me to Canterbury and Folkestone where I watched the accomplished Kent batsmen with great fascination – Luckhurst and Woolmer and Denness and an ageing Cowdrey and the dashing Asif Iqbal and the brilliantly eccentric Alan Knott – and cut out the match reports from the *Daily Telegraph*.

Brian Luckhurst captured my imagination. He had opened for England and fended off Lillee and Thomson, and there was something simple and straightforward about his method. He hit the ball crisply and always made runs when I watched, including several centuries. I also liked the fact that his bat was different from the rest. It was a Lillywhites and the black sticker glinted impressively in the sunlight when he brandished it at the crease.

I opened the batting for the school team and drew a black Lillywhites logo on the back of my Ben Warsop. I overheard opponents wondering what was that 'weird black smudge on that show-off's bat'. Undeterred I made a few decent scores. I painstakingly recorded every innings in a book, kept a cumulative total and calculated my average to two decimal points.

I got to 50 against Alleyn's and was clapped by the opposition as I held my bat aloft. The umpire, Alleyn's cricket master, patted me on the head and said well batted. The pitch was easy and the bowling friendly. I got to my highest score, 84, when I noticed there were three fielders behind square on the leg side. I knew that was illegal so I had a big slog and was bowled. I pointed out the three men behind square. 'That's not allowed,' I said. 'It's a no ball.'

'Are you arguing with the umpire?' the Alleyn's cricket master challenged.

'Yes!' I replied indignantly.

'*That's* not allowed,' he retorted, 'now bugger off, you cocky sod.'

Shame my dad hadn't been umpiring.

A Room with a View

I played a few games for Middlesex colts and ended up in the county Under-19s. I was picked as an all-rounder and batted at No.8. There wasn't much chance to make a decent score from there. But someone must have liked the look of me because I was selected for a national Under-19 trial match. It was a two-day game at Lord's. This was my chance to get noticed.

I whitened my pads and boots that night and practised my backlift in the bedroom mirror, as Boycott said he did in *Play Cricket the Right Way*. I looked down the list of England's Test hundred-makers in *Wisden* – Cowdrey and Hammond (22), Barrington (20), and further down Luckhurst (4) and wondered if I'd ever be on it. I checked my bat rubber and the protective tape on the inside edge and tarted up the Lillywhites logo which had faded a little.

I had watched many games at Lord's – Tests and one-day finals – but only once been in the pavilion. The scale of the building and the shiny, squeaky floors strike you when you walk in. And the obvious disdain of the stewards if you are not immaculately dressed. 'Straighten your tie, boy,' a whiskery bloke said as I entered.

I was playing for the National Association of Young

Cricketers XI and we changed in the home dressing room which Middlesex and England used. It was the size of a church hall, with a spectacular view of the ground. There was a table laden with chocolate bourbons and custard creams in the centre of the room, a large fluffy white towel hanging over each seat and a big red payphone in the corner. I changed next to it. It rang several times before play and I answered it. First it was a slushy-sounding girl called Trace, then another who referred to herself as The Minx. They asked if 'Wayney' was about. I realised they were referring to Middlesex's fast bowler Wayne Daniel and I was in his spot.

The batting order was read out. I was disappointed to be down at No.8. I reminded myself that Luckhurst began life as a left-arm spinner batting at No.9, and so indeed did Garfield Sobers. (I didn't know then, of course, that Kevin Pietersen would bat at No.8 when he first played for Natal.) When it was my turn to bat, our match manager said we needed to get on with it a bit. I descended the pavilion stairs excited at the prospect of traversing the famous Long Room on my way out. But it was closed for cleaning so I had to exit through a side door. The pitch was on the extreme edge of the square on the Grandstand side. The boundary on one side was barely 40 yards.

The pitch was beautiful and the ball seemed to ping off my bat. I clipped some singles, flicked a two and swept a couple of legside fours off a left-arm spinner. I felt confident and was enjoying myself. Then out of the blue we declared. A sprinkling of spectators – the parents – clapped us off.

The pitch was faster than anything I had ever seen before and I took some wickets with the ball. I had a spell of four for

10. Driving home my father was a bit grouchy about a couple of no-balls and thought I had 'played across the line a bit'. I could tell he was pleased though. I had had a good day. The following morning, as I was loosening up on the outfield, the match manager approached me accompanied by a little old man with a stick. He was introduced as Gubby Allen, Middlesex stalwart, former England captain and Test selector. I knew his name from reading about the Bodyline series. He was the one who had refused to bowl leg theory.

I thought he was going to compliment me on my batting, offer a couple of tips and perhaps promise me a county contract. Middlesex were looking for a new opener to partner Mike Brearley. But, in a surprisingly thin, reedy voice, he said: 'Hughes! Pitch it up more and don't warm up like that – it makes it look like you chuck.'

I played some games for Middlesex 2nds towards the end of the season, taking quite a few wickets. (I wore long-sleeved shirts to dupe any doubters about my action.) I didn't get much of a chance to bat. I played 81 games of cricket that year, batting 52 times (average 31.76) and bowling 784 overs. Yes, 784!! With our current health-and-safety obsession limiting juniors to six-over spells, endless school exams, not forgetting family holidays to Marbella, modern teenagers don't even get through a quarter of that. (At least they will have decent knee joints when they are 40, but is that so vital?)

At the last match of the season, playing against Cross Arrows on the Lord's Nursery, a man came up and introduced himself as Arthur Flower, Middlesex secretary, and asked if I would be interested in accepting professional terms 'for my lively fast bowling'. I was delighted. It was what I had craved from the age of about eight. But the excitement was tinged with frustration. I had witnessed from my brief encounters with the pros that batsmen got all their gear sponsored and a car with their name on the side. Bowlers had to buy or borrow kit and drove round in old jalopies. I would have to work my way up the order.

Track-suited and Booted

That's when the trouble started.

Having spent part of the winter in Sri Lanka, staying with my friend Dilip's family, in an attempt to sharpen my game, I arrived at Middlesex the following season full of optimism. Playing or practising every day, my bowling had got faster. More importantly, I had broadened my batting experience against an assortment of feisty quick bowlers uttering strange phrases – I discovered too late that *bumpa ekak danna* meant 'stick it up his nose' – and clever spinners with weird double-jointed actions. (Murali was about five at the time.)

I was ready to be challenged by the exciting world of county cricket and to fine-tune my skills with intensive practice and specialist coaching. Quite apart from bowling at some of the world's great players, I would learn how to convert skittish twenties into sparkling hundreds. I would get the sponsored car and a limitless supply of new bats. I'd need them, too. While I was away my father had used my old ones as the legs for a new bed he had made me.

I met all the Middlesex stars on my first day as a pro – Gatting, Brearley, Emburey, Edmonds, Radley, Selvey, Barlow, Downton, Gould – England players all. I was looking forward to watching how these men prepared for the game, picking up valuable technical tips, and showing what I could to the craggy-faced coach, Don Bennett.

But there was no sign of a cricket bat or a ball in my first week. We attended a boot camp and all we did was shuttle runs and strengthening exercises in the airless, Barclays Bank gym. The England spinner Phil Edmonds spoke for all of us when he said: 'Are these burpees *really* necessary?' We finished the sessions off with five-a-side football when I became acquainted with the stern demeanour and crunching tackles of Don Bennett, who had also played full back for Coventry City. He made Chelsea's Ron 'Chopper' Harris seem like a poodle.

When we reported to Lord's for the second week (me with slightly bruised ankles), the captain Mike Brearley divided us into groups of six for net practice. Theoretically that meant a 20-minute bat for each of us in the two-hour session. But the senior batsmen had nearer half an hour each, leaving the rest ten minutes at the end. By then most of the squad had gone in for lunch, leaving a couple of exhausted quick bowlers to lob down a few spinners at me. Trying to impress, I danced up the wicket to one and attempted a lofted straight drive. The ball skewed off the inside edge, ricocheted off a wooden upright and narrowly missed the head of Bennett, who was throwing extra balls to Mike Gatting in the next net. 'Come out, you prat,' he said severely.

I thought after lunch the situation would be reversed and those who hadn't had much of a knock would go in first in the afternoon. But the order remained the same, and when, after 90 more minutes' net bowling I thought I'd get a proper bat, we were summoned for fielding practice instead. It went on like that all week.

Even if you did get a ten-minute knock at the end of the day, it was against knackered bowlers to the accompaniment of chuntering groundstaff who wanted to take down the nets and get off home. Plus the pitches, which had been used intensively for four hours, were now treacherous, the ball constantly darting off a bump to locate some unpadded piece of flesh. There was no coaching. Just about the only comment on my batting from Don Bennett was: 'You don't see Gatt wearing his thigh pad outside his trousers in the nets, do you, son?!'

The first Middlesex 2nd XI game of the season was a one-day match against the Royal Navy at Portsmouth. We batted first. I was down at No.9 just ahead of Bennett, who doubled as 2nd XI captain. I got in with about four overs remaining. My heel was still a bit sore from all the net bowling (and the crunching tackles), so I wore comfortable rubber-soled shoes to bat in instead of boots. I got a few runs with some decent shots, but off the last ball of an over my partner was out.

Bennett walked in at No.10. He was at the non-striker's end. I had been told he enjoyed his little bat. Conscious there were only a couple of overs left, I thought it would be a good gesture to give him the strike. I pushed the ball to mid-wicket shouted 'yes' and set off. I overestimated a 50-year-old's speed off the mark however, and he was slow to respond. I tried to stop, slipped on the hard, grassy pitch and partially lost my balance. Seeing me falter, Bennett hesitated, then, as I regained some forward momentum, he continued. In vain. The throw went to his end and despite a desperate lunge he was run out without facing. 'Sorry, Coach!' I called out as he hauled himself to his feet and stomped off.

I thought I redeemed myself by taking ten off the last over

and returned to the dressing room expecting a few well-played back slaps. Instead, there was embarrassed silence as a crimson-faced Bennett sat in the corner brushing dirt off his neatly pressed whites. 'You stupid fucking idiot. Wear spikes when you bat!' he said eventually, eyes blazing. He hit the ball so hard at us in catching practice before we took the field several of us had bruised fingers for a week.

Runs, Rabbits, Runs

There was even less opportunity to bat in the nets after that. It was as if the batsmen had a divine right to bat for as long as they liked, while the bowlers rumbled in ball after ball making light of people obstructing your run-up, disintegrating foot-holds and complaints if you bowled wide or aggressively short. And if your ball was hit out of the net you had to go and fetch it yourself. I realised it was the only way to get a breather, but sending down a pie every few balls does not endear you to coach or captain.

When the batsmen had had their fill and towelled them-selves off, they went back in an adjacent net for throwdowns with the coach while the tired bowlers attempted to give each other bits of batting advice. It was the blind leading the blind. None of the last four in the Middlesex batting order averaged over 7 that season.

Most old bowlers tell the same story. There's a 'them and us' mentality in cricket teams, with batsmen getting all the pref-erential treatment and personal tuition and bowlers doing all the hard labour. It is ridiculous. Everyone in a cricket team has to bat at some stage and, in truth, the worse you are at it the more practice you need.

Yet this myopic attitude – that batsmen get all the serious rehearsal time and specialist attention and bowlers are left to scratch around and pick up whatever crumbs of batting assistance they can find – prevailed until well into the last decade. It was only the arrival of Duncan Fletcher as England coach that transformed the lives of tailenders and as a result prolonged Test match innings.

Fletcher set aside a lot of time to help the bowlers with their batting – helped by the rapid swelling of team entourages allowing each player to receive one-to-one attention (you'd often see the fielding coach throwing balls to Stuart Broad or Jimmy Anderson in the nets, for instance). The advent of the 'sidearm' – Graham Gooch's clever adaptation of that stick that projects tennis balls yonder for dogs to chase – means you don't need decent net bowlers any more either. Using it, batting coaches like Mark Ramprakash can reproduce anything Dale Steyn, Morne Morkel or Mitchell Johnson can unleash. Not that it makes them much easier to play.

The idea of buddying – pairing up a specialist batsman with a lower-order player – was also Fletcher's. Andy Flower continued this approach – about the only facet of the game on which the two Zimbabweans see eye to eye. It converted many dubious positions into dominant ones and contributed hugely to England winning the Ashes in 2009: the work that Anderson and Monty Panesar had done with Alastair Cook and Paul Collingwood respectively, enabling them to bat out 11 overs in the first Test in Cardiff and save the game. (Odd that Panesar's last-ever home Test should be remembered for his batting.)

When Fletcher took over as India's coach in 2010 he

instigated the same dynamic. He banned the word 'tailender', referring to the last five batsmen as the 'lower order' and ensuring they had as much, if not more, time in the nets as the more recognised batsmen. (That suited someone like Virender Sehwag, who hated nets and preferred a few gentle half volleys he could bash into the advertising boards.) The off-spinner Ravi Ashwin said he had never batted in the nets on India duty until the arrival of Fletcher. Now he has two Test hundreds to his name.

Fletcher, a coach who applies common sense to the often bewildering science of cricket, initiated a general realisation that it is easier batting against an old ball when the bowlers are exhausted – bleedin' obvious really – and therefore every man in the team must develop a reputable batting method. Although no Test No.11 has yet made a hundred, it is no coincidence that the record for the tenth wicket in Tests has twice been broken since 2012, and now stands at 198.

The flipside of improved batsmanship down the order is the loss of the genuine 'rabbit'. Seeing the No.11s Wasim Akram liked to call 'my walking wickets' – men like Courtney Walsh (batting average 7.5), Devon Malcolm (average 6.05) and Alan Mullally (average 5.52) – hopping, jabbing and jerking at 90mph bowling was an oblique highlight of a Test match innings. It was where sport met circus. Coco the Clown struggled for the laughs Phil Tufnell incited when he was trying to avoid being nailed by one of Wasim's missiles, especially when, after surveying his shattered stumps, he said: 'I wasn't backing away too much, was I?'

In defence of Tufnell, who actually had a good eye, the batting practice he received was negligible – 'no one *ever* told me what to do!' he lamented recently – and the protection he had was flimsy. The thigh pads of the time were like pillow slips and helmets frequently disintegrated on contact. Anyway, Wasim made perfectly decent batsmen look just as hopeless. And his pace was so extreme it could have penetrated concrete never mind the tentative defence of a novice. But in this era of 'multi-dimensional' cricketers, rabbits are more or less an extinct species now. Will there ever be another Chris Martin, who recorded 36 ducks in 71 Tests for New Zealand, averaged 2.36 and comfortably took more Test wickets than he scored runs? Sadly not.

TOP 10 WORST TEST MATCH BATTING AVERAGES (Qual: 25 innings)

	M	I	NO	HS	Runs	Ave	Wkts	Ave
M.Mbangwa (Z)	15	25	8	8	34	2.00	32	31.43
C.S.Martin (NZ)	71	104	52	12*	123	2.36	233	33.81
R.D.King (WI)	19	27	8	12*	66	3.47	53	32.69
Manjural Islam (B)	17	33	11	21	81	3.68	28	57.32
Maninder Singh (I)	35	38	12	15	99	3.80	88	37.36
A.N.P.R.Fernando (SL)	17	29	10	17*	75	3.94	42	46.50
B.S.Chandrasekhar (I)	58	80	39	22	167	4.07	242	29.74
D.R.Doshi (I)	33	38	10	20	129	4.60	114	30.71
B.A.Reid (A)	27	34	14	13	93	4.65	113	24.63
A.L.Valentine (WI)	36	51	21	14	141	4.70	139	30.32

Nature or Nurture?

The question is, could any of these inept batsmen have made a hundred with the technical advice and support given to players now? In Martin's case, almost certainly not – that would be like trying to train Pavarotti to dance *Swan Lake* – but possibly in other cases. Tufnell (highest first-class score 67★) was no worse a batsman than Jimmy Anderson, and he made 81 in a Test match recently. The dishevelled-looking New Zealand spinner Daniel Vettori was a resident No.11 when he first played for his country in 1997. He didn't look as if he could hit the ball off the square. He finished his Test career with six centuries.

What this suggests is that becoming a successful batsman is not just to do with ability. Opportunity and dedication are key factors, too. How otherwise do ungainly-looking club batsmen make unfathomable amounts of runs? I played with a bloke at Ealing C.C. who only had one shot – christened the 'axe' because he jammed down on the ball as if he was chopping wood. But he knew how and when to use it and scored many valuable fifties. (I tried to copy it, of course, and succeeded only in chopping the ball onto my stumps while creating a large divot in the pitch.)

The key is to convince someone that you have at least a small portion of batting ability and a large dollop of determination. That earns you the three As – attention, assistance and advice. It generally helps to be shortish of stature. Of average height at most. The ten leading run-makers in Test cricket are all under 6ft tall (only just in Jacques Kallis's case.). Of the 25 men in the history of the game to have scored 100 hundreds, only Graeme Hick, Frank Woolley and W.G.Grace were over 6ft.

Why? Shorter men are generally quicker on their toes. Stands to reason: the brain is closer to their feet. Their balance is better, too. The lion is more agile than the giraffe. It also helps (and this might sound silly) that the eyes are nearer to the ground. This means a shorter player doesn't have to tilt his focus down as much when the ball pitches and temporarily lose sight of it. Tall batsmen are invariably vulnerable to fast yorkers. (Goalkeepers' weakest point is near their feet.)

Tall batsmen also don't generally play the bouncer as well, as they have a larger frame to move and are a bigger target to hit. The compensation is they have a greater reach (something Kevin Pietersen makes brilliant use of) and longer levers enabling them to hit the ball further with minimal effort. No modern ground is big enough for Chris Gayle. Some of his hits should be worth 12.

Actually, with the general dearth of really fast bowling in the world game right now – that demanded super-slick reactions and movements – and the increasing emphasis on power, being tall as a batsman is less of a disadvantage than it was. But still the ideal height would be about 5ft 10in. Think Ricky Ponting.

In some the talent is immediately obvious. An 11-year-old Ponting, whose father was a decent club player and whose uncle, Greg Campbell, played for Australia, scored four centuries in five days in a junior cricket competition in Tasmania in 1986. He had gone one better than Don Bradman, who made his first hundred aged 12. Mind you, the Don had recorded a triple hundred for Bowral 1st XI by the age of 17. He was soon recruited to a trial for New South Wales. Of course he made 110.

On a self-prepared pitch in Antigua, the batting of the youthful Viv Richards was already revered, and at 12 he won a sports scholarship to the local grammar school. He made his debut for Antigua at 17 and the local schools were given a half-day's holiday to watch. When he was (wrongly) given out first ball, there was a mass invasion of the pitch and he was re-instated. Ironically he was (correctly) given out again three balls later. But there weren't too many failures after that.

Sachin Tendulkar began hitting a ball with a broomstick aged two and a half, and at six practised, like Bradman, with an erratically bouncing golf ball. He was adept at manoeuvring it around the family living room without damaging anything. He scored a hundred at school when he was just 13 and a century in every innings he played in the season after, averaging over 1000 in the Harris Shield, a domestic tournament for Under-16s.

OK, we're talking about the immortals here. Men with God-given talent. Or perhaps we should say the God-given opportunity to *develop* their talent. They would have been prodigies in any era. They got preferential treatment and they deserved it. Tendulkar, for instance, was taken under the wing of the esteemed cricket coach Ramakant Achrekar. There were five nets on his local *maidan*, Shivaji Park. He was afforded the special privilege of batting in each of them against an assortment of bowlers in the morning, then after batting in a club practice match in the afternoon, he was back in the nets for two more hours that night.

For the last 15 minutes, Achrekar would place a one rupee coin on Tendulkar's stumps and get everyone to bowl at him. If he remained not out, he got to keep the coin. 'It was a serious challenge and winning the coin gave me intense sat-isfaction,' Tendulkar says. And after that he was made to run two complete laps of Shivaji Park – the size of a small common – in his pads. He did all this virtually every day in the summer holidays. (Achrekar, of course, ended up broke.)

You can see where Tendulkar got his incredible dedication from. It was instilled from an early age. Scoring 326 not out (aged 14) in his famous partnership of 664 with Vinod Kambli in the Harris Shield was just the ultimate extension of his daily routine. Having a half-brother, Ajit, who was ten years older, was a massive bonus as he escorted Sachin everywhere. Many a young sporting career has been afflicted by a parent's general ennui at another outrageously early Sunday morning drop-off. 'They want you there at *what* time?!!!'

But not every eventually prolific batsman was so precociously gifted. For instance Andrew Strauss (21 Test hundreds) didn't distinguish himself in his first couple of years in the Radley School team and, aged 20, averaged only 12 in a half-season of matches for Middlesex 2nds. Kumar Sangakkara was, as he admits on page 244, not especially good with the bat as a teenager. The 18-year-old Kevin Pietersen was initially regarded more as a bowler in South Africa and spent much of his first season at Notts batting at No.6. The arch sledger-in-chief Steve Waugh began his first-class career for New South Wales batting at No.9, was originally picked for Australia as an all-rounder and took 42 innings to make the first of his 32 Test hundreds. When once he questioned the right of the young Surrey bowler Jimmy Ormond to be representing England he was famously told: 'You're not even the best batsman in your family!'

Batsmen are like golfers – the mental torture and loneliness of their job mean they often mature later than other sportsmen. A dismissal in cricket – the closest thing to death in sport – is so terminal, so final that its spectre places unique pressure on a batsman. Failure results in endless soul searching and technical tinkering (just like golfers), which often just exacerbates any problem. It is only when they become more self-aware, learning to be more comfortable with themselves and their precarious existence, that they are fully formed.

The age of 30 seems to be a critical point for both batsmen and golfers. It is from here where the best truly flourish. Despite Brian Lara's two record-breaking innings in 1994 aged 25, he scored two-thirds of his Test centuries (21 out of 34) after he reached 30. England's two most prolific run-makers, Graham Gooch and Alec Stewart, both made significantly more Test hundreds after their 30th birthday than beforehand (four before and 16 after for Gooch, four before and 11 after for Stewart). The older they got, the harder they practised, the more runs they scored.

No matter how early in the morning you arrived for a county match at either Chelmsford or The Oval, you would always be greeted by the sight of Gooch or Stewart in the nets facing the men they had commandeered as their personal ball-feeders – Alan Lilley or Geoff Arnold (the reason Arnold is considerably shorter than he used to be). The more they tasted success, the more they wanted.

The greatest golfer who ever lived – Jack Nicklaus – won seven major titles before turning 30 and 11 after. Arnold Palmer secured six of his seven major victories after his 30th birthday. A similar win/age ratio applies to Tom Watson, Lee Trevino and Gary Player. Their best years were in their thirties. Only one of the truly great players, Tiger Woods, confounds this theory (winning just four of his 14 major titles after turning 30). And we all know why that was.

All these men became more and more obsessed about seeking technical perfection, and had an insatiable desire for success. Well, apart from Tiger, who apparently had an insatiable desire for something else. Interestingly, many top batsmen become addicted to golf in retirement. It satisfies their eternal quest for technical and mental superiority. They're too old to combat the moving ball so they settle for taming the stationary one instead. And, what's more, in golf you never lose the strike or get run out by a partner's stupid call.

I Dedicate the Award to ...

I didn't know any of this when I was starting out in county cricket. All I knew was that I was the right physique to be a batsman – 5ft 10in and around 12 stone (think Ricky Ponting!) – had a reasonable technique and decent reflexes (all that table tennis with my dad). I knew to watch the ball and play straight when I got to the wicket and try to keep my head down. Oh yes, and to 'wear spikes'. I don't recall ever being given any other bits of (sensible) batting advice. I never tinkered with grips or backswings as you see batsmen (and golfers) do. The only 'trigger movements' I knew were in episodes of *Hawaii Five-O*. No one ever highlighted the faults I needed to work on. They probably didn't know where to start.

The bowling machines were always monopolised by the senior batsmen (and anyway had an alarming habit of interspersing programmed half-volleys with the odd random beamer straight at your head). The team video camera – provided to film matches or net practice – was used only to record Wayne Daniel, clad just in a large white towel, speaking on the red dressing-room payphone to some female while casually fondling his genitals. (Lucky for him there was no YouTube.)

I wanted the chance to face Daniel in the nets, to test my reflexes against a genuinely fast bowler. But he tended to send down only a few looseners on practice days before repairing to the dressing room to do an inordinate amount of sit-ups and stretches (and make phone calls) in his jock strap. The one guy who did bowl at me was Mike Gatting. He was a bundle of restless energy who, once he had finished his extensive diet of throwdowns, wanted something else to do. He loved the opportunity of what he called 'a trundle' and would bustle enthusiastically in to bowl at anyone who was still standing. The trouble is he always kept a hard, highly polished ball in his bag and he swung it prodigiously at a brisk pace. Half his deliveries I couldn't lay a bat on. The other half nipped back and rapped me painfully on unprotected inner thigh to much guffawing.

Actually when you've run in and bowled for an hour or more in practice, you lack the energy to focus on batting for long. You might block a couple, bat sensibly for five minutes, but then you tend to be inhabited by the desire to express your-self and have a bit of fun. This manifests itself as a succession of big yahoos to see how far you can hit the ball. One flies off the top edge out of the net, bounces on the roof of the grounds-man's house and into the road, just as the coach, who has been gathering up the practice balls, looks up. 'Those new knackers are twenty quid a pop,' he says, 'we'll dock the next one off your wages.' That would have been a third of my earnings.

He had a point, but name me a fast bowler who was able to play long, dedicated, careful innings. I can think of one –

Imran Khan. He had exceptional powers of mental resilience, underlined by an eight-hour century against Australia, continued, in later life, by his unstinting commitment to banishing corruption in Pakistan. He is the exception that proves the rule. None of the other quickies who could bat – Botham, Hadlee, Marshall, Kapil, Wasim, Flintoff or Shaun Pollock – played safe for long. Batting was their release from the physical ordeal of bowling.

Not that I am comparing myself to any of those legends, just making the point that the exertion of fast bowling leaves you aching and footsore and unable to apply yourself with the bat for long periods. If these men were going to make a hundred, they would do it in a whirr. Their main objective at the crease was to make as many as possible WITHOUT HAVING TO RUN. It made great viewing, except for the next man in.

Botham had just produced the most extraordinary performance in Bombay. He had taken 13 wickets in the Test match, bowling 26 overs unchanged in India's second innings in stifling 33°C heat. And that after a barnstorming 114 (from only 144 balls) coming in when England had slumped to 57 for four. We learned later he had also stayed up practically till dawn each night necking the ample supplies of Foster's lager they had brought from Australia (1980s Indian beer was undrinkable).

I cut out the match report and stuck it on my bedroom wall. That was the way to play cricket (though I preferred Fullers). And HE began at No.9 for Somerset. That, clearly, was the place to start.

CHAPTER 3

Getting Ready

Swimming Against the Tide

The next opportunity I had to demonstrate my batting prowess was in a Middlesex 2nd XI match against Essex. It was early August. I had completed the summer term at Durham University and joined the 'Dinky Doos' (Twos) for the game at the Barclays sports centre where we'd done pre-season training. It was a mixed bag of a team, with one or two more experienced players such as the opener Wilf Slack seeking a bit of batting practice, and an assortment of younger lads, some of whom might make it – like the all-rounder Kevan James who subsequently had a successful career at Hampshire – and one or two of whom certainly wouldn't.

It was a good pitch that Essex didn't make the best use of. Having bowled 12 overs, I was down to bat at No.9. It was a good omen (Luckhurst and Botham's original spot) – and I watched the game keenly while Middlesex batted. A rain interruption meant we declared behind, so I didn't get in, but helped bowl Essex out just before the close of the second day. We required just over 100 to win.

The third morning was beautifully sunny, and after the warm-ups the coach Don Bennett left one of the senior bats-men in charge while he caught up with some admin indoors. 'You can bat number eight this time,' he said, 'not that you'll be needed.' As soon as the openers set out to knock off the target, someone suggested having a dip in the sports centre's heated outdoor pool. The water looked inviting, especially to ease the tired muscles from bowling the day before. Four of us jumped in.

We had just started a game of frisbee polo when James – nicknamed 'Spikes' for his habit of being 'so far up the coach's arse that's all you could see' – approached looking worried. 'Lads, we're eight for three!' he exclaimed. 'Coach will be spewing!' We all leapt hurriedly out of the water and dashed to the changing room, relieved to find Don Bennett still absent. We couldn't see the pitch from our changing position. We sent a padded-up Spikes out to check on the score. Soon afterwards he scurried back to pick up his bat. 'It's thirteen for five now!' he said. 'It's swinging all over the oche,' and he headed out to the middle.

I was standing there in nothing but a pair of soaking wet, stripy underpants and I was next in. There was no option but to drag on my whites over my soggy Y-fronts. I had just got one pad on when another wicket fell. I did the other pad's straps up, shoved a damp towel down my trousers as a thigh pad and put a white sunhat on to cover my wet hair (yes, I had some then).

I walked out to bat trailing straps and laces and carrying my batting gloves under my arm. I had to stop on the way out to do everything up, just as the coach emerged from the office indoors. The score was now 20 for seven. I hoped no one had noticed our extra-curricular activities, but the Essex captain – the veteran Brian 'Tonker' Taylor – said: 'Been swimming, son?' The blue stripes of my wet pants were visible through the seat of my whites.

I somehow survived for a few minutes, but a sequence of lower-order batsmen – one with water from his dripping wet afro running into his eyes – had no answer to the late swing of left-armer Gary Sainsbury. I was last out caught at slip by Derek Pringle. We were all out for 29 and Sainsbury had taken eight for 8.

We sat in the changing room afterwards, shame-faced, still wet-haired, waiting in trepidation for Bennett to vent his wrath. It wasn't so much the hairdryer as the whirlpool. He was wheeling about the room, almost foaming at the mouth, ranting – 'You idle, useless fucking toe rags! Going swimming!! What do you think this is fucking Butlins?!' Just at that moment there was a knock on the door. It was the janitor. 'Excuse me, someone left their sunglasses by the pool,' he said. Bennett grabbed them and flung them furiously against the wall causing the lenses to fly out of the frames. 'Well, don't think you're getting any time off this week, or next! Report to Lord's tomorrow with your running gear at nine am sharp!'

There have been examples of worse preparation for a sporting event – the Jamaican bobsleigh team practising on sand dunes, for instance, or Wayne Larkins spending 12 hours in a pub before opening the batting in a one-day match (he was out immediately) – but not many. Graham Gooch was fond of the phrase 'if you fail to prepare, prepare to fail' (coined originally by Benjamin Franklin) and adhered to it throughout his career.

Gooch's one lapse was unavoidable. Playing for Essex he attended a party thrown at home by the one and only I.T.Botham, then playing for Durham. When Botham said 'drink ...' it wasn't an invitation, it was an order. Châteauneuf-du-Pape was his interpretation of 'the spirit of cricket'. Gooch failed to extricate himself until gone 4am. The morning after he was utterly incapable of locating the ball with his bat. (I was the lucky beneficiary, although Gooch had the last laugh as Essex won the match.) The nation lost more than just a brilliant all-rounder when Botham retired. There are fewer incidents now of England's star opponents requiring stomach pumps.

Trigger Happy

I came to realise as my career progressed that there was one thing common to all the best batsmen (apart from their perennial claim that 'that ball wouldn't have hit another set!'). It was their meticulous preparation. Again it is very like golf, with its obsession with gear and technique and spectators being told off for breathing or twitching an eyebrow.

Batsmen/golfers are fastidious about how they stand – feet precisely 25.6cm apart at an 85.7 degree angle to the pitch/ fairway – and fiddle endlessly with the position of their hands. Some are so obsessive they look behind themselves before every ball to check they are precisely right. (This could be exploited by a bowler craftily taking a shorter run or letting go of the ball by the umpire.)

You can judge a man by his handshake. There's the Cruncher (bully), the Wrencher (control freak), the Wet Fish (introverted or intellectual), the Clasper (manipulator – putting their other hand over the top of handshake), the Clammy (nervous), the Backslapper (bullshitter). So you can often tell a lot about a batsman from his grip. The Bottom Clencher (bat held low down the handle) is a gritty, nuggety player with a compact method, getting as close to the ball as possible, playing the ball under his nose with minimum risk – say Justin Langer or Shivnarine Chanderpaul. (I try to resist using the term 'bottom hand' after a girl wrote in some years ago asking why a player's ablutionary habits were relevant to his batting style.)

The High & Mighty (bat held at the top of the handle) is liable to be a more expansive player, maximising his potential leverage. A dasher, in other words (eg Adam Gilchrist). It is why that type of batting is sometimes called giving it 'the long handle'. The Slicer (the face of the bat angled towards mid-off) is a batsman who favours hitting through the offside – sometimes known as the 'posh' side. He will like to cut and carve (eg Nasser Hussain, Brendon McCullum). The Worker (bat face closed towards the pads) will be someone prone to hitting the ball to leg (which is regarded as more workman-like – hence 'working' the ball – eg Steve Smith). The New Zealand opener John Wright used to glue one glove to the bat handle to ensure his top hand was in exactly the correct position. Presumably he didn't change his gloves (or bat) often.

The stance (and backlift) is rehearsed endlessly in the bedroom mirror or any other reflective surface he can find. Australia's David Boon recalls the time he was woken at dawn the morning before a Test match by the sight of his opening partner and room-mate Geoff Marsh 'standing in the nuddy apart from his gloves and helmet' practising his set-up in front of the wardrobe mirror. Pre-match, Mike Gatting would stand before the Lord's dressing-room mirror in mock stance, thumping the floor so relentlessly with his bat it disrupted MCC committee meetings in the room underneath. (Irritated bangs on the ceiling from the gin-swiggers below just made him tap harder.)

Stance-styles come and go in vogue. In the 1930s, Bradman confounded the MCC coaching manual by resting his bat between his feet (rather than in the orthodox manner on the back toe) and spawned a number of imitators. At the outset of the fast bowling age (early 1970s), Tony Greig stood upright at the crease, bat held aloft, a method borrowed subsequently by many including Graham Gooch, Graeme Hick and Ian Botham. If it looked as if they did this so that their bat was brandished for attack against the quick men, it was only partly true. Greig said the reason he stood tall with his bat up was because, as he was 6ft 6in, his bat couldn't rest on the ground or his toe unless he stooped. Having your eyes level is crucial.

The England all-rounder Peter Willey took this to extremes, by also ensuring his eyes were both facing directly down the pitch. This meant standing front on to the bowler, left shoulder pointing to the square leg umpire. It looked bizarre, though he justified it by saying it gave him a perfect, two-eyed view of the ball. I would have argued that his subsequent shift to a conventional side-on position as the ball was coming down nullified the advantage. But as he clubbed numerous runs off the all-conquering West Indies and had forearms like Popeye, I kept quiet.

A slightly crouched style of stance evolved in the 1980s and early 1990s, largely to make yourself as small a target as possible for all the ferocious bouncers flying around. Lower backlifts were also a consequence of the vicious inswinging yorkers perpetrated by the likes of Waqar Younis and Wasim Akram. (Paul Collingwood finished up with no backlift at all. After his international retirement he should have enlisted for the French cricket team.)

Brian Lara bucked this trend with an up-periscope backlift like the baseballer Babe Ruth. In some of his most extravagant shots, the bat made a full 360-degree revolution. Adam Gilchrist and Virender Sehwag were similar. Chris Gayle would be too, except he doesn't believe in wasting any energy lifting his (enormous) bat up before delivering the payload. He doesn't believe in wasting any energy after clobbering the ball either. His incredible, record-breaking 30-ball century in the IPL contained 98 in boundaries (eight fours and 11 sixes).

At the start of a season (or tour), batsmen spend many waking hours getting their 'trigger movements' properly grooved. Most use this trigger to get themselves going, a sort of prelude to hitting the ball, a little pre-shot warm-up. For some this is a little step back and across as the bowler reaches his delivery point. Alastair Cook likes his front foot to be 'floating' – ie hanging just above the ground – as the bowler releases. For others the trigger might be a little shuffle two-footed across the stumps, or, in the case of Kevin Pietersen, a jump across and a slight step forward (unless the bowlers are obviously in bouncer mode).

The timing of these movements is absolutely crucial. Too quick or too early and the batsman is in position too soon, front foot anchored, and there is then a risk of getting stuck. Slightly too late and they might not get in line in time. We are talking nanoseconds here. The transfer of weight ideally needs to happen almost simultaneously with contact with the ball. That is what you might call perfect timing.

When a batsman is out of form it is often because these 'triggers' have become corrupted for some reason. They are out of sync. It will usually be something that has crept in without them noticing, like biting your nails or saying 'Look ...' at the start of every sentence (the inevitable effect of any time spent in Australia). When Cook's front foot is floating fractionally too high (ie his weight is back a shade too much) he can't get forward properly, resulting in many of those tame dismissals to relatively innocuous full deliveries and subsequent insults from Piers Morgan.

During the 2005 Ashes, Australia's bullying left-hander Matthew Hayden was making his big forward lunge too early, planting his front foot just before the ball arrived and then having to work around it. He was out LBW or bowled six times in the series playing across the line. The Incredible Hulk became the Intolerable Sulk.

A few batsmen – Sachin Tendulkar being one – stand stock still, bat slightly raised as the bowler releases. Since a 90mph ball gives them less than 0.4sec reaction time – to move forward or back, line up the ball and hit it – this suggests remarkable reflexes and supreme confidence. Or, in the case of some tailenders, a transfixing fear – the original rabbit in headlights.

The intimidating South African left-hander Graeme Pollock stood with his feet far apart and barely ever moved from that position, leaning forward slightly to drive powerfully or rocking back to pull. It worked for him because he was tall (and incredibly good). It wasn't suitable for legions of South African 11-year-olds I coached who tried to imitate him. I pointed out that doing the splits at the crease before the bowler bowls wasn't ideal. 'OK sir,' they said politely, and then carried on exactly as before. The power of TV, eh?

Perhaps the greatest left-hander of them all, Garfield Sobers, neither moved a muscle *nor even* picked the bat up before the fast bowler delivered. He barely twitched as the ball was released. But the whirl of willow as he dispatched it was helicopter-esque. The kinetic energy generated during his pulsating 254 for Rest of the World against Australia in 1972 – an innings that Donald Bradman described as the best he had ever seen – would have powered Sierra Leone.

I had no idea which of these styles would suit me, so I experimented. I tried Pollock's rigid, wide stance and found myself completely unable to reach anything wide and a sitting target for anything short. More importantly my protective box tended to slip out of my underpants and down the inside of my trousers. I tried Peter Willey's front-on method in the nets and bowlers kept aborting their run-ups thinking I wasn't ready. A couple of attempts to swivel my body around to a side-on position as the bowler let go left me feeling slightly dizzy.

Another successful player around that time, Derbyshire's Kim Barnett, had a similarly unconventional method, taking guard a foot outside leg stump and then almost leaping across and into line at the point of delivery. Bowlers said he was very off-putting to play against because he was a constantly moving target. But as soon as I tried that in practice, the coach said: 'If you're not going to take nets seriously, 'op it.' I realised in the end that the main thing is to feel comfortable at the crease and be as stable and balanced as possible as the ball is released. Whatever you do, make it second nature so you're not thinking about it, just concentrating on the bowler.

Image Conscious

A real growth area in batting philosophy is the art of visualisation. If you had mentioned that word to a pro in the 1980s, they would have assumed you were talking about sex – 'Yeah, I visualise Kim Basinger every morning when I wake up, and I turn over and see Gatt!' (England players shared rooms on tour in those days.)

Everyone dreamt what they might do that day on the big stage, of course. Those who were self-confident, anyway. Mike Gatting himself imagined any delivery sent down by a spinner as a big fat bacon roll. Those of a more anxious disposition had nightmares about facing big, marauding fast bowlers, or looking like a new-born foal on roller skates against mystery spinners. Nasser Hussain was so nervous before Test matches he kept himself awake virtually all night to ward off the likelihood of unpleasant dreams and to drag out the period before having to actually perform as long as possible (his argument being if he went to sleep the reality of walking out to bat was virtually upon him when he woke up).

His Sky TV colleague David Lloyd helped solve this dilemma. When Bumble was England coach in the mid-1990s, he was highly enterprising. Quite apart from playing 'Rule Britannia' tapes in the dressing room and wearing Union Jack vests, his innovations also included involving a fitness trainer and a sports psychologist for the first time, and he also ordered video highlights of each player's best performances. These were cut together into a film to be played to the team in the lead-up to the match.

Hussain, a man prone to self-doubt (I know you won't believe that from his forthright observations on TV, but it's true), didn't truly believe he deserved to be in the Test arena at that point. His insecurity came out in his clashes with authority and a bolshy attitude. He was identified as a member of the 'brat pack'. He rarely socialised and had a reputation as someone who never bought anyone a drink. Despite his obvious talent, he was dropped four times in his first five years as an international. He didn't feel part of the England set-up. It probably didn't help that when once at an England camp he produced a tape of his batting to the coaching staff, and pressed 'play', it transmitted an episode of *Neighbours*. Unbeknown to him, his girlfriend had recorded over his material.

But seeing video clips of assorted boundaries taken from a century for Essex made him not only more confident of his own ability but also drew approving comments from the other England players. 'Shot, Nass!' they purred as he fizzed another drive backward of square. It gave Hussain a better sense of belonging. 'Quite a few of my England team-mates hadn't really seen me bat much before that,' he said. 'Now some of them could see from the video that I could play a bit. It made me feel better about myself.' His response was a battling, match-winning, maiden Test hundred against India on a tricky Edgbaston pitch and another two matches later. He still didn't buy a round after, but extravagant demonstrations of happiness were never his thing.

Video is now a key part of a batsman's – indeed every top sportsman's – preparation. Their laptops will contain short highlights of some of their best performances that they look at whenever they need to check on one or two technical issues and, most importantly, get themselves in the right frame of mind for the match. In his last few years, Andrew Strauss, for instance, always liked to replay his Ashes hundred in 2009 at Lord's, an initiative-stealing innings studded with scorching drives and pulls. It had the added bonus of seeing Mitchell Johnson as an aerosol-bowler, literally spraying it everywhere.

All the current England players have software installed on their laptops that enable them to pull up scorecards, click on a decent individual score and watch edited highlights of that innings. They can even isolate certain shots and watch just their cover drives or their nurdles to leg if they so desire. These videos are a sportsman's 'bottle of confidence' – something he can carry with him and drink from whenever he needs a little pick-me-up or reassurance.

None of these batsmen's films ever feature a dismissal or a play and miss. The message is eternally positive which, thinking about it, is sensible given the fragile existence of a batsman where one tiny false move can be fatal. I guess this is where I went wrong. Every time I went in to bat I was thinking only about all the possible ways of being out.

It is harder, even in the days of camera phones, for the keen amateur to have decent video of himself to refer to before he goes out to bat. In which case, get your eight-year-old to lob you a few half volleys in the park or back yard and, remembering that he/she is probably much better with technology than you, get them to film that on your phone and edit it to 'Mambo Number Five' for future match-day use.

A lot of sport is played in the mind. The coaches and psychologists call it The Penthouse and its strange inner workings are often to blame for some crazy shot by a player who should have known, or thought, better (eg Kevin Pietersen). Why did a supremely gifted batsman like Mark Ramprakash, for example, often look so constipated at the crease for England? Because he cared too deeply, it all meant too much. Though he was naturally aggressive – and nicknamed Bloodaxe as a young player in the Middlesex team – he played for England as if he feared the worst and finished up batting in a straitjacket. His natural flow was inhibited by his anxious mind-set. Eventually he would either have a rush of blood and get out or just silently succumb. More of that later.

The modern tactic to banish these negative thoughts is time spent visualising your innings. It's a sort of controlled dreaming – imagining the bowlers you are going to face, the field settings there will be, and transplanting the video-enhanced memories you've retained into the shots you're going to play. Some do this quietly sitting in the hotel or somewhere else they can't be disturbed.

More often you see players doing this in the middle – either the day before the match or, with Alastair Cook, Ian Bell and Gary Ballance, early in the morning after the stumps have been put in, but before too many commentators are standing around the pitch pontificating. Although he means well, Geoff Boycott coming up to you and saying 'My moom could make a ton against this lot' is probably not that helpful.

Matthew Hayden used to do his dress-rehearsal in his socks, tiptoeing on the pitch as lightly as he could as if it were a precious ornament, practising his defence and his big stride forward, imagining which bowlers he was going to intimidate. The idea is to get yourself acclimatised to the environment, absorb the feel of being out in the middle, hear the buzz of the assembling crowd, get into a batting mindset to be ready for the duel ahead.

Three hours before the 2015 World Cup final, Michael Clarke was a lone figure standing in the middle of a predominantly deserted MCG mentally preparing himself for his most important (and final) one-day match. The rest of the Australian team hadn't even left the hotel. Clarke stood on the pitch and looked around and absorbed the environment and visualised himself out there later, in charge scoring match-winning runs in front of 93,000 people. Ten hours later his vivid imaginings had become reality.

In Sachin Tendulkar's case, his pre-match appearance in the middle would also be to check the sightscreens (crucial in India where often they appear to be turmeric-stained hotel table cloths draped across a line of seats) and make sure they are high enough, wide enough and not liable to flap in the breeze. The screens at the Nursery End at Lord's were too low for his liking, and he conducted a constant campaign to get them raised. Failing that, he asked for the adjacent staircases to be painted white (even in the Lord's Bicentenary match in 2014, after he had officially retired from cricket). The source of his faultless play was his fastidious preparation.

Visualisation is part of the routine many batsmen feel they must go through to achieve the right karma for the day ahead. They feel more vulnerable without it and more empowered with it. Having never made a Test hundred in Australia in 24 attempts, the West Indian Desmond Haynes went to the lengths of striding out to the middle the day before a Test in Perth, shadow batting at each end for a while, and then walking back to the empty WACA pavilion raising his bat in mock-appreciation of the applause for his century. Four days later he was doing precisely that, caught Healy bowled Hughes for exactly 100.

The modern method to help visualisation is to rehearse 'scenarios' a day or two before the game. It's a specific form of middle practice. Pairs of batsmen are set targets. For the openers it might be getting to 20 in ten overs without being dismissed by the team's new-ball bowlers with attacking, Test match, field settings. Middle-order batsmen might be challenged to make 35 from ten overs of spin. It's a good way of imagining various match situations. Whatever batting scenarios Brendon McCullum instigates for New Zealand before one-dayers, they must need a few boxes of spare balls.

The nature of sport is that nothing makes you bullet proof. So visualisation is also a way of absolving mistakes, banishing yourself from blame to keep your own self-belief intact.

Batsmen who return to the pavilion having missed a straight one saying 'that swung in a mile, how could I play that?' are subconsciously using this technique. Botham was the master of it. Once playing for Durham at Hartlepool, he was clean bowled having a wild swipe at the ball. He marched off glaring angrily at some spectators by the sightscreen. 'Bloke's flashing a mirror right behind the bowler's arm,' he ranted when he came in, 'bloody blinded me!'

'How would you know?' I countered unwisely. 'You were looking at the sky.'

I am lucky to be alive to tell the tale.

Potty Time

Many batsmen are incredibly superstitious. This ranges from such basics as never eating duck the night before a match (Michael Atherton) to always putting on their kit in a certain way, to wearing a lucky shirt (Rahul Dravid), or keeping the same frayed, red handkerchief in a hip pocket (Steve Waugh). There are some who play certain music on the way to the ground (a regimental march in the case of Jack Russell, whose potty pre-match habits also included stewing Weetabix for exactly 15 minutes before eating). Others ensure the car radio volume is set to an even number (Alastair Cook).

Opening the innings, Atherton *had* to be first onto the field, sometimes barging past a surprised partner at the boundary rope to ensure he was. Mark Ramprakash kept the same piece of chewing gum in his mouth throughout an innings, and if he was not out overnight, stuck it to the top of his bat handle and popped it back in his mouth on the resumption of play the following morning. The England team nutritionist might put the block on that nowadays.

Other celebrated batsmen are unable to take to the crease before spending time on the toilet (which is why you sometimes see an unexpected change in the batting order after a couple of quick wickets). One former colleague of mine developed a strange compulsion for pleasuring himself before going out to bat. It gave an alternative meaning to the familiar term 'wristy player'.

South Africa's Neil McKenzie took superstition to extremes, taping his bat to the ceiling overnight (initially to make sure it wasn't moved by the cleaners, afterwards because it brought him some success) and, even more absurdly, making sure he never stepped on any white lines when batting. It's the cricketing equivalent of the innate childhood fear (imparted by wicked older brother) that a terrible fate will befall you if you tread on the cracks in the pavement. Although not many batsmen indulge in such eccentricities, most develop some unusual mannerism or other reflecting the unique stresses of making runs for a living. Two words sum that up: Jonathan Trott.

Hit and Polish

Their OCD tendencies extend to their pre-match practice. Some like their net at an exact time with pre-arranged bowlers or feeders. Kumar Sangakkara and Ian Bell are extraordinarily meticulous. They like their routines just so. A change in practice schedule will have to be practically advised in writing, a week in advance.. Sangakkara plans his practice forensically, asking for certain bowlers for certain lengths of time to bowl in certain ways. He analyses it all on video afterwards, checking for virtually undetectable variations in his footwork. Everything is monitored to the millisecond.

On the morning of a game, Bell will specify precisely how many balls he wants to be fed, at what length and from what angle. 'Throw me six, hard length, from close to the stumps,' he'll say. 'Then six from wide of the crease. Then six round the wicket, back of a length' and so on. It is all designed to replicate the bowlers he is likely to face in the middle. He and others have further simulated the action in the middle by facing the Pro-batter bowling machine, which has the run-up and delivery stride of a specific opponent projected onto the front. There's also Merlin – a device that looks like a soft-drinks dispenser – which can reproduce any known spinning delivery (bowled or thrown).

The advent of the 'sidearm', or 'dogstick' as the players now call it, has marginalised the traditional bowling machines. With it top coaches can now produce all manner of different deliveries at varying trajectories and paces, and from a short run-up, which gives the batsman more scope to get into his natural batting rhythm than a machine that suddenly catapults a ball out like a shot from a gun with little warning. Using the sidearm, Ramprakash can swing the ball both ways and even propel a reputable version of the back-of-the-hand slower ball. The continued employment of a team's batting coach is not now related to his technical acumen or man-management skills but how versatile he is with the 'stick'.

On the morning of a Test match 'throwdowns' – TDs for short – are generally preferred to net bowlers. Pacemen are invariably reluctant to bowl in the nets – they'd rather warm up in the middle – and the benefit derived from facing an assortment of academy lads, batsmen and journalists (me) is dubious. This was obviously the reason I was politely relieved of England net-bowling duties during the 2005 Ashes. (I was only sending a few friendly ones down to Matthew Hoggard and can consequently claim some distant credit for his wonderful, series-seizing cover-drive off a Brett Lee full toss at Trent Bridge.)

Ricky Ponting was one of the few who preferred a serious net before a match, against a proper attack. It probably helped that his side had some of the best fast bowlers in the business. 'I always wanted to face McGrath, Gillespie, Lee and the others on the morning, bowling with new balls. It was what I was likely to face in the match so I wanted my preparation to be as close to the real thing.' If he got through that on juicy early-morning practice surfaces he believed he could survive anything.

It was fascinating watching Pietersen in the nets before a Test. No modern batsman practised harder or more thoroughly or with a greater flamboyance. (He admits, intriguingly, that his younger brother Bryan was a better cricketer than him. 'He just didn't apply himself as much as I did.') There'd be a few throwdowns first to get his rhythm. Then a full-blown net against all the available bowlers, taking his time between deliveries, carefully readying himself for every ball, bat jabbing at the ground, feet precisely placed, the stride (invariably) forward, the bat brought strongly through, the ball studiously defended or strenuously dispatched.

After a brief water break, he was back in another net with one of the coaches to scrupulously hone his repertoire: straight drives first, the ball feeder often in mortal danger such was his power, then the whips to leg, then the pulls off the front foot, a few deft sweeps both conventional and reverse, then to finish a sequence of monumental drives soaring out of the nets and landing among the distant camera crews or into the seats beyond. It was a potted version of one of his innings, an exhilarating demonstration of his art that made you relieved you were not an opposing bowler. Or, having read his book, a coach or team-mate.

Before the 2006 series against Sri Lanka, Pietersen requested a bowling machine with cut-down legs to replicate facing the 5ft 8in slinger Lasith Malinga. He spent hours working against this lower trajectory. The England team analyst Mark Garaway had spotted that Malinga looked to bowl his wicked yorkers early in a Test innings, so Pietersen prepared for that by standing deeper in his crease against the machine. He also practised a lot of switch-hitting to combat Murali. He had never rehearsed more thoroughly.

In the second Test at Edgbaston, Pietersen was batting at No.4 and in early. Malinga tried a yorker first ball. It dipped in dangerously, but Pietersen, well back on his stumps, turned it into a leg stump volley, picked up two runs and was away. He dominated the bowling, making 142 and even, famously, switch-hit Murali for six, though he was out trying to repeat the shot next ball. This all confounds the notion that Pietersen's batting was pure spontaneous bravado. It was in fact the result of careful thought and planning.

Preparing for a one-day match requires a different approach. There will be more rehearsal of the innovative shots in the nets and time spent in the middle assessing the dimensions of the ground and likely wind direction. Then, especially the middle-order hitters, players such as Paul Collingwood, Eoin Morgan or Jos Buttler, will stand close to the actual pitch and a coach will under-arm them waist high full tosses. They will attempt to smite every one for six – in different directions – fine-tuning their timing and acquiring an understanding of which boundaries are easily clearable and which are not and how the wind helps or hinders. Borrowing the idea from golf they call it 'range-hitting' – the twisting of the torso, the use of the hips to drive through the shot and the extended follow-through are all adapted from the golf swing. It's dangerous if you happen to be conducting an interview with another player in the stand. There is unfortunately no tractor-drawn device to retrieve all the balls afterwards. A large slice of the £28 million annually spent on the England team probably goes on practice balls. Brendon McCullum actually works with a specially recruited baseball coach to practise his big hitting before T20 matches.

Immediately before the start of a game, what a batsman ultimately wants is to feel bat on ball, to hit a few in the middle, to hear the coach crooning 'shot, shot, fantastic!' and thus enter the match in confident mood. Gentle, structured throwdowns are their preference. Little appetisers, you could call them.

I never acknowledged this. I thought easy half-volleys were pointless. What an opening batsman needed was a dose of realism – a few inswingers and outswingers and the odd short ball to simulate what they might face in the first few overs in the middle. The proper main course, in other words. So when I was asked by one of the Middlesex openers to chuck him a few in the morning, I grabbed a new ball, held it seam up and, from close range, curved a few away and then bent one or two back in towards his unpadded legs. The yowls of 'you fucking idiot!' as he inside-edged one into his unprotected shins soon got me out of that job.

Enter Stage Left

Once all the practice routines and visualisation have been done, the batsman is, he hopes, ready for action. The game is about to get underway. What's the scene? Dressing rooms are always hives of activity, especially at tense times such as the first morning of a match. There will be some players eating to settle their nerves, others shadow batting or getting their kit ready or perhaps discussing the match with a team-mate or coach. In the Middlesex dressing room at Lord's Wayne Daniel was invariably still on the red payphone, half-dressed, even if we were bowling first. He was always lacing up his big boots while everyone else was halfway out onto the field.

The England dressing room, adorned with 'feel good' pictures of players in full flow or celebrating landmarks, is festooned with players' bags and kit, and shirts and programmes and miniature bats to sign. There are coaches' flip charts to look at, the team analyst's laptop displaying opposing bowlers' 'heat maps' (where they are likely to pitch the ball), a food bar for sandwiches and energy snacks, and a physio's couch on which one of the bowlers will be having a rub down. The increasing buzz of expectation in the ground is reflected in the dressing room.

Amid the general hubbub it is not always easy for the opening batsmen to get the few minutes of peace and calm they generally require before taking the field. Most like to start immersing themselves in their 'bubble' – playing out the first few deliveries in their head – well before the five-minute bell rings. This is particularly hard if the opener is also the captain, and – before a Test match anyway – has had to conduct several post-toss media interviews, perhaps present a first cap to a debutant and then address the team. They have barely ten minutes to prepare themselves for their own vital job.

Andrew Strauss sustained his excellent record as a Test opener throughout 50 Tests in charge, which, with the extra demands of Test captaincy nowadays, shows phenomenal focus and ability to compartmentalise, as well as succinctness in answering Jonathan Agnew and Mark Nicholas's questions. Having practised a lot of meditation, he became very proficient at taking a few deep breaths and getting into the 'zone'. Only twice did he emerge to open looking stressed – on the first morning of the 2009 Ashes Test at Headingley when the toss had to be delayed because Matt Prior suffered a back spasm. And in Brisbane in 2011 when, as well as the interviews, he had to endure lengthy renditions of the national anthems before making his way to the middle. On each occasion he was out immediately.

Openers rarely have much time to prepare. The start of the match is usually chaotic and if their team are batting second, they're dashing off the field, undressing, dressing, wolfing a cereal bar and an isotonic drink, donning the batting gear, daubing on the zinc ointment and dashing out there again in seven minutes flat. At least there's no time to get nervous.

Wayne 'Ned' Larkins, one of the most naturally gifted openers ever to play for England, kept it simple. Stroll off field, remove cap, quick fag, brush hair, helmet and pads on, finish fag, stroll back out to middle. He was completely unfazed about the state of the match, the time remaining in the day or which fearsome fast bowler he might be about to face. The quicker they hurled it down, the harder he hit it back. (He once smote the first ball of a match from Malcolm Marshall over extra cover for six.)

Ned treated a difficult and often dangerous job as if it were as straightforward as, well, lighting a cigarette. Having flayed a ferocious opening over from the strapping fast bowler David Millns for 12 on a green flier at Grace Road, he sauntered up the pitch towards his trembling partner (me – the night-watchman), patted down a divot, grunted 'Piece of piss', and sauntered back. He had the perfect countenance for an opener. Perhaps the reason he was frustratingly inconsistent was because he found it all too easy.

Law and Order

The worst position to bat is No.3. You might be in to the second ball of the match or not till the second day. South Africa's Hashim Amla had to wait literally 24 hours to get to the wicket in 2008 after Graeme Smith and Neil McKenzie's record opening stand of 415.

Ideally No.3s are – like openers – relaxed, unflustered types. Michael Vaughan was perfect (and believed No.3 was actually the *best* position to bat as you could control the innings from there). Another excellent No.3, Jonathan Trott, exuded calm-ness on the outside. Behind the scenes his obsessiveness was his way of dealing with the responsibility and uncertainty of his position. He is fastidious about arranging and laying out his kit, his bats are all numbered and positioned carefully next to each other, just touching, but deliberately not in order. His favourite (No.1) bat is in the middle of the line so that it is *not* the one on the end that others subconsciously pick up and fiddle with. If a mischievous bowler deliberately knocks one of his bats slightly, tilting it out of alignment, Trott methodically puts it back again. 'To me if I see my gear in a mess then I feel underprepared going out to bat,' he says.

His addiction to computer games could be seen at the wicket in the mechanical re-marking of his guard. It was the equivalent of clicking 'play again' on *Temple Run*. His colleagues take the rise out of him for this relentless scratching at the crease, even sometimes when a match is over. But it is part of his essential routine, to shut out all the peripheral stuff – the pitch, the match situation, the ball before – and focus on the next one. 'My front spikes have titanium tips so they never wear down. All the other spikes at the back are really short. You'll see me going round the changing room saying give me your old spikes. If they're too long at the back my feet get stuck at the crease.' Trott takes being scrupulously organised to extremes. That chiefly accounts for his success – the most reliable No.3 England had had for decades, until his sudden withdrawal in 2013.

'Batting number three you've got to expect anything so you can't be surprised by anything,' he reflects. 'You just go with it. I don't think about my innings or going out to bat until I'm actually doing it. You can work yourself up in the dressing room. Imagining things are there that they're not. You have to back yourself and trust your method.' Contrast that with Philip Tufnell who, watching an opposition fast bowler from the pavilion, admitted he got himself out in 'the dressing room.'

The most prolific No.3 in Test history – Sri Lanka's Kumar Sangakkara – is also the most meticulous. Quite apart from his carefully programmed practice, his self-analysis, his visualisation, he also studies the play intently once it is underway.

'Do you think it's swinging?' he will say.

'Yes,' replies the coach.

'Are you sure?'

'Yes.'

'How much?'

'A bit.'

'But *how much*?'

He wants the answers in millimetres and degrees and will minutely adjust his stance, backlift and angle of stroke as a result. Batting, to him, is applied science. We will get to the specifics of his approach in Chapter 10.

Sangakkara is at one end of the preparation spectrum. The approach of Middlesex's last three – Hughes, Fraser and Tufnell – was at the other. While the top-order batsmen were making hay on a balmy summer's day at Lord's, we would relocate to the Nursery End in T-shirts and shorts to get some rays. It was the perfect plan until there was a sudden crash of wickets and we had to dash back to the pavilion. The added problem was that we had to sneak round the back of the Mound and Tavern stands (out of sight of the coach and captain) which made the journey longer. There was barely time to get dressed and padded, never mind the throwdowns or the visualisation. Once I only avoided being the first batsman in

County Championship history to be 'timed out' by going out to bat without wearing any socks. When I got to the middle I realised that I had two left gloves. 'I thought the National Village final was next week,' said Alec Stewart, who was keeping wicket. I'm glad my father was too far away in the Warner Stand to see.

Stewart was another who was always scrupulous about his kit, numbering his sets of batting gloves (bowlers normally had only one pair anyway) and watching the game intently, while defusing the occasional tense atmosphere in the dressing room with a timely wind-up. With considerable stature and a wicked eye for detail, he would have been a healthy influence on Kevin Pietersen, whose bravado batting style belies a highly insecure character. Before batting he paces about anxiously and frequently visits the toilet. 'You should get sponsored by Boot's Incontinence pants, Kev,' he might have said, unaware of a potential bullying accusation further down the line.

Ian Bell sits quietly watching the play. He is the closest equivalent to Sangakkara in the England team, laying out all his equipment neatly, getting padded up early and switching his focus between the live action and the TV. The four-second delay on the transmission means he can watch each ball twice, helping him to accurately understand what the ball is doing and how the pitch is behaving. He wants to absorb the action for a while and get a feel for it before appearing on stage. Throughout his career Bell has been mainly the antithesis of Pietersen, his approach being dictated *by* the play rather than dictating *to* it.

You can tell a lot about a batsman by how he walks to the

middle. Strauss and Cook are functional, unflamboyant, Trott almost robotic, Pietersen a touch manic, striding out briskly swinging his arms, Bell more demure, at times slightly uncertain. Your arrival conveys a powerful message to the opposition who, especially if they are Australian, place a lot of emphasis on body language. A meek-looking young batsman will be greeted in Queensland with 'Hey Bruce, this one's still on the tit!' The confident, statuesque arrival of Greg Chappell oozed authority and inspired a thousand imitators, not least the fantastic New Zealand batsman Martin Crowe, a man who should be mentioned in the same breath as all the great runscorers but rarely is.

As stage entries go, Viv Richards' was peerless. He swaggered out, leisurely, taking his time, aware of the impact his arrival had on opponents' heart rates. His head was held high, the cap slightly askew, the bat brandished two-handed across his rippling torso, accentuating his impressive biceps. He chewed furiously, as if he was already devouring the bowler before he had even delivered. He took guard – 'gimme two legs please' – in his basso profondo – and surveyed the field casually, almost disdainfully. 'No one's gonna stop ME!' his demeanour seemed to say. Fielders in one-saving positions edged a couple of yards deeper. His aura was truly intimidating. He smiled to himself and took a couple of steps up the pitch to prod an imaginary bump. The suspense was intolerable. At that moment you, the person about to bowl, would rather be anywhere else. The dentist's chair, a torture chamber, being interrogated by Jeremy Paxman. You just want to close your eyes and get it over with. I would probably have done better if I had.

Deadly Serious

My first significant entry onto a county field with bat in hand was slightly less impressive. I had played several games for Middlesex without getting a knock. Rain or declarations curtailed our innings. Finally, at the St Lawrence Ground, Canterbury, my spiritual second home, I had an opportunity to wield the willow. It was an excessively dry end-of-season pitch and the Kent spinners bowled almost unchanged.

It was strange watching Derek 'Deadly' Underwood wheeling away from the pavilion balcony rather than from the Frank Woolley Stand where I'd sat clutching my scorecard for many summers before that. I knew intimately the long, waddling run up, the sideways pivot, the vigorous action and the imploring LBW appeal. I was acutely conscious of his relentless accuracy and his clever changes of pace. I was also aware he was a decent chap. I was confident that he wouldn't be too hard on me.

The score was 229 when the ninth wicket fell, bowled Underwood. This was it. 'Good luck, Yoz boy!' the dressing room chorused, as I exited the room. 'Plenty of time! Sock it to 'em.' I descended the small flight of pavilion stairs, my spikes (yes I had remembered to wear them) clicking on the concrete.

I cannot claim I walked purposefully to the crease. It was more of a nervous shuffle and I stumbled slightly as I crossed the boundary rope. I felt totally self-conscious and uncomfortable in my pads, as if I was wearing somebody else's clothes. It seemed to take ages to reach the middle. When I got to the wicket all the Kent players were still in a huddle. 'Man in, lads!' the England wicketkeeper Alan Knott said. None of them moved very far.

I suddenly didn't know what guard to take. Normally I asked for leg stump, but with Underwood turning the ball sharply away from the bat, I wondered if that position exposed too much of the wicket. I had noticed some of our batsmen standing further over to him. (Years later, Michael Atherton did this to Shane Warne.) But if I took middle I might get bowled behind my legs (as Atherton actually was). The umpire was Roy Palmer, a tall West Country man who toured the county circuit in a motorhome, often parking it by the boundary. 'What do you want, son?' he said in his Wiltshire burr.

'I don't er . . .I'm . . .er . . .two please,' I stammered.

'That's two,' he said. 'Left arm round the wicket, three to come.'

I didn't have to look round the field. Most of them were less than three yards away, staring straight at me. There was a slip and a gully, and a second gully and a silly point, and a short leg and a backward short leg. And a silly mid-on. Six close fielders. A good batsman would think – Great! That means only three men out so lots of gaps for runs. Even a Graeme Swann would be itching to get up the pitch and biff the bowler back over his head into untenanted space. I thought – Shit! One slight misjudgement and I pop up a simple catch. I settled into my stance. 'Right Deaders, let's finish this off!' boomed one of the short legs.

I knew they called Underwood 'Deadly' because of his quicker ball. With no apparent change of run-up or action it was twice as fast as anything else he bowled. It arrowed in on the stumps, hustling past many an unsuspecting batsman's defence or pinning them leg before as they hung back thinking it was something to cut. He used it a lot against tailenders.

I was determined not to fall for it. So as he ran in to deliver the first ball I had faced in county cricket I shifted forward slightly, kept my backlift low, and brought the bat down early. It was a regulation ball which pitched a yard in front of me and spun past my groping bat. There were some oohs and sharp intakes of breath and the short leg said: 'Bad luck, Deaders! You'll have 'im next ball.'

'Look for the quicker one,' I said to myself again, stepping forward and prodding hard at the ball. Again it spun past my edge. 'Wasted on 'im, Deadly!' they chorused.

One ball to go in the over. 'This must be the quicker one,' I reasoned. I lunged forward almost before Underwood had let go of it. It was even slower and shorter and I finished up reaching out far in front of my pad to try to meet it with the bat. It spun and bounced and struck my glove, but I had pushed at it so hard it ballooned over the close fielders to safety. 'Overrrr,' Roy Palmer called. I can still hear the laughter of the fielders now. It's the worst thing you can experience as a sportsman. Worse than losing or getting injured or being sacked. You recover from those. Laughter highlights ineptitude. It haunts you forever.

Graham Johnson was bowling off-spin at the other end. He was an opening batsman who turned his arm over when persuaded. It staved off the boredom of fielding anyway. He was a handy spinner but certainly no wizard. My last-wicket partner Mike Selvey took nine runs from the first four balls of his over, leaving me two to negotiate. This was potentially straightforward. My parent's lawn sloped from off to leg a bit (like Lord's from the Pavilion End) so I was always better playing the ball angling in. The Canterbury pitch is on a similar angle.

There were still five men round the bat. I should have been

thinking – Good, there's lots of space on the leg side for my first first-class runs. But I wasn't. I was still thinking about the humiliation of the previous over. It was the only thing on my mind. The laughter was ringing in my ears. I was sure I could see the close fielders about to crease up again.

Johnson sent down an innocuous ball. It was slow and straight and a fullish length. Unthreatening. I played vaguely inside the line, expecting a bit of turn. The ball did nothing. It went straight on, stole past my bat and, with a clunk, took out my off stump. The furniture had not just been re-arranged, but demolished. By a part-time spinner. I was out for a four-ball duck. I was utterly mortified. The simple scorecard entry S.P.Hughes b Johnson 0 concealed the devastating dashing of a childhood dream.

There were two minor consolations. First, my father was not present to witness my haplessness (he was away, ironically, filming a TV comedy show: but I was the one getting the laughs . . .). Second, as the innings was now over, I could leave the field relatively inconspicuously, as part of a group. I can understand why Phil Tufnell said he preferred batting No.11 because it meant he never had to walk off on his own. It was a sunny afternoon and as the 13 players strolled towards the pavilion, gaggles of boys ran onto the field – as I had done at that very ground – to get a glimpse of their heroes. As opposed to now when it would be to take a selfie.

I stayed close to the Kent players as we walked off, got a few random pats on the back from over-excited kids and even one autograph request from a boy who presumably hadn't been watching. Buoyed along by the applause for the Kent team I was feeling slightly less dejected as we reached the pavilion, reasoning that we were all part of one big family to which I now belonged, however tenuously. As I made to climb the stairs to the dressing room another boy approached me. I was expecting a pat or a handshake or a scorecard to sign.

'Can I have your bat?' he asked.

'Why?' I said, dumbfounded.

'Because you aren't using it,' he replied.

CHAPTER 4

Believe!!

Don't Look Too Closely

'Watch the ball.' It's the first thing they tell you. 'Why do you think you missed that one?' the coach says. 'Because you took your eye off the ball! Watch it *all the way*.' You can lip-read batsmen saying it to themselves as the bowler is running in. Watch the ball. Right on to the bat.

But have you ever tried to actually do that?

It's impossible. An 80mph delivery – an average pace for a fast bowler – travels at 117ft per second. So it takes about half a second to travel 66ft (22 yards) – the length of the pitch. That is almost 12ft (3.65m) per 0.1sec. Sharp eye movements – called saccades – take about 0.3sec for the brain to generate and process, which means that in the case of an 80mph delivery, by the time you have focused on it the ball will be in a different place.

That explains why, when I came to face the great New

Zealand pace bowler Richard Hadlee in my second season of county cricket, the ball was past the bat before I got it down. I 'saw' the ball all right. Well, sort of. I caught sight of it leaving his hand. Then I was just conscious of a red blur zipping down and up and past my outside edge followed by a malicious-looking scowl from the bowler.

What batsmen really do is keep their eye on where the ball is *expected to be*. Experience and expertise enable them to work out from the information received – the bowler's release, the trajectory, the speed of the delivery, the perceived movement in the air, the point of pitching – where the ball is likely to end up. And the good players are quick enough to fashion a response. The best seem to anticipate where the ball will be even before it's released.

In fact research demonstrates that the better players actually watch the ball for *less* time out of the bowler's hand, shifting their focus to the expected bounce point earlier than lesser players, giving them a fraction more time to play their shot. The young Bradman achieved this naturally through his endless repetition of hitting a bouncing golf ball with a stump.

Obviously you can sharpen your reactions, not just with practice against fast bowlers and bowling machines, but with other techniques too. Andy Flower improved his eyesight by deliberately following a bird in the sky. He would really focus on it as it flew past, watching it carefully, monitoring its movement as it veered about, his gaze locked onto it until it was just a distant speck. He chose birds like swallows that changed direction sharply in flight. He was convinced it enhanced his ability to focus on and respond to the moving ball. He also ate a raw egg at 2am every night (mixed into a protein shake) setting his alarm specifically to do so. (Flower averaged over 50 in both his Test and first-class careers.)

The Indian legend Sunil Gavaskar went to the lengths of watching the ball as it was fed round the field and back to the bowler. It helped him maintain focus and also, over time, gave him little clues about what the bowler might bowl. 'Michael Holding always used to set off on his right leg instead of his left when he was going to bowl a bouncer,' he remembers. 'One hundred per cent!'

Ricky Ponting focused on the ball three times as the bowler was running in. 'Once at the top of his mark, once half way through, once at delivery. I wasn't able to stay zoomed in all the way through the run-up. I found that too intense.' Kevin Pietersen stared intently at the ball throughout the bowler's approach. He was particularly good at playing reverse swing because he could detect the shiny side. Both he and the West Indies opener Desmond Haynes were so sharp-eyed they zeroed in on the seam of the ball in the bowler's hand and Haynes even tried to read the manufacturer's small print. It made him the only batsman in the world who could hook a lame bouncer out of the ground and cry: 'Made in England, sent to Barbados!'

Batting in a club match recently, I tried the Ponting technique of focusing on the ball intermittently as the bowler ran in. An immediate problem was that one bowler had an irregular run-up and changed the ball from hand to hand as he advanced. It made me wonder what Ponting did when someone like Wasim Akram shielded the ball from view to hide the shiny side. Still, I made sure I watched the ball like a hawk on release and as it came towards me.

I found I was so concerned with *watching* the ball that I couldn't hit it properly. I was transfixed with the *idea* of focusing intently on the ball in the bowler's hand and was unable to move quickly into position to play a shot. (Is this another example of men being unable to multi-task?) I was late bringing the bat down and twice inside-edged past leg stump. Staring at the ball throughout the bowler's jolting run-up actually made me feel vaguely giddy. Clearly it takes time to adjust to a different visual method, and in the end I went back to my old approach.

This is the one most batsmen use. They talk about looking at the 'general area' of the ball in the bowler's hand rather than anything more specific. Many are not even conscious what they are focusing on. They are more concerned with making sure they are in the right frame of mind to face the delivery. This – a state of relaxed alertness – is akin to the feeling of driving a car on a familiar road. You are calm, your body is at ease, your mind is clear, you are not worried about what is in your peripheral vision, but you are ready and able to react to something dangerous veering in to your path – a stray vehicle or a swinging ball.

In fact Gavaskar, India's record runscorer before Tendulkar came along, believes that driving through the chaos of an Indian city was very valuable in his cricketing development. His theory is that if you can negotiate your way between wobbling bikes, weaving cars, belching trucks, blaring buses, wandering pedestrians and meandering cows, and get to your destination with your car, and your wits, intact, then you can certainly handle a small ball coming towards you with a few men hanging around close by.

There are other ways of enhancing your reflexes apart from hiring a car in New Delhi. Peppering someone with 90mph bouncers from a bowling machine is a common method. This is fine if they are tennis balls. They sting a bit if they hit you, but nothing more. It is not so fine if the feeder slips in one of those hard plastic machine balls without you knowing. Not only do they fly off the surface faster, but when they strike you it is like being hit by a cannon ball. If you want to simulate fighting in the Napoleonic wars, try it. I still have a faint discolouration on my left shoulder from this excruciating experience (courtesy of Phil Edmonds) 28 years ago.

You will see current England players facing a succession of yellow rubber balls hurled at them at high speed, or tennis balls fed out of the bowling machine at 90mph-plus. Michael Atherton was subjected to a series of rookie fast bowlers slinging them down at him from 18 yards in an indoor net for a couple of winters during his late teens. He felt that stood him in good stead for the bumper barrage he endured during his dozen years as a Test opener. In the case of the Australian batsman Dean Jones, he and his brothers used to wet the concrete driveway of his home, making the hard rubber ball fly at your throat.

Repetitive exposure to rapid fire is not, however, a guarantee of better batting performance. Nurture cannot always override nature. Scientists have done tests on dedicated club players of different standards and detected varying reaction times. More and more analysis is applied now to the cause of that – how your stance and general set-up affects your speed and accuracy of response. Your movements are governed by your 'motor eye' – the one that monitors moving objects.

There was real live evidence of differing reaction times every day in a back garden in Durban. There the Smith brothers of Hampshire and England practised against a bowling machine. Both Robin and Chris were highly talented ballplayers. The quality of both was clear when the machine was set at 80mph. The feeder – usually another Hampshire player cordially put up by the Smiths – would be crooning 'Shot, Judgey!' when Robin crunched another square cut into the side-netting or 'Top drawer, Kips!' as Chris unfurled his elegant off drive.

The machine was then cranked up to fire 90mph tennis balls. Fuller deliveries both batsmen handled comfortably. But when the ball was fast and short it was a different story. While Robin pulled and cut ferociously with lumberjack forearms – clouting them into the netting with a resounding thwack – the main sound when Chris faced the same deliveries was a splat of ball on flesh and a wince of pain. He just did not see the short ball as quickly and finished up having to take evasive action.

Endless practice never really solved this hand-eye glitch and he suffered because of it. Fast bowlers knew he had a blind spot and bombed him. His resultant footwork was suspect. He was utterly determined and still made stacks of runs (more than 18,000 for Hampshire), but at some cost to his body. In county matches even I scored the odd strike on his shoulder. (Although when I foolishly tried the same delivery to Robin it was the spectators and local wildlife that were in danger.)

Though a more perky and driven character who worked assiduously at his game, Chris looked out of his depth against international quick bowling and was exposed at Test level.

Robin, oddly less confident, less focused but also less naturally intimidated, was one of the only batsmen to tame the fearsome West Indian attacks of the last two decades and his square cut should have been issued with a national health warning. Two peas from a pod with an identical upbringing illustrating that however hard you to try to watch the ball it doesn't mean you can always see it.

Head Examinations

Hadlee soon found my blind spot. Well, it was anywhere between him and me to be honest. His short, stealthy run-up exuded menace. It was like the remorseless tread of an executioner. He seemed to hang briefly in the air as he pivoted his body sideways at the wicket, drew back his right arm and then, in one slick motion, brought down the guillotine. He was the eighties equivalent of Dale Steyn, with the same ruthless efficiency and terminator's stare.

The ball seemed to fly out of his hand and for a split second it was there. Then it zipped off the pitch and was gone, leaving you groping at thin air. Geoff Boycott called him 'slippery'. It's a good description.

His deliveries were like a non-stop express train that you see clearly coming towards you, but then whip past the platform much faster than you expect. Boycott's simple batting philosophy – 'You have six decisions to make in a third of a second: do I play or do I leave; front foot or back; defence or attack?' – fizzed past like the ball. All I seemed to have time to do was pick my bat up and the ball was through to the keeper.

I'm immensely proud to have scored my first legitimate runs off the bowler who many people would have in their all-time

World XI – the first man to pass the milestone of 400 Test wickets. It was a boundary, too. All along the ground through the off side. But when I say it was an attempted block back down the pitch that scooted off a thin edge between first and second slip, who dived and got in each other's way, you probably get the picture.

I wasn't conscious of any applause (unlikely, as it was on Hadlee's home ground at Trent Bridge). I *was* conscious of his aggrieved expression and irritated Kiwi tone. 'Put mud-off at lig gully,' he said tartly. I knew the next one was going to be short. He wouldn't have put a second short leg in otherwise. I was ready for it. I shifted back and across my stumps just as I'd been practising in the hotel bedroom mirror.

I saw his shoulder dip slightly and the ball dug in short. The next thing I knew it had thumped into my left knuckle. I had instinctively turned my head away and have no idea where the ball went. Not to a fielder anyway. I wasn't hurt. My glove had done its job, but so had the ball.

I was freaked. Not by the prospect of being injured, but by the feeling of helplessness, of being incapable. The realisation that a ball that you see leaving the bowling hand can *disappear* like that is extremely disconcerting. Especially when you suspect that the same thing is going to happen next ball.

Hadlee came gliding to the crease. I was back and across again, getting a little lower this time, trying to minimise the target. I was peering at the ball in his hand as hard as I could. It was a beamer! A flat one! It was going straight for my head without bouncing. 'Don't turn your head away!' I said to myself, turning my head away. I braced myself for the clang of ball on helmet. Instead I felt it rap into my left shin, followed by a shuddering LBW appeal that froze my blood. It had been a beautifully disguised slower ball and it had struck me on the pad right in front of the stumps.

From my slumped position I looked up at the umpire, Don Oslear, expecting, probably even hoping for, the finger of doom. Hawk-Eye would have said it was knocking all three out. It ought to have been the first time a batsman had ever walked for an LBW. Amazingly Oslear's hand stayed down. I have no idea why. Maybe he liked my father in *Last of the Summer Wine*. Somehow I remained 4 not out at the end of the innings.

Despite regular practice against bouncers, to the delight of whichever Middlesex player got the chance to hurl a few at my head from close range, it wasn't the last time I got into trouble against the short ball. I wasn't alone in that, of course, especially against the terrifying Sylvester Clarke at The Oval. A barrel-chested Bajan, Clarke was colossally strong (he once struck a six into the gasholder, fortunately not off me). Despite a hobbling run-up, his pace was extreme and his natural length short. When he put in a bit of extra effort, the ball made an alarming *splat* on the pitch, reared up throat high from nowhere and cut back as well. It was the cricketing version of one of those heat-seeking missiles from which there is no escape.

He 'sconned' many a top-order batsman, but really came into his own against the lower order. This was not because he was malicious, more because he knew the quickest route to a nice hot bath with rum and coke in hand was to bounce out the tail. No amount of sympathising about the chilly weather or the dodgy footholds from the non-striker's end diluted his intent. If he ever needed motivating, one of the Surrey fielders would rile him by calling out – 'Hey Syl, did you hear what the batsman called you? – A fat black *git*!!' Such an accusation would these days arouse the ire of the Race Relations Board, of course. Then again, if given the choice, most batsmen would infinitely rather have faced it than him.

Clarke's natural lift and angle pinpointed a batsman's most common weak zone, a ball into the rib cage. It's a strange phenomenon in a way, as the shorter the ball, the more it loses pace off the surface. A full-length 85mph delivery will arrive at the batsman's end at about 78mph. An 85mph bouncer will decelerate to 75mph after pitching. The problem is more to do with the rapid-eye movements – we're talking those saccades again – to look down from the release point into the surface and then abruptly up again as the ball rises off it. It's the change in the vertical plane that's the difficulty.

A Clarke bouncer was truly wicked. At his rapid pace it was not short enough to hook or high enough to duck. The best option was to try and weave out of the way, but, because he often made it swing or cut back sharply, you finished up doing a sort of limbo to try and avoid it. When a snorter suddenly appeared in front of your chin there was no option but to throw your hands in front of your face and punch it away, hoping it lobbed to safety.

As time went on, I realised that many celebrated batsmen also struggled to deal with a good rib-tickler. Steve Waugh was very jumpy against the short ball, often flinching nervously or parrying it over the short-leg fielder, Brian Lara never looked convincing when the bounce was high. Nor sometimes, whisper it quietly, did Little Lord Sachin (he was hit in the mouth in his first Test). Even the greatest of them all, Donald Bradman, obviously didn't fancy it. (Mind you, he still averaged 56 in the Bodyline series.)

The main difference between them and lesser mortals was they didn't allow this supposed fallibility to affect them. You couldn't tell from their post-delivery demeanour if they had just been struck on the head or slapped a long hop for four. Waugh seemed to actually relish being hit. It psyched him up (as did sledging). His greatest innings – 200 not out against the West Indies in Jamaica – which finally wrested the title of world champions from the Windies – was compiled in defiance of a bouncer barrage featuring over 150 short balls and his body took quite a battering.

The most prolific batsmen excel at erasing the previous delivery from their mind and focusing only on the next one. Perhaps this is one reason why the autobiographies of most of the greats are so boring – because they can't remember anything. Especially not the bad stuff, which is usually the interesting bit.

Watch batsmen between balls. There are those who can clear their head – with a little walk to square leg and a gaze into space before tuning in again. Alastair Cook is a master of this, so was Jacques Kallis and of course Sachin Tendulkar, despite the expectations of a billion Indians. Then there are those who fret constantly between deliveries and can't help replaying the last ball again – eg Ramprakash, Hussain or Pietersen. This achieves little except advertising to the bowler that you are agitated and expends vital energy. But at least they write better books.

The A & E Years

The eighties was the Golden Age of Fast Bowling. Perhaps we should call it the Black and Blue Age given the number of batsmen who were repetitively struck on the body. Here's a list of the bone-breakers who were knocking around in county cricket at the time:

Michael Holding
Andy Roberts
Malcolm Marshall
Joel Garner
Wayne Daniel
Colin Croft
Sylvester Clarke
Courtney Walsh
Winston Davis
Tony Merrick
Ezra Moseley
George Ferris
Hartley Alleyne (all West Indies)
Garth le Roux (SA)
Clive Rice (SA)
Imran Khan (Pakistan)

Followed by:

Curtly Ambrose
Patrick Patterson
Winston Benjamin

Tony Gray (all WI)
Wasim Akram (Pak)
Waqar Younis (Pak)
Allan Donald (SA)

Not forgetting (from England):

Bob Willis
Jonathan Agnew (when young)
David 'Syd' Lawrence
Devon Malcolm
Graham Dilley
Greg Thomas
David Millns
Paul Jarvis
Darren Gough

All these men were capable of touching 90mph and pro-jecting a serious bouncer. At least 15 of them were prowling around the shires at any one time. It made the 1980s the toughest decade for batsmen in the history of the game. Well, let's say the toughest since the cabbage-patch pitches of the 1780s when lethal underarm bowlers (that is not an oxy-moron) like David Harris of Hampshire could land the ball on a molehill (yes really) and make it leap into the batsman's unprotected fingers. Harris and his ilk forced batsmen to step forward for the first time to try to smother the threat (every-one played back before that time, or stood their ground and swung) and a score of 25 was regarded as a major achievement.

The fast bowlers of the 1980s drove batsmen back on to

their stumps. There was no official restriction on the number of bouncers – the Laws of Cricket stated only that 'the bowling of fast short-pitched balls is unfair if it is constituted as an attempt to intimidate the striker'. It was left to the umpires to intervene, taking the 'relative skill of the batsman into consideration', but they rarely took any effective action. When Sylvester Clarke was politely informed he was overdoing the short stuff for Surrey against Middlesex, he retorted 'What do you think this is? A ladies' game?' and continued frightening the life out of everyone.

Of course short-pitched bowling was meant to intimidate. Why else would you bowl a ball at the batsman's head? In fact in the West Indies a bouncer was a thing of joy, of excitement, of opportunity. It was a macho statement – like flexing your biceps – a challenge, provoking an aggressive response from the batsman. 'Give it some licks, man!' the spectators would shout, and the batsmen often did.

Whereas in England a bouncer incited awe and apprehension. The sight of one delivery head high from a previously unknown Barbadian had everyone in the dressing room scurrying around for their arm guards and chest pads and all the toilets were suddenly engaged. The bowlers escaped censure largely because many of their deliveries weren't actually bouncers. They were dug in and rose up chest high. They exploited the unevenness of 1980s pitches and made a batsman's life both miserable and painful. Graham Gooch had his hand broken by a lifter from Ezra Moseley and another, from Malcolm Marshall, removed part of Mike Gatting's nose. My colleague Roland Butcher, a daring hooker, had his face completely rearranged by a bouncer from his compatriot George Ferris.

The problem wasn't just self-preservation. It was how to make runs. If four or five balls an over were banged into the surface and lifted above the waist, the only scoring areas were behind the wicket. There was invariably a long leg and often a deep square leg, making hooking risky. (The boundary was the fence, rather than a sponsored draught-excluder 15 yards in for 'health and safety' reasons, and bats weren't tree trunks, so top edges tended not to sail for six then.) The short leg was waiting for a catch from the one you tried to turn to leg that 'got big on you'. Cutting, on a surface of variable bounce, with a keeper, four slips and a gully in attendance, was also not advisable.

The best option was to hope for something 'in your half' to push through mid-wicket or cover. But with another paceman whistling them through chest high at the other end, and, in the case of the West Indies, two more ready to take over for the rest of the session, it could be a long wait. As a result the Test records of the best players of the time were significantly poorer than those of today.

Of all the leading batsmen whose careers straddled the Evil Eighties, only two – Allan Border and Javed Miandad – averaged over 50 in Tests. (Viv Richards did too, but didn't of course have to face his own bowlers.) Batsmen of the highest calibre – men like Graham Gooch, David Gower, Mark Waugh, Martin Crowe and Mohammed Azharuddin – an absolute genius (bowling to him was like hurling a sock at a ceiling fan on full speed) – had to be satisfied with Test averages in the early to mid-40s. They would undoubtedly have filled their boots in the post-millennium run-spree in which all but one of the top ten batsmen average 50 and above. But, like Vietnam vets, they probably prefer the special bond their traumatic experiences imbue.

The Long Walk Back

It wasn't a great time to try to become a batsman, or at least contribute vital runs. Like my father, who often went for the best television parts and was turned down by some heartless director, I wasn't put off though. Fast bowling was so exasperating. You would charge in ball after ball, jar your ankle landing on the edge of a foothold someone else had dug, strain every sinew to get the ball down the other end, practically falling flat on your face with the effort, and then watch as the batsman, barely moving a muscle, would deflect the ball wide of the immobile slip fielders – 'cardboard cutouts' we called them – to the boundary. 'Why can't you make the ball lift like their blokes?' my team-mates demanded, failing to notice 'their blokes' were two 6ft 5in West Indian hulks and I was a 5ft 9in honky. Then, when you got off the field at the end of a fruitless and exhausting day, and all you could think of was soaking in Radox, you'd invariably find the batsmen had nicked all the baths.

The batters got all the free gear – the bats, the tracksuits, endless pairs of trainers – watches, sunglasses, cases of wine, food hampers, free made-to-measure suits, complimentary holidays and the swanky sponsored cars. The bowlers got the odd T-shirt if they were lucky, had to buy their own bowling boots (£170 a pop) from a bloke in Sutton Coldfield, and got to drive the kit van. It's not easy pulling blondes in a Ford Transit full of fermenting shirts and jock straps.

My bowling had got me tipped to play for England, and I

was selected for a Test trial. I knew if there was a choice between two quick bowlers, the one who could bat would get the call. So I waited my turn to practise in the nets, persuading people to bowl at me with offers of a date with my voluptuous 17-year-old sister, Bettany. I kept a low backlift and worked hard on defending the short ball, copying a number of decent players who turned their top hand further round on the bat handle (with the knuckle now facing gully) to enable them to get their hands higher and keep the lifters down.

It paid off to some extent. I stayed in and picked up a few runs, mainly behind the wicket, and proved hard to dislodge. A few double-figure scores initiated a climb up the Middlesex order (to No.10). The trouble was, with my new grip I now couldn't drive the ball (on the rare opportunity that a drive was feasible). My left hand was too far round on the bat so when I tried to stroke (OK, nudge) the ball through the off side the blade twisted in my hand and the ball skewed back down the pitch off the inside edge. The technical adjustment was strangling any natural ability I might have had. Many, far more illustrious players than me recognise that issue.

This all came to head as I'm sent out (now in the heady position of No.9) to help secure victory in a one-day match against Sussex at Lord's. There are 20 balls to go and 14 runs to win. Straightforward really, especially with the inimitable Clive Radley, a master stealer of runs, 50 not out at the other end.

'Good luck, Yoz, keep calm, give the strike to Rad,' my colleagues call out as I leave the dressing room. I have bowled effectively earlier in the match, so am feeling good and confident of getting us home. It's the first time I have batted in any sort of critical situation and I'm excited at the chance to prove my worth. I descend the famous pavilion stairs and enter the Long Room. It does feel like walking through a museum (and some of the people in it belong in one).

You shuffle (then) past a huge portrait of W.G.Grace in action and are immediately struck by his enormous size and the silly, little cap perched on his massive head. There are unflattering paintings of Len Hutton and Douglas Jardine and of course Bradman, looking down a touch sternly from his central position on the back wall. You are acutely aware of the history of Lord's (200 years and counting), the grand expectations and some of the terrible artists knocking around cricketing circles.

There is a little ripple of applause as you pass through the Long Room and the relics wish you good luck. 'Play straight, young man,' they say encouragingly. You exit, imagining a return in 15 minutes to rousing applause at a victory nervelessly secured with a cool 10 not out. You click-clack down the concrete pavilion steps and the kindly steward holds the gate open for you with a smile and none of the insensitivity of his Old Trafford counterpart who was wont to remark – 'I'll keep it open, eh? You'll be back in a minute.'

It's quite a way to the wicket at Lord's, due to the rectangular shape of the ground with its extra-long straight boundaries. If you're in good spirits the walk is uplifting, the goodwill of the members, the buzz of the crowd and the hallowedness of the surroundings giving you a feeling of self-importance, almost invincibility. You take your time, invigorated by the atmosphere, hoping an England selector might be surreptitiously watching from the committee dining-room balcony.

BELIEVE!!

'Come on, laaads – into the tail now!' the Sussex keeper, Ian Gould, shouts out from his position – disconcertingly 25 yards back – as I take guard at the Pavilion End. I chuckle to myself. He is a former Middlesex colleague. He's just having a laugh. 'Ach, don't listen to that Teflon!' my partner Radley urges, just loud enough for Gould to hear the reference to non-stick utensils. 'Come on, Yoz-boy, you can do it!'

The bowler is the giant blond South African paceman Garth le Roux, a man who looks like he could have kept the Zulus at bay single-handedly. He has a chest like Tarzan and a stare that could crack stone, but he telegraphs his bouncer with a dip of the shoulder and they tend to balloon harmlessly over your head. I feel sure I can handle him. I am imagining flicking him over square leg for the winning runs.

But I haven't batted at Lord's much and I look down the pitch suddenly realising that practising in the flat, level, Nursery End nets does not remotely prepare you for the slope across the main square. It is the only Test venue in the world with the playing surface on an angle. Oddly, the more you play on it, the more its unique geometry affects you. The slope away from the right-handed batsman at the Pavilion End makes you more vulnerable to edging the ball. The track slopes *in* towards the stumps if you're batting at the Nursery End, meaning more likelihood of bowleds and LBWs. (Prior to the Lord's Test, the England team analyst actually illustrates this to the players on a coloured graphic. It doesn't stop batsmen getting out this way. Sometimes too much knowledge is worse than too little.)

Le Roux is at the end of his curving run. 'Come on chaps, let's make it hard for this fellow!' John Barclay, the ex-Etonian captain of Sussex, chirps, bringing in a short leg. From feeling certain and confident of my approach, my mind is now foggy. I check my newly developed grip on the bat to deal with the bouncer, glance at the short leg staring quizzically at me, hear Gould's cockney suggestion to 'get it up 'is 'ooter' from behind the stumps. I contemplate Le Roux's strength and speed and natural movement away – enhanced by the Lord's slope – which has taken the previous wicket. I wonder if he is going to repeat the delivery or go for the bluff and the inswinging yorker. I remember that there is no reputable batting left and reflect on the match situation: 14 to win from 3½ overs, with Radley itching to get back on strike for the last two balls of the over. I *must* get a single. But suddenly there seem to be fielders everywhere.

I take a deep breath and try to pull myself together. I see a decent gap at extra cover and imagine, if the ball is around off stump, I will knock it there for a single. Le Roux sets off and comes galumphing in to bowl. His advance is colossal, like the approach of a T-Rex. The ball is fast but I've guessed right, it's on off stump. I move smartly to block it into the offside space, playing slightly outside the line to allow for possible movement down the slope. I call 'yesssss!' immediately and set off. Radley responds.

But my unnatural grip on the bat and over-compensation for the slope has nudged the ball slightly straighter than I intend. It goes straight towards mid-off. On a nondescript Monday afternoon at Northampton, there would be a weary paceman stationed in that position and the single would have been easily completed. But this is a cup match at Lord's and the man at mid-off just happens to be the best outfielder in England. Possibly the world. It is Paul Parker. A Ponting of the

1980s (without the hair transplant). He swoops on the ball and throws down the stumps at my end. I am run out by two yards.

If you're out for a first-ball duck at Lord's, the walk back takes an eternity. It's even worse if you have been run out at the Nursery End and have to turn and walk all the way back down the pitch in the full glare of the celebrating opponents. However quickly you try to shuffle to the sanctity of the pavilion, it seems like a mirage, retreating tantalisingly out of reach. You feel lonely, conspicuous, embarrassed, a total let down. Finally you reach the steps. The steward dolefully holds open the gate without looking up, and the other spectators in those sought-after pavilion seats tut and avert their eyes.

In the Long Room, not a word. A deafening hush. Everyone hiding behind their newspapers. Bradman's stern expression on the wall has deepened into something bordering on disdain. You console yourself with the thought that there will at least be some sympathy in the dressing room. But no. Not the familiar 'well tried' or 'bad luck' or a reassuring 'great bit of fielding!' in sight. Just an awkward silence, one or two deep intakes of breath, an accusatory look. Eventually the captain Gatting looks at me in exasperation. 'Oh *Yozzer*!' he says with an unconscious mixture of annoyance and pity. 'Thought he was effing Carl Lewis!' chimes the coach.

We still won the match. I couldn't watch. Because that was the day I realised that in this perplexing little world Love and Hate are just one ball apart.

Ground Zero

Nought. A duck. A blonger. Didn't trouble the scorers. Is there any worse feeling in sport? The object of batting is to make runs. Each run is a brick, building towards an imposing structure that can withstand the opposition's advance. No runs is just flatness, a desert. Nought equals hopelessness, inadequacy, total failure. And if you are a batsman there is no way to compensate for it. Not in a one-innings match, anyway.

In tennis, if you lose 6-0 6-0 and haven't returned a single ball, you have still served a few yourself. You have contributed something to the match. In football, unless you score an own goal with the last kick of the game, you have got time to atone for any mistake you might have made. Hell, even if you have shanked every drive into the bushes on the golf course, there is always hope that you will nail one down the middle on the 18th. Failing that, you have at least kept your opponent(s) company for a few hours and held the flag while they putted.

But nought in cricket. What has that achieved? Zero. Nil points. Rien. Just a boost for the bowler (or fielder in the case of my run out) and a waste of everybody else's time. Very occasionally there are good noughts, such as the time during Australia's remarkable 729 all out in a day at Southend in 1948 when Keith Miller came in at No.4 and took pity on Essex, standing aside to let his first ball clean bowl him. He departed with a 'Thank God that's over' and apparently headed to the races. Recently England's No.11 James Anderson stuck it out for a courageous 55-ball nought against Sri Lanka, in a desperate attempt to save the match and the series. Cruelly, he was bounced out with just one ball remaining, so it was futile in the end. 'Nothing will become of nothing,' says King Lear. You have to hand it to the Bard. He's got a point there.

The spectre of getting nought makes everybody nervous. I've not heard of a batsman who wasn't when he walked out.

BELIEVE!!

All the swagger and arm-swinging is just a façade. In Kevin Pietersen's case it is a total giveaway (and perhaps partly due to his consumption of cans of Red Bull before batting). The hectic first few balls of his innings as he seeks his first run – usually a madcap single – are worth the admission money alone. Everyone is anxious to get 'off the mark' – so named because at the origin of the game in the late 17th century, the scoring of runs was recorded with notches on a stick, starting from a 'mark' delineating zero at the bottom.

The key is *not to let on* that you're anxious, regardless of the dryness of your throat and the butterflies in your stomach, and Mitchell Johnson revved up at the end of his mark. But that is easier said than done. After all the hype and posturing and Glenn McGrath perennially forecasting a 5-0 whitewash, how do the England openers walk out to bat on the first morning of an Ashes Test without quivering lip and uncertain tread?

Graham Gooch, England's most prolific Test batsman (until his protégé Alastair Cook overtook him in 2015), found a strict pre-match routine on the morning of the match worked to get him in the right mindset. Initially this would involve a diet of fairly gentle throwdowns – 'a controlled environment to get my feet moving and find my batting rhythm'. This would last about 20 minutes. Then he would go back to the dressing room to get prepared.

Having got all his batting gear on, he would then spend the 15 minutes before the start playing out his innings in his head. 'I didn't want to talk to anyone. I just wanted to think about the bowlers I was going to face and the shots I was, and was not, going to play. Any memories of failures against those bowlers I put to the back of my mind. You discipline yourself to do that. You must only take positive thoughts with you on to the field. That makes your general body language strong.'

In his prime, Gooch's stride to the crease was confident, purposeful. He obviously expected to make runs. At the crease he bristled with intent. But it wasn't always thus. He had a disastrous start to his career, which makes him an interesting case study. As a 21-year-old he was selected to make his Test debut against the 1975 Australians, featuring the demons Dennis Lillee and Jeff Thomson. He shuffled apprehensively to the crease at No.5 and made a pair. 'Well, it's no bad thing having your Test debut scores in your surname,' G00CH quips. He adds: 'I wasn't in long enough to get out of nick.'

He is only half joking. This is a top batsman's default mechanism. To regard failure as a sort of strange anomaly. An aberration. It's going to happen sometimes, that's life, but don't worry about it. Think positive. This must be hard though, if you have just got a pair of noughts, and on your Test debut.

'I'm philosophical,' says Gooch philosophically. 'I'm not a party person. I don't celebrate wildly when we win. But I don't get too down when we lose. When I came back in the dressing room people agreed, you couldn't tell whether I'd got nought or a hundred and fifty. Of course I was disappointed with that pair in my first Test, but I had already scored seventy-five for MCC against those Australians so I knew I could play.

'I had talent. What I didn't have was structure. I was a bish, bash sort of player. Some days it might come off. Some days it might not. As well as tightening my technique, I had to acquire more discipline, especially when I was asked to open the batting. I had to evolve a method, deciding which balls to play, which ones to leave, what shots were OK in any situation.'

He realised that to concentrate for long periods he had to be fitter. So began a lifelong commitment to eating doughnuts and jogging. Gooch had a sweet tooth, but it had a beneficial effect because he always felt obliged to work the calories off by pounding the streets after scoffing a couple of iced-fancies. He became a habitual bun-runner.

The other change was induced by Viv Richards. 'The presence he had was so powerful. His body language said "This is my crease, I own this place," and he projected himself onto the situation. He eyeballed the bowlers and imposed himself on them.' (My figures of one for 99 after Richards' bullying 135 for Somerset at Lord's in 1985 are hard evidence of that.)

'I started to think I *will* be successful instead of *might be*,' Gooch says. 'I imposed that thought on myself and it helped me feel and look more confident at the wicket. The image you convey in the middle is *what you think about yourself*. It's one of the main things I repeat to all the batsmen I work with like Jonathan Trott and Ian Bell. You have to believe in yourself and manage your self-doubt.'

Why? Because bowlers sniff out uncertainty as sharks detect blood. If you play and miss, don't hang your head. Smile, stand up straight, pretend it never happened. The bowler will soon wonder if it actually did. The motto is – have confidence in yourself. Or be a good actor.

Through most of his career Gooch was intimidating to bowl at. He was a burly figure who stood upright at the crease, stern faced, eyes narrowed, chest puffed up, chunky bat brandished menacingly stump-high ready not just to defend the ball but to dismiss it. You knew he would larrup anything short so you tried to err on the full side. But his big forward stride and meaty swing of the bat met a good length ball on the rise and pinged it back straight with hand-stinging power. And that was just his block.

He was clinical and merciless. Once, when I was having some follow-through trouble with an officious umpire who claimed I was running on the pitch, I lost my rhythm and inadvertently fed Gooch a few half-volleys. When, after my five overs for 30, the captain Mike Gatting said he'd seen enough, Gooch wandered up the pitch towards me. I was expecting him, peerless batsman, to sympathise with the plight of a poor bowler burdened by a heartless umpire. 'Oh, are you coming off?' he said totally deadpan, 'I was rather enjoying that.'

Graham Gooch: from binary numbers to not just England's leading scorer, but the world's greatest run-maker. His 67,057 runs (in first-class and one-day matches combined) are the most *anyone* has ever made in the history of the game (5,297 more than Jack Hobbs). A triumph of talent and will.

Didn't he ever get bored batting? I asked him once. 'I don't come to the game to watch other people bat,' he replied matter-of-factly.

CHAPTER 5

Immortal Lessons

Delusions of Grandeur

I'm bowling from the Pavilion End at Lord's. It's early June and it's a lively green pitch. It is rumoured that an England selector is about, though I haven't seen any. I have just produced a nasty lifter to the Somerset opener, Nigel Felton, that reared up and jammed his fingers into the bat handle causing him to retire hurt. Viv Richards is in next. He saunters out, slowly, deliberately, lingering over his entry. He wanders up the far end to take strike, it seems to me a touch sluggishly. I wonder if someone has just woken him up and told him he is in.

He takes guard, a little gruffly, looks casually about the field, contemptuously ignoring the short-leg fielder the captain has posted. Invigorated by the helpful conditions, I am feeling confident and have good rhythm. The great Richards might have recently decimated England's attack with an extraordinary 189 not out in a one-day international at Old Trafford (do you remember, he put Derek Pringle over long off onto the railway line?), but this is a run-of-the-mill County Championship match with a smattering of spectators. He is unlikely to be motivated today.

I set off on my run, easing to the wicket – not rushing – hit the crease hard and send down a pacey delivery, around about 85mph, aiming at the same spot as the previous ball. It is about a middle-and-off stump line, slightly short of a length and, as if to order, it lifts towards Richards' rib cage. It is an awkward delivery, which would have most batsmen fending or flinching or wringing their hands after being struck. I took many wickets with that type of ball.

From his half move forward and across, Richards rocks smoothly back and flips the ball insouciantly from under his armpit. It flies over the ducking short leg, over the neck-cricking square leg, and beyond the Mound Stand fence, landing about ten rows back. Six! It is an astonishing stroke, of lightning reflexes and silky movement and outrageous non-chalance. As the ball is retrieved from under a seat, Richards leans on his bat contentedly. He knows what he has done. He has reminded me who I am (a jobbing county cricketer) and who HE is (the Master Blaster). My optimism has been obliterated at a stroke. My edge has been blunted. I'm just a spoon-feeder now. Richards is unstoppable after that, until he gets bored an hour or so later and flicks a sharp catch to mid-wicket.

None of us can ever hope to demoralise a bowler quite like he could, but perhaps he could offer a word of advice to us ordinary mortals grappling to make runs. I grabbed him briefly in the bar later, as he stood surrounded by adoring West Indian fans. What's the most important thing for a batsman to possess, I asked. 'A guy gotta have shots,' he replied. 'If he got shots I can teach him defence. If he got no shots he ain't no good to me.'

I couldn't get these words out of my head the following day when Middlesex batted. 'A guy gotta have shots.' They echoed around my mind incessantly and built into a sort of feverish intent so that when it came to the tea interval and I was next in to bat, I tore into the ham sandwiches like a rabid dog. When the seventh wicket fell, I marched out of the dressing room, making light of my indigestion, and nearly fell down the pavilion stairs in my eagerness to get out there. I completely ignored all the portraits on the Long Room wall and strode to the middle with aggressive intent.

The bowler was the Somerset off-spinner Vic Marks, as wily a cricketer then as he is shrewd commentator now. He was an accurate spinner but seemed almost to bowl in slow motion. I'd seen other batsmen advance up the pitch and thump him over the top. It didn't look too hard. I blocked my first two deliveries easily. The ball wasn't turning. There was nobody back straight, so I thought using my feet was a good assertive option. I could plant one over his head and make him push the fielders back. Then I would be in control. The sight of Richards looking on from slip gave this idea the seal of approval. I wanted to impress him.

Marks sashayed in to bowl. Just before the point of release I made my move. Perhaps he saw me coming because he tossed the ball a little slower and wider outside off stump. Instead of hitting straight, I was obliged to try to strike it over extra cover, a much harder shot to attempt, especially against the spin and with my weight going towards the bowler rather than the ball. It was a shot at which Richards excelled – in fact he probably invented it. I didn't quite get to the pitch, the ball turned a fraction, floated past the vague waft of my bat and bowled me middle stump.

'I always told you Hughes was a useless bat,' said one spectator to another on the Lord's pavilion balcony, unaware that my father was in earshot behind them. He was mortified. He didn't say a word to me over supper that night. (Yes, aged 26 I was still using the free lodging, canteen and laundry service that was my parents' home.) In fact I had learnt an important lesson. As Richards' words continued to reverberate around my head, I realised that it was not just a matter of 'having shots'. The key to batting was having shots *you can actually play*.

Wanna Be a Batsman Rule No.1 – Realise your limitations. Or, as Ricky Panting, was fond of saying, 'Swim between the flags.'

I was reminded of this watching the England–India Test at Lords in 2014. Just before lunch on the fifth day England were 173 for four, with at least an outside chance of chasing the 319 for victory. But after Moeen Ali was bounced out, the innings subsided in a blaze of ill-judged shots, the last five wickets disappearing in just nine overs. Bob Willis summed it up perfectly on Sky's *The Verdict*. 'There were more hookers in the England team than on a Soho street corner,' he said.

India's post-lunch tactics were telegraphed. The wild-haired Ishant Sharma repetitively pummelled the middle of the pitch with three men positioned for a mishook. Like lemmings England fell for the bait. Big bats and better helmets have emboldened batsman to have a flap at most bouncers, irrespective of their ability. It has prompted a kamikaze attitude. So Matt Prior pulled and hooked compulsively and was soon caught in the deep. Two overs later, Ben Stokes skied an attempted hook. Three balls afterwards, Joe Root, who had been paddle-hooking repetitively, hit one straight down deep square leg's throat.

The batting was not just foolish and condescending, born of a macho who-are-you-to-think-you-can-bowl-bouncers-at-us? mentality. It was technically flawed, too. Ricky Ponting had given a superb hooking masterclass on TV during the lunch interval. He emphasised the importance of coming from 'high to low' when hooking or pulling. In other words, getting your hands as high as, or higher than, the ball as it arrives when playing the shot to enable you to keep it down. As soon as he saw the ball short, the hands instinctively rose to almost chin height. He demonstrated a range of hook and pull shots hit in an arc between fine leg and deep mid-wicket, all along the ground. Clearly no one in the England camp watched it.

When Prior and Stokes hook, the bat and hands start from slightly *underneath* the ball, therefore they are doing the opposite of Ponting – ie going from low to high. It is almost impossible to keep the ball down. Playing it that way with three men posted for the shot is suicidal. They might smack the odd one into the stand, and everyone says great shot, but the humiliation of a miscue ending up in the fielder's hands is imminent. As Willis might have said, it's a bit like being caught emerging from a dingy doorway in Wardour Street with your flies undone. Remember that bit in the Lord's Prayer – 'and lead us not into temptation'? It could have been written for a batsman

Go in head first …

A human head weighs about the same as a 5kg bowling ball. It's your heaviest individual body part (except in the case of Katie Price and Dolly Parton). It stands to reason, then, that if your head goes towards something, your body (ie your feet) will follow. That is the principle behind one of the oldest laws of batting – 'head over the ball'.

All the greats abide by it. Hobbs, Bradman, Compton, Sobers; the phrase 'Get your head over the line' is all over Geoffrey Boycott's *Play Cricket The Right Way* – much more so than the words 'footweerk' or 'techneek'. It's a mantra that straddles eras. Kevin Pietersen says: 'It's all about head. I've got no interest in feet. I know I'm batting well when my head is to the ball. I call it kissing the ball.' In the huge statue of W.G.Grace batting in the Coronation Gardens at Lord's, stretching forward, head down, it looked as if he was trying to head it rather than hit it.

Monitoring Gooch on a dressing-room TV make an imperious 183 for England against New Zealand, I was struck by the repetitive wobble of his head in his stance, ensuring it was upright and inclined down the pitch, jaw jutting in to his left shoulder, as the bowler ran in, before striding into position. We mimicked it slightly disrespectfully, waving our heads about like rag dolls. And then it all made sense. It was his way of making sure his eyes were level and his weight going forward, head leading the way. Despite much piss-taking from colleagues, I copied this in the nets, when there were any nets in a wet summer, and his bat brandished–aloft method.

Around this time another master batsman hoved into view.

Between Tests, New Zealand played against Middlesex allow-ing us a close-up view of Martin Crowe. He was a smooth operator who glided about the crease, his bat appearing to be an extension of his arms, the button-down sleeves enhancing the effect. He was depressing to bowl at, because he seemed to have so much time and make batting look as natural as breath-ing. His balance, his alignment, the dynamic way he moved to the ball, you couldn't imagine anything more perfect. Every shot was beautifully controlled and efficient, yet not in a boring, mechanical way. He exuded fluency and rhythm.

He capitalised on anything off line, off either foot on either side of the wicket, with a minimum of effort. His footwork was so slick, his positioning so precise and his timing so immaculate, there was very little margin of error. His head remained incredibly stable whatever shot he played. Even when you did get a ball in the ideal restrictive spot – at a decent pace, on a good length, hitting the top of off stump, maybe moving away a fraction – he defended it so deftly late, right under his nose, stunning the ball into the ground a yard in front of him, that he could steal a quick single. The best delivery you could bowl. And he still got a run.

Crowe seemed impenetrable. He was totally in control. There was no way through. Every ball he had an answer for, almost as if he knew what you were going to bowl before you knew yourself. Even when he was at the non-striker's end, I could feel his eyes on me running in, giving me a body scan trying to pick up clues. Playing against him was like being forensically examined. He made a flawless, stylish 78 against an assortment of international quality seam (Cowans and Fraser) and spin (Edmonds) and me before realising that some other

New Zealand batsmen needed practice before the Test series. I could see why he was so revered.

Watching has to be the best way of learning in sport. Especially now, when you get so many incredible close-up slow-motion replays and players' techniques are microscopically analysed by annoying pundits who couldn't do it themselves. So I absorbed every little detail of Crowe's method – his straight bat and hands working together and his compact movements and lovely flow into the ball – and I tacked it onto Gooch's pronounced head position and bat-aloft stance. Call me Graham Crowe.

Believe it or not it worked. Well, sort of. It kept me side-on and in line, and helped me transfer my weight into the ball and I found some fluency. I made a few runs at last, and had a fruitful spell with the ball. I was briefly top of the national averages. A spate of injuries to bowlers, and Botham's banning for admitting to smoking cannabis, weakened England's attack and I was talked about as a possible replacement. It helped that my county captain, Mike Gatting, was now leading England as well. I thought if I could get a few decent scores with the bat that would put me ahead of my rivals, such as Gladstone Small and the emerging Phillip DeFreitas.

On a flat Uxbridge pitch against a Warwickshire attack including Small, I benefited from a fast outfield, keeping to a compact method of clips and glides and the odd firm straight drive. The bowlers were tired and the ball was old and I was into the forties and approaching a first fifty. I was beginning to think about my celebration. Should it be a vigorous point to the dressing room, arm and bat outstretched to thank them for their eternal support?(!) Or a leap in the air and an ecstatic whirl of the bat, or a proud little fist pump, or a traditional bat raise, blade reversed with personal sponsor's name facing all the photographers? As I didn't have a personal sponsor and there were no snappers that I could see, I decided on the fist pump.

But then the eighth wicket fell and in waddled Philip Clive Roderick Tufnell. His least favourite bowlers were anyone with a run-up longer than four paces. Despite being an excellent timer of the ball he seemed a bit jittery, even though the bowler who was on at that moment – the former Leicestershire quick Gordon Parsons – actually ran in faster than he bowled. I said I'd face him and he could take the spinner. 'Good idea, mate,' he said. Over confident and completely forgetting my game plan, I gave myself some room to try to carve one through the covers to bring up my fifty. I fell over to leg and was bowled for 47.

This wasn't just a case of over-ambition. It was a case of ignoring the basics. Irrespective of all the crazy body positions adopted by the modern batting bullies, and the violent shots they play, the head stays rock solid, eyes level and resolutely locked onto the ball's path. Watch Chris Gayle muscle one miles into the stand or A.B.de Villiers jump outside off stump and sweep a 90mph length ball over deep square leg. Once they have established a stable position, feet planted, the head never moves. They clear their front hip out of the way, their arms swing expansively through the ball, the bat creates a wind speed beyond the Beaufort scale, but you could balance a wine glass on their bonce. They never overbalance.

This vital ingredient is confirmed by Ted Dexter, a batsman famous for his audacious assaults on the fearsome West

Indies quicks Wes Hall and Charlie Griffith. He was an ultra-attacking player in the 1960s, a pioneer of the one-day game, and later chairman of selectors. He still takes a passionate interest in the game. He says: 'Hold your position. Once you've got stability and positioned yourself at the crease, you can hit the ball as hard as you like and wherever you like, but you must hold your shape.'

Wanna Be a Batsman Rule No.2 – Keep your head still.

Slave Driving

Time to interrupt my haphazard attempts to grasp the art of batsmanship with a news flash. It is November 2014 and someone has just scored 264. In a one-day international! On his own. Two hundred and sixty-four!!! Ten years ago that was a decent, not to say winning, *team* score in a 50-over game. Twenty years ago it was a standard first-*day* total in a Test match. New Zealand's Chris Martin didn't score that many runs in his entire (71-Test) *career*. And now one player – India's Rohit Sharma – has got there on his own in a session. What's more, after the first seven overs he was only on six (from 20 balls) and by the halfway point had just 60. He took 204 from the last 25 overs. It rather ridicules Alastair Cook's recent promise that if he batted the full 50 overs he'd make a hundred.

Rohit wasn't slogging either. Most of his 42 boundaries were conventional strokes, pulls, sweeps and drives, some lofted over the infield. Sometimes he made room to hit a straight ball over the off side and he swung a few legside deliveries into the stand over square leg. But it was all done with a minimum of movement and an easy, almost languid, swing of the bat. It was a stunning performance.

Some of the Sri Lankan bowling was an insult to international cricket – the medium-paced waist-high full tosses on leg stump would have been easily dispatched by Boycott's mum with her rolling pin. But you have to feel for the bowlers. The new fielding restrictions for 50-over cricket are absurd. Only four men are allowed out of the 30-metre circle (and only three during the five-over batting powerplay). With the colossal bats that batsmen wield and the extraordinary repertoires they have developed – the scoops and ramp shots and switch hits, never mind the more authentic biffs and scythes – bowlers need *more* boundary fielders, not fewer.

It has made a mockery of bowling at the death. Where teams used to look to double the 30-over score by the end of the innings, now they look to do this after the 35th. It is not that hard. If you divide the outfield into six segments – three scoring areas on each side – a maximum of four deep zones can be patrolled at any one time. There are always two boundary avenues open. As soon as the bowler sets the field, the batsman has a good idea where the ball is going to be. If all four boundary fielders are behind square, for instance, he knows the ball is likely to be short. Similarly if most of them are in front of the bat and straight, it is likely to be full. The element of surprise – such a vital weapon for bowlers – is lost.

A run-rate of 12 an over from the last 15 overs is feasible. With two new balls in use per innings, hits travel further as the ball remains hard throughout. And with boundaries now as short as Jeremy Clarkson's temper, clearing them is easy. In fact, a lot of the biggest hitters don't pay any attention to where the boundary fielders are. They just wallop the ball over them. In the two years since the introduction of these new restrictions, there have been 25 totals of more than 350. There were three of over 400 in the 2015 World Cup. How long before we get a total of 500 in a 50-over match (and a triple hundred by an individual)? And how long before a beleaguered one-day *bowler* goes home with a 'stress-related' illness? At least pre-2000 we trundlers only sustained physical injuries.

Syd (Not So) Vicious

Come August, professional cricketers start contemplating winter. Nowadays it isn't such an issue, as many are on full-time contracts and, after a short break, return to training in early November. The dreaded (fat-measuring) calipers are invariably in a fitness-coach's holdall near you. Back in the day, the off-season was either an opportunity to venture abroad, or an opportunity to sit on your arse. I once asked the Glamorgan seamer Steve Barwick what he was doing for the winter. 'Absolutely nothing!' he replied and he was proud of it.

Aged 26, I was thinking about Australia. People always say the mark of a decent cricketer is one who can handle all conditions and Down Under was where the pace was fastest, the bounce highest, the light brightest and the sledging loudest. It still is. It's the oven of the game, to bake your technique hard. Whatever standard you're at it's the place to go if you want to be considered a 'real' cricketer.

There was an England tour Down Under that October and they would have to take at least four fast bowlers and two all-rounders. None of the seven pace bowlers tried against New Zealand had set the world alight and England had lost the series 1–0. Botham was still suspended and no one knew quite what state he would be in when he returned. Meanwhile, in front of Gatting the England captain, I had just taken a career-best seven for 35 at The Oval, gone past 60 wickets for the season and played an important role in Middlesex winning the Benson and Hedges Cup (I managed to keep the number of knee-high leg-stump full tosses on offer to just two in the final over and we won by 5 runs). I had half a chance of being considered.

I had to make runs though, as well as take wickets, and Gatting gave me the perfect opportunity. He promoted me to No.3 against Gloucestershire. OK, he asked me to be night-watchman. It was a dubious honour as Gloucestershire's attack featured David 'Hissing Syd' Lawrence and Courtney Walsh, the fastest, nastiest pair of opening bowlers in the country that year.

Walsh was one of the most deceptive fast bowlers who ever played the game. They called him 'Shorty' but he was 6ft 6in and lithe. He didn't look all that quick from the dressing room and he loped in to bowl with an unthreatening ease. But something happened at the wicket. The gangliness of his long arms flying in different directions was confusing and the ball seemed to suddenly appear from an odd angle and at unexpected speed, invariably at an awkward height. He had subtle changes of pace and his bouncer was pinged down with no apparent change of action or extra effort, and it kept coming at you like a heat-seeking missile. He was exceedingly good at pinning the batsman back with a few well-directed short balls and then finishing him off with the perfect leg cutter. It took him just three balls to finish me off in an earlier encounter. It was some consolation to discover that many of the best batsmen of the last two decades agreed he was the hardest quick bowler to face.

There was nothing subtle or deceptive about Hissing Syd. Of Jamaican extraction, he was a strapping 6ft 4in with a huge barrel chest and vast thighs that made his trouser legs strain at the seams. He thundered in from the sightscreen like an enraged buffalo, made a giant leap at the crease and hurled the ball down with all his might, and a grunt like Maria Sharapova on acid. He had only two lengths: short and very short. What he lacked in control he made up with total intent. He was another England hopeful out to impress the captain. Being a nightwatchman facing these two on a lively pitch late at night was the job from hell.

In fact, the whole concept of the nightwatchman is insane. Why send out some poor, petrified tailender to face fast bowlers armed with a new ball in dim light who smell blood and know that they have only got to bowl three overs each before they can put their feet up? We are lucky that someone has not been seriously maimed. There should be a campaign to outlaw nightwatchmen or oblige batsmen who ask for them to donate £100 to the Bowlers' Knee Replacement Fund.

Inevitably Middlesex lost a wicket before the close. So out I toddled, protecting who? Well, Gatt himself. Couldn't exactly say no, could I? In fact it wasn't that bad. The bowlers tried too hard. It's often the way. I watched a succession of bouncers balloon over my head or sail down the leg side. Behind the stumps Jack Russell was more Jack in the Box. Only about three of the ten balls I faced required a stroke. I managed to steal a leg bye off the last ball and walked off at the close with my wicket and body intact, the first time I had ever experienced being not out overnight. It is rather a satisfying feeling and I got a few claps and pats on the back when I walked in. It was a sign. This was my time. Even Bradman's grave expression on the wall seemed to have lightened a bit.

The following morning was bright and sunny. 'A good day for battin',' Boycott would have said. I thought I would be nervous, but actually I wasn't. I knew I had done my job and now anything else was a bonus. In fact I was looking forward to the challenge. If I could get through the first ten overs, and see off the opening bowlers, there were runs to be had. The pitch was good and the rest of the Gloucestershire bowling wasn't too demanding. Fifty beckoned, hopefully more.

Preparation was vital. I knew what I was going to get in the first half hour. So I had Angus Fraser and his brother Alistair hurl bouncers at me in the Nursery End nets from close range. Exclusively bouncers. I didn't even bother to wear pads. Just a helmet, gloves, chest pad and arm guard. I practised the duck and the weave and the sway and the fend and the jumping jackknife – the one where you start going up with the rising ball, feet off the ground, and then suddenly double-up and duck your head towards your knees when it gets too big on you. I got lower and lower – almost crab-like – in my stance with every projectile. This trial and error went on for about 40 minutes and drew quite a crowd.

When I got back to the dressing room, I found Mickey Stewart, father of Alec, talking to Gatting. He had recently been appointed as the first England manager and he was there in a selectorial capacity. He took the job extremely seriously, too. He was telling a story about being at Trent Bridge the previous week to check on the form of Chris Broad.

'I got there about ten-thirty am and the Notts chairman invited me into the committee room,' Stewart was saying.

'"Would you like a gin and tonic, Mickey?" he said. "No, no," I replied, "I'm here on official business." When the match started he came up to me again. "Gin and tonic now, Mickey?" "No thanks, I've got to keep an eye on the game," I said.

'I watched the game until lunch and then we sat down to eat. "Red or white, Mickey?" "No thanks, a glass of water's fine," I said. Then after lunch he said, "Can I pour you a glass of port with your cheese, Mickey?" And I said, "Look, that's very kind but I need to keep my wits about me and watch the game!" And the Notts chairman looked me in the eye and he said, "Are you *sure* you're an England selector?"!'

I tried to laugh along with them, but the thought and responsibility of my imminent task made it tough. I managed a weak chuckle.

'Yozzer's up the order then, Skip!' Stewart said, seeing me in pads, donning my arm guard. 'Good luck, my son!'

'Yes!' said Gatting, 'he's going to bat all morning, aren't you, Yoz?! Here you'll need some sustenance . . .' And he handed me a cup of tea he'd poured from the giant dressing-room urn and a plate of chocolate bourbons (stealing one for himself). 'Shall I tell Nancy you want lunch down here?!' (The not out batsmen often had it brought to the dressing room.)

The five-minute bell rang. 'Umps on the way!' called out the twelfth man and there was a scrap for the last packet of custard creams, while John Emburey and Angus Fraser were having an argument over the comfy armchair in the double-doorway looking out over the ground.

'Oi, why are you sitting there you lazy toe-rag, you did fuck-all yesterday!' Fraser exclaimed.

'Well, if you'd bent your fackin' back, I might have had a

fackin' chance, Fack-face!' Emburey retorted. It was always like that between those two. It was their way of showing mutual respect.

I donned my helmet and prepared to leave. 'Go orn, Yoz boy!' people chimed as I exited.

'See you at lunch!' Gatting called out encouragingly, though I noticed he had his pads on, and gloves and helmet at the ready.

I walked out with my partner, Wilf Slack, noticing my player number on the big scoreboard (9) with the little light above it signifying I was on strike, and a 1 below it giving my not out score. I looked up at the dressing-room balcony. It was full of my team-mates, an unprecedented occurrence with me at the crease. *Another* sign.

I walked to the far end and took guard. I felt good. I looked at the field – two short legs, four slips and two gullies and a man at cover – and at the distant, still gargantuan, figure of Hissing Syd at the end of his run, about five yards from the pavilion rail. I didn't feel quite so good. 'Don't disappoint him, Syd!' Jack Russell called out in his thin voice from so far behind the stumps he needed a loud hailer. It's good to remember the rules of standing on precipices in these situations: don't look down/back.

I regained my composure. I had handled him in the dark the night before when the pressure was on, now I was free, I had a licence, a golden opportunity to impress the two most important men in English cricket. An hour's batting here, with this field, and I'd have fifty already and a ticket to Australia almost guaranteed.

Lawrence started his run. It was a bit stuttery at first before it gained some momentum. He pounded up behind the umpire and leapt jerkily into his delivery stride. My heart was beating hard, but I remembered the drill. I took a step back and across and was already half ducking as he let go of the ball.

What I had negligently forgotten was that early in the morning Syd was so muscle-bound he was as stiff as a board. Until he'd loosened up a bit he was like a machine that hadn't been oiled. His co-ordination was all wrong. He was like a dad dancing. Instead of a rapid rib-tickler, the ball floated out of his hand at about medium pace and landed on a half-volley length on leg stump. It was a dream delivery to get, the definitive buffet ball. Help yourself to four down the hill through the completely unprotected leg side.

But because it was so unexpectedly slow and I had got so low down and far across, I was off balance and flicked at the ball too early. I was almost through the shot by the time the ball arrived and succeeded only in spooning up a dolly catch to short leg off the leading edge.

I made my forlorn way off, passing the incoming Gatting in front of the pavilion. 'Better cancel that lunch order!' he said sympathetically. There was an eerie silence when I returned to the dressing room, until someone failed to suppress a snigger and then they all burst out laughing. I sat down in my seat, reflecting on my fate, and picked up my unfinished cup of tea. It was still warm.

Wanna Be a Batsman Rule No.3 – Play the ball, not the man.

You're No Mate of Mine

Australia. The Auld Enemy. Amazing what they've achieved really (not least three 5-0 whitewashes over England) considering it is mainly a vast useless desert full of spiders. The Australian teams of much of the 1980s were not, of course, some of their strongest outfits. The selectors, it was said, 'couldn't pick Bill Lawry's nose' – not that they had much to pick from. The Aussies were so bad that after they had lost the Ashes to Mike Gatting's England team one local headline asked: 'Can Pat Cash Play Cricket?'

I made it on the Australian tour. Not as a player, predictably. I covered the latter part of England's victorious series for the *Independent*. I hadn't given up my day job though, and planned to play some cricket after the Ashes series was over. I was still intent on self-improvement as a cricketer, exploring the boundaries of my potential. All right, I was fed up with Gatting's general exasperation having seen me let a batsman off the hook with a couple of leg-stump half-volleys after four searching outswingers, or throwing away my own wicket, shaking his head sadly and muttering that I was 'such a waste of effing talent'.

An Australian with Irish parents had been playing for Middlesex 2nds and he invited me back to play for his club in Sydney. Despite their poor Test performances, Australians were still hugely respected in English cricket for their commitment and dedication and intrinsic positivity (and their capacity for drinking lager). You witnessed it every day when you asked an Australian how he was. 'Good!' he'd reply, or 'Bonza!' It was so much more optimistic and uplifting than an Englishman's traditional response – 'Not bad,' or 'Mustn't grumble.' A 'decent catch' on the BBC commentary was 'an absolute ripper!' on Channel 9.

Batting-wise this was what I thought I needed: some

expression and assertiveness in my game. These days you'd seek out the team psychologist and do a Myers Briggs questionnaire and he'd interpret the results and tell you that you suffered from an intense fear of failure and give you some exercises to do, such as imagining all your opponents in women's underwear or something.

Two decades ago, talk of psychologists was taboo. There was a genuine fear that if you went to see one you'd end up like Jack Nicholson in *One Flew Over the Cuckoo's Nest*. You had to find practical solutions. Justin Langer's grandfather did just that. He collected his straggling 23-year-old grandson from home at 5.30am one morning. Intent on curing Langer's fear of heights (ergo failure), he drove him to the city centre and took him to the 20th floor of a construction site. He made him stand on the edge of a 200ft drop and look down. Langer was terrified. Then he told him to look up. Langer was mesmerised by an amazing sunrise. 'You must always look at where you want to go, rather than where you don't want to go,' said his grandfather, who could clearly have established a lucrative career lecturing at business conventions, especially ones in high-rise city centres. 'See the sunrise, see the sunrise,' he said. And, based on Langer's subsequent record of 7696 runs in 105 Tests, he was cured.

My grandparents were long dead, but I could see from my father's unpredictable acting career that his undoubted skill could have achieved deserved stardom if he'd believed in himself more. He avoided the limelight and was reluctant to put himself out there and butter up a few casting directors. He didn't think they'd be interested in him. I shared a similar reticence. Deep down I didn't believe I was good enough.

Australians were perpetually upbeat and self-assured – OK strident – and I believed being surrounded by their eternal optimism and encouragement for a few months would have a beneficial effect on me. I'd develop greater confidence through osmosis. It would do my cricket the power of good, even if I annoyed people by inheriting a habit of saying 'Beaut!' all the time.

My first game for my Sydney club was on their 'country tour'. We had driven into the interior of New South Wales for a few hours and arrived at Young, a small town not far from where Bradman was born at Cootamundra. The ground was on the outskirts, a fairly rough-looking unfenced paddock surrounded by gum and wattle trees. The heat rose up visibly from the red dirt of the outfield.

The two teams warmed up together near the changing shed and, being a 'tour' match, there was an air of jolly conviviality between the players – 'Hope yous are not too crook after the journey, mate?' …. 'Want some sunblock, mate, fuckin' scorchin' here!' … 'There'll be some Sheilas down the pub to look after ya later, mate.' (Funny how Aussies always call everyone 'mate'. Must be their Cockney upbringing. Or perhaps they're just bad at remembering people's names.)

We batted first, the pitch was fast and true and the standard decent, as good as English premier league club cricket is now (and Young was a town of just 6,000). The opening bowler was tall and brisk, his partner whippy and insistent. The fielding was sharp. Stumpy, the keeper, was energetic behind the stumps. Runs flowed and wickets fell. It was a typically entertaining tour match, full of positive intent. Just what I needed.

I went in at No.7. A small, red-faced man they called Blood

Clot was bowling nagging medium pace with Stumpy stood up to the stumps. If my pallid skin wasn't enough of a giveaway that I was a Pom, my plummy request for 'two legs please, umpire', was. As I surveyed the field, I thought Stumpy might have said, 'What part of the mother country are you from then, mate?' or 'Good luck cobber, remember this is the Land of Opportunity!' and wished me well, as we might have done in England to a visiting Aussie playing in a Sunday afternoon club match. You know, sort of, 'Sorry about the cold fella, but at least there's no flies in Finchley!' But Stumpy waited until I was about to settle into my stance. 'Mate,' he said through his bristling moustache, fixing me with a cold stare, 'you're as welcome out here as a fuckin' turd in a swimming pool.'

The generally held view is that you only sledge batsmen who look fragile, temperament-wise. You try to get under the skin of players who look technically OK but unsure of themselves and susceptible to wry observation or acerbic comment. The idea is to get a reaction, try to engage the player in idle – or occasionally challenging – banter, and thereby disrupt his concentration.

It was pointless sledging someone like Michael Atherton. He was confident, knew his game from a young age, and completely self-contained. He wasn't chatty or particularly sociable, except with people he knew intimately, and crucially wasn't desperate to be liked (a flaw in many young batsmen who crave a feeling of 'belonging' and are unsettled by simple remarks like 'One more failure and you're Test history, eh?'). But Atherton revelled in being an annoyance to the opposition, and any verbal abuse only made him more defiant.

Me? I tried to turn the Australian 'welcome' to the crease

to my advantage. I clenched my jaw and gritted my teeth and jabbed my bat on the ground more vigorously. I'll show 'em, I thought. I'm not that much of a pushover. In a sense, though, the sledge had already worked. It had startled me, and stopped me from playing my natural game. Whatever that was. In my determination to prove myself, I pushed too hard at my fourth ball and chipped a return catch. Stumpy yelled 'Yaay!' as the ball nestled in the bowler's thick hands, followed, with indecent haste, by 'Next!' And this was the equivalent of a club 'friendly' in England.

It set the tone for the next three months: tough, abrasive, noisy cricket; arch rivalry between Sydney club sides. Perhaps because they bat or bowl only every two weeks (they played two-day games spread over two Saturdays) each ball was bowled or each stroke played with just a bit of extra intensity. Brawny medium pacers with bustling run-ups would thrust the ball into the pitch at no great pace, but it would bounce insistently and hit high up the bat, jamming the handle repetitively into the V between thumb and index finger: the definition of bowling a 'heavy ball'. Your hands were bruised if you stayed in any length of time, without being actually hit on them.

Spinners would flick the ball menacingly from hand to hand before fizzing it down with vigorous body actions, making it zip off the surface, accompanied by vociferous appeals for LBW or bat-pad catches. They didn't spin the ball much but they were at you all the time. Short legs with big walrus moustaches and tattooed forearms would crouch in your eyeline and grunt 'time to fuckin' clean him out, Sumo!' without apparently moving their lips. There was the occasional 'Bowl him a pie, this joker looks hungry!' if the batsman was on the skinny side. Wit was non-existent. It was mostly just basic abuse, enhancing their earthy, no-prisoners-taken attitude to sport .

Your game can't fail to be enhanced by a season in Australia. The heat, the light, the pitches, the practice ethic, the standard of play and the cacophony of noise on the field. So many have benefited: Gatting, Stewart, Smith, Collingwood, Strauss, Bell and Pietersen are just some of many who have returned from a summer Down Under fitter, sharper, hungrier, cockier, with a new vocabulary of words like 'arsewipe' and a tendency to start every sentence with 'Look . . .'

Wanna Be a Batsman Rule No.4 – Close your ears.

CHAPTER 6

Flicking the Switches

Mr Whippy

Look ☺, the year 1987 was a whirl. At the start of it, England returned triumphant from their all-conquering tour of Australia and prosperity ruled. Maggie Thatcher was elected for a third term, eventually making her the longest-serving British prime minister since the 19th century. In their trendy London flats with their Conran furniture and designer girl-friends, my City mates celebrated with coke spritzers (a few lines of cocaine washed down with Bollinger) while listening to *The Joshua Tree* or watching *Rocky* movies.

Two months later, literally without warning, came the Great Storm, causing death, widespread destruction and reducing the town of Sevenoaks to Oneoak. It was followed immediately by Black Monday and the Great Stock Market Crash. Several of my friends lost their high-flying jobs and went back to beer and fags, and people who had gambled a lot of their money with Lloyds were ruined, sold up and moved to France.

On the cricket field, the Pakistan team was our Great Storm. Their arrival was tempestuous as they complained about schedules and the home umpires appointed for the series; later there was acrimony as they were accused of time-wasting and over-use of substitutes by the English press; and their pace bowlers, led by Imran Khan, produced devastating spells to win a first Test series in England.

The atmosphere became seriously inflamed when England returned to tour Pakistan that autumn, culminating with Mike Gatting's famous spat with umpire Shakoor Rana. Gatting began the year as a national Ashes-winning hero, and ended it in disgrace. The incident made history. It was the first time the c-word – emitted by the England captain to the Pakistan umpire – had appeared in the national press.

Pakistan ruined my season, too. Trying to build on my Player of the Year status from the previous summer and emboldened by playing in Australia, I practised hard in the Lord's indoor school (it was too wet outside). There was a new breed of young batsman at Middlesex dedicated to feeding the bowling machine for each other. That was great for everyone: the batsmen grooved their techniques, the fast bowlers did lots of stretching and strengthening (ie sleeping), and Phil Tufnell lounged around the dressing room smoking. Occasionally, Gatting sent us all off on a run round Regent's Park, which he mysteriously avoided, saying he had 'some business to attend to'. We never established if this 'business' involved eating, but he rarely went longer than an hour without putting something in his mouth.

As usual, there were a number of England bowlers injured and I still dreamt idly of a Test opportunity if only I could find consistency and make significant contributions with the bat. I was given an early chance to impress for Middlesex against Pakistan a week before the first Test. They fielded their strongest side and, with Mickey Stewart again in attendance, I managed to get three of them out, including the dangerous Salim Malik and Imran himself.

Against not especially demanding bowling on the second day (Imran wasn't fully fit) Middlesex eased to 116 for three and we middle/lower-order batsmen luxuriated on the balcony in a rare bit of sunshine and had an extended lunch of our favourite lamb cutlets and roast potatoes followed by apple pie, ice cream and custard in the players' dining room. It's at the rear of pavilion with no view of the pitch but, looking down on the back door, is always a useful vantage point to check if there are any tasty-looking girls hanging about waiting for autographs.

We were just enjoying a post-prandial coffee and mints when we were summoned by the twelfthy. 'Quick!! Gatt, Butch and Nobby [Paul Downton] are all out! It's 122 for five. Yozzer, you're next in!' Actually I was next but one, but we dashed downstairs to find a dressing room in panic and Gatting puce in the face wondering where we'd been. I hurriedly got padded up, looking up to spot John Emburey being trapped LBW by a whippy left armer we had never seen before.

The No.8, Neil Williams, walked out and was caught at slip first ball. The bowler with the floppy hair and fast arm wreaking havoc was now on a hat-trick. It was Wasim Akram. And

I, still hurriedly arranging my equipment at the crease, was facing him.

I took guard surrounded by close fielders, Imran in charge, moving players a yard this way, a yard that, ordering everyone about in his statesmanlike way. There was a general commotion round the bat with everyone calling out 'Shabash shabash! Iski wicket chahyeh!!' or something. (Mostly I am amused by Asian languages randomly incorporating English words, but not then.)

Still, having remained undefeated in my previous two innings and with lots of practice against the bowling machine in the bank, I was confident of survival. There was no time to get nervous anyway, as I had made it from dining room to crease in nine minutes flat. Wasim's run-up was short and brisk. He hustled to the wicket, legs pumping, unruly hair flapping. I initiated my back and across trigger movement. From a blur of arms and legs the ball suddenly shot out. I saw it for a split second, then it disappeared. The next moment I felt it cannon into my pads and ricochet somewhere accompanied by a frenetic appeal for LBW, bowler and fielders all in unison. 'HOWZAAAAAAAAAAAATTTTTTTTTTTT!!!!'

'Thaat's not owwt!' said lofty umpire Roy Palmer in his Wiltshire burr.

'Oh my god, how could that not be out?!!' enunciated Imran in his pukka accent from short mid-on.

Was I relieved? Well, no actually. Batting against Wasim was the most difficult thing I have ever had to do, and that includes understanding quadratic equations, reading *The Satanic Verses* and persuading a girl to go out with me. I had faced all the overseas quicks – Holding, Marshall, Garner, Clarke, Lillee,

Thomson, Hadlee, Walsh and in later seasons Donald, Waqar and Ambrose. They were all fast. But with each of them you could at least *see* the ball out of the hand, even if you weren't good enough to hit it. None hid the ball from view or made it duck and dive like Wasim. His deliveries were the original disappearing act. Now you see it – a bit – now you don't.

His bowling arm juddered as he ran in, and he often switched the ball from one hand to the other, making it impossible to focus on. At the crease his body was only briefly suspended in motion before his left arm whipped over and the ball flew out. There were no cues – a slightly more purposeful run-up, a bigger jump at the crease or a more pronounced duck of the head (suggesting a bouncer) – to judge what the length of the delivery might be.

As for the line, well, he had this unique ability to make a delivery dip or curve late in flight, in or out. You did not see the ball for long enough in approach or release to work out what it was likely to be or detect the shiny side, and there was no discernible change in action. Just a subtle variation of pressure from his fingers. And his superb co-ordination meant the ball was projected at considerable pace. Even if you had lined up the occasional delivery, it seemed to skate off the surface much quicker than expected, meaning you were invariably late on it. You were reduced to a series of hopeful jabs and jerks at the ball with little certainty of contact.

That was before he went round the wicket, scurrying up behind the umpire, invisible except for a pair of elbows, before jumping out to ping one down, sometimes, but not always, angling in towards your pads and then curving away at the last moment. This was a deadly tactic against tailenders – people he liked to call 'walking wickets'. (His favourites were Devon Malcolm, Phil Tufnell and Courtney Walsh.) YouTube features numerous examples of lower-order batsmen wandering across the crease looking absolutely clueless as a Wasim exocet bends past their hopeful prods and uproots their off stump. It was like being shot by a sniper.

I made 7 not out that afternoon. I have no idea how. It was mostly a case of ball hitting bat (or person) rather than bat hitting ball. Several whistled past but somehow missed the stumps. The way I batted it should have been minus 7. Wasim took six for 10 in his spell and polished off the innings, as he so often did throughout his career. Whatever means he used to make the old ball swing, you still have to bowl it in the right place, at speed, and get your angles right, and he was an absolute master of the art. He was only 20 then, just starting out, but he taught me a vital fact. I realised that day I would never be a batsman. And, if I had to face people like him every day, I didn't want to be.

New Kid on the Block

Something else important happened in 1987. I am not thinking of the Swedish invasion – IKEA opening its first UK store (in Warrington) thereby consigning Britons to an adulthood of poring over unfathomable assembly diagrams. No, it was the first-class debut of a suave-looking, brilliant 17-year-old who appeared destined to capture a million batting records on the field, but ultimately captured the hearts of a million housewives on the dance floor: Mark Ramprakash.

There was a spate of injuries at Middlesex early season, and Ramprakash, voted Best Schoolboy Cricketer in 1986 and who had made three hundreds in pre-season friendlies, was drafted in for the first Championship match against Yorkshire. He had to duck out of school to play. He didn't own a helmet and batted in the first innings – against the decidedly lively Paul Jarvis and the decidedly niggardly Arnie Sidebottom – in a colt's cap.

Initially he was taken aback by the pace of the pitch and the bowling, groping at his first ball from Sidebottom and was nearly sconned by the next – the inevitable bouncer. If there's one thing that riles gnarled old pros the most, it's a kid batting in a cap. 'I didn't see much of it!' Ramprakash said later. 'I thought nobody in the world could have hooked that!' He battled his way to 17 before being bounced out by Jarvis.

He looked discouraged, but we all said he had played well and I offered him my helmet for the second innings, which he gratefully accepted. He held the innings together, making an accomplished, surprisingly mature 63 not out. 'That lad will play for England,' Sidebottom said afterwards with grudging acceptance of his talent. It was the best performance my helmet had ever produced, if you will pardon the expression. When Ramprakash returned to play in the school holidays – scoring a composed 71 out of 166 all out on a tricky pitch at Chelmsford on his next appearance – he had one of his own.

Now here was a proper batsman. He had balance and poise and a whiff of arrogance. He had an immaculate defence, played resolutely straight, hit in the 'V' between mid-on and mid-off, but also could pull and cut and hit outlandish shots over the top with an extravagant follow-through. He idolised Viv Richards and had just a hint of his style and strut. He could mimic him (and others) brilliantly.

He was strong for his age, too. I was trying to regain some confidence after a poor match for Middlesex and thought that bowling at this teenager in the nets would do the trick. He moved smoothly about the crease, negotiating the swinging ball adeptly, defending respectfully. I went past his edge a couple of times and was starting to regain some rhythm.

Completely out of the blue, he suddenly took a step up the pitch and, with a massive arc of the bat, launched one of my better deliveries way over my head. It flew across the Nursery and into the indoor school car park. There was a loud crash as the ball landed on corrugated iron. Unfortunately, it alerted the attention of the captain Mike Gatting, practising nearby. He tutted when he saw the identity of the dispatched bowler. I wasn't selected for a while after that.

The only aspect of Ramprakash's personality that betrayed his youth was a tendency when dismissed for the bat to precede his person on re-entry into the dressing room. He was generally a quiet, mildly spoken lad, but it was occasionally wise to take cover when he returned from the wicket and had an angry rant at himself and took out his ire on a chair. He had an intense streak and it earned him the nickname Bloodaxe.

He was highly motivated in practice and took nets very seriously, treating them like a match, taking his time between balls and rehearsing each stroke carefully. Because my bowling had quite a lot of variety (OK, I lacked control), I became valuable to give him the full range of deliveries he might face in a game. Inswingers, outswingers, bouncers, slower bouncers (a euphemism for long hops), half-volleys and even the odd good-length ball. I enjoyed bowling to someone who appreciated it rather than just tried to slog you into Wellington Road. We netted a lot together and I, ten years older, and remembering how little guidance I'd had when starting out, offered him little bits of advice and tried to help him fine-tune his game. Not that he needed much help. Some players are just born with the necessary attributes.

That was abundantly clear in the NatWest final between Middlesex and Worcestershire in September the following year. On a tricky Lord's pitch made more awkward by a 10.30 start, Worcestershire managed only 161 for nine from their 60 overs. (That's an average 20-over score now.) Then Graham Dilley reduced Middlesex to 25 for four. But Ramprakash, who again had played for the county only in the school holidays, held firm. He negotiated the team out of trouble, elegantly riding the movement off the pitch, timing the ball beautifully where everyone else had struggled.

He looked in complete control. He seemed to instinctively understand how to pace his innings and when to attack. Once he daringly launched the imposing Dilley back over his head for four. We marvelled at the audacity of the shot from an 18-year-old against an Ashes-winning Test bowler. 'I just sensed he was going to pitch that one up,' he said afterwards, matter-of-factly. Again batting in his cap, he took Middlesex to within three runs of victory and deservedly won the man of the match award on his first appearance in the competition. None of us had ever seen a young batsman of such precocious talent, and that included the 19-year-old Sachin Tendulkar who I bowled at two years later. He was a *wunderkind*.

Ramprakash's first full season in county cricket coincided

with the arrival at Middlesex of the West Indian batting maestro Desmond Haynes. He was hugely influential. All the other batsmen copied his slightly chest-on stance, his preference for bats with longer blades and the little punch of gloves with his partner when a boundary was struck (yes, *that's* where it started!).

He was ultra-competitive and would stride confidently into the lively Nursery End nets announcing to our battery of fast bowlers: 'I'm going to give you some *drives*!' The customary response was 'If you want to drive, buy a Peugeot!' at which Haynes would laugh mockingly, and crow, 'What you guys got then, huh? Come on, give it to me, and I'll give you some *licks*!'

Bowlers are easily riled, and this would initiate a pulsating 20 minutes of rearing deliveries from the likes of the rapid Ricardo Ellcock (also Barbadian) and the relentless Angus Fraser and some spanking cuts and pulls – and the odd top edge into the road over the groundsman's house – from Haynes in retaliation. (I noticed he never got told off for losing balls.) He cherished his wicket, even in the nets, but looked to impose himself on the bowlers, too. He made practice challenging, and all the more enjoyable and rewarding as a result.

Haynes was a fantastic player. Resolute in defence but devastating in attack with a flamboyance that only other West Indians could match. He had a bristling presence at the crease and his strident call of 'YES!!' after he'd struck a drive exuded authority. He could play all types of innings and loved the individualism and self-expression of batting, but was never selfish, happily protecting lesser players from difficult bowlers, always batting for the team.

He was insatiable for runs, and exceeded even Ramprakash for vehemence when he was out, violently haranguing himself with a deafening 'AAARRRRGGGGHHH DESSY!! What were you DOING!!!!' when he was back in the dressing room, slamming his pads down, his eyes blazing. Once, when he had fought hard for an hour on a difficult Headingley track and then dragged a cut into his stumps, he was so incensed he whacked his bat on the side of a glass shower cubicle and accidentally demolished the whole thing. Everyone in the ground heard it.

With a Guyanese father, Ramprakash grew up watching the great West Indies sides of the late 1970s and early 1980s on TV, and hung on Haynes's every word. 'I was lucky to have both Dessy and Gatt in the Middlesex side,' he reflected later. 'They both really liked to *bat*, and they always said: "When you get in, cash in." They made proper big scores. Gatt might have a couple of low ones but then after that he'd go and get a hundred and eighty not out.'

Ramprakash made his maiden first-class hundred in that shower-exploding Headingley match. The dry pitch was very unreliable but he never seemed troubled, gliding about stroking the ball around with ease and elegance, occasionally emerging from his composed accumulation to crunch a drive or a pull to the fence. There was something cat-like about his method, as he moved stealthily about the crease and pounced on any decent scoring opportunity. The hundred was celebrated with a double arm-raise and a broad smile. We knew it would be the first of many. What we didn't know was that he'd make 113 more, but only two for England. Why the massive discrepancy? Well, we will come to that.

Ball-by-ball Coverage

My attempts at making serious runs, meanwhile, were becoming more and more futile. Against anyone but really world-class bowlers, I had a decent method and could stay in for a while. 'I knew where my off stump was' to use a horrible, modern cliché. I would pick up a few runs through the leg side or down the ground, mainly off the front foot. I'd get into double figures, even into the twenties. But I couldn't get any further.

Mainly this was because of a lack of concentration, though colleagues and opponents would have explained it more simply as a lack of talent. Reaching 20 took me, say, about 40 minutes. I was starting to relax and enjoy myself and consider what shots to try. I'd done the glance to fine leg, the open-faced guide to third man, the nurdle past mid-wicket and the nicely timed straight drive. Now I wanted to hit one on the up through extra cover like the best players did. Make a statement. That would force the bowler to pitch shorter and then I could dispatch him past square leg.

Who did I think I was, Don Bradman?

Well, yes actually. It's amazing the feeling of invincibility you get when you've been out there 45 minutes and your feet are moving and the balls hitting the middle of the bat and your partner's punching your gloves and saying: 'Looking good ... keep going, fella!' You might only have 20 on the board but it feels like 60.

Fatal.

So, on 21, I sidle up the wicket to the steady Surrey seamer Martin Bicknell, giving myself a bit of room, and aim to hit him 'inside-out' through the covers. I've done it in the nets and I'm seeing the ball well. It's a short boundary to the Mound Stand as well, down the hill, and there's a few mates in down there having a beer.

Bowled off stump.

At Leicester, I dig in against a spicy attack featuring George Ferris (90mph), Jonathan Agnew (86mph), Chris Lewis (occasionally 88mph) and Les Taylor (84mph). After 45 minutes cobbling together 15 runs, I pull a bleary-eyed Lewis for four. I am early on the shot, swivelling onto the back foot and rifling it through mid-wicket. It feels good. I think I am seeing it big. I try to do the same to Agnew in the next over.

Bowled middle stump.

Against the Australian tourists, I'm leaving the nagging Terry Alderman well, ducking Merv Hughes's bouncers and ignoring his unintelligible curses when I play and miss. I drive the pace bowler Geoff Lawson (86mph) back past him for four. He smiles wryly. I am friends with Lawson, known to everyone as 'Henry'. I have played against him in Sydney and been to his house for dinner. I know how he thinks and what he's going to bowl.

I am back on my stumps waiting for the bouncer. It arrives, a bit quicker than I expect. I hook it off my chin, make good contact over the head of the square-leg fielder. But the pace of the ball has disturbed my balance and as I swing round with the momentum of the shot I flatten the wickets with my bat.

It's as good an example as you can get of what happens when you don't adhere to Ted Dexter's first principle of 'holding your position'.

As the ball crosses the boundary I am surveying my shattered

stumps, much to the amusement of Allan Border who is guffawing at second slip. It was about the only time he smiled all
tour until the Australians won the Test series 4-0 and regained
the Ashes.

My county colleagues underlined what they thought of my
batting at Trent Bridge one day. We were playing for a draw,
and, with about 12 overs left to survive, I came in at No.9.
With the memory of fending off Malcolm Marshall for a session to save a match fairly fresh in my mind, I felt quite
confident of achieving the task. As usual I walked out to the
middle putting my gloves on, my bat under my arm. It was
only when I arrived at the crease that I discovered a condom
stretched neatly over the bat handle. I removed it, half amused
half irritated, and handed it to the square-leg umpire, Nigel
Plews, a former policeman. 'At least it's not a used one!' he
said.

I settled down to face Franklyn Stephenson, the gangling
West Indian pace bowler with a brilliant change of pace. He
smelled victory, but I was determined to keep him out. I
blocked the first delivery, but the bat slipped out of my hands.
The lubricant from the condom had got onto the bat handle
and I couldn't grip it. It was the middle of the over, so I went
down the wicket to my partner John Emburey and swapped
bats till I could call for a replacement. But the lubricant was
now on my gloves and *his* bat twice slipped out of my hands
during the remainder of the over, although I managed a couple
of runs. I gripped the bat tighter for the last ball, but the force
of the delivery knocked it sideways and I dragged the ball into
my stumps.

I returned the bat to an agitated-looking Emburey and

retrieved mine as I walked disconsolately off. But the lubricant had now transferred itself to *his* bat handle via my gloves. It rendered his bat ungrippable and he was bowled off a bottom edge shortly afterwards. We were bowled out with ten overs left. The dressing room was not a happy place.

Getting into the Zone

In fact, despite this catalogue of errors, the fundamental difference between me and a proper batsman wasn't basic ability. It was attitude. People will say there were issues of hand-eye coordination and eyesight. Possibly. But if I was quick enough to hook a fast bowler like Geoff Lawson to the boundary, there was not a lot wrong with my reflexes (even if I did overbalance onto my stumps). In any case, the professor of physics at Adelaide University tested Donald Bradman's eyesight and discovered his reactions to be slightly *slower* than the average student's.

What Bradman, and all other great players, had from an early age was an ability to focus, *and stay focused*, on the job. Scoring runs was their mission, not entertaining people, or themselves. (Although they drew deep satisfaction and enjoyment from scoring lots of runs.) They were blessed with a natural ability to concentrate and developed a system to maintain it. They would not be distracted by a desire to look good or show off. It became part of their DNA. As Bradman wrote, 'Concentration must be cultivated by anyone who wishes to rise to international standards.' An intense, unwavering focus – at the appropriate moment – was/is the essential ingredient of any prolific batsmen. It is also what makes many of them –

Bradman, Boycott, Gower, Atherton, Tendulkar, Kallis, Cook – slightly impenetrable characters.

What actually is concentration? It's a state, a mindset. It's the ability to focus on one object or thought, and exclude from your mind anything that's unrelated. It's the ability to do one thing at a time. It's the opposite of multi-tasking, which is probably why men who are especially good at batting (therefore concentrating) are useless at looking after three kids. And vice versa.

Some were born with it (Boycott, Atherton). Some acquire it (Gooch, Strauss). I've definitely not got it, as in the course of writing these last two paragraphs I've answered the phone, checked my emails, tweeted, watched a bit of Professor Brian Cox's *Human Universe* with Billy, my supposedly 'ill' 11-year-old son, looked up prices of flights to Barbados, and been to Sainsbury's where I had a ten-minute discussion with the fishmonger about Kevin Pietersen calling young county pros 'muppets'.

I have trouble writing my 600-word analysis of a Test match day in a commentary box, with Michael Vaughan planning his social engagements, Mark Nicholas humming songs from his favourite Springsteen album and Geoffrey Boycott telling us – for the 20th time – what Fred Trueman used to say to women after he'd had sex with them ('That all right for thee, then?!' – it's funny when he tells it), while Di, our long-suffering Channel 5 producer, keeps reminding us that the game is still going on. Whereas Atherton has no problem knocking off his 1200-word *Times* match report despite similar late-afternoon distractions.

The longest I ever batted was about two hours (the match

against Nicholas and Marshall's Hampshire, luckily on a feath-erbed of a pitch). It was just as well the umpires called 'time' there when they did. I couldn't have lasted one more minute. If there had been another ball, I would have had a massive slog. I was mentally spent. I have no idea how anyone can concen-trate in the middle for longer. So here I will defer to the man who, aged just 21, batted for more than ten hours to make the (then) record Test score of 365 not out: the remarkable Garfield Sobers.

I chatted to him recently on his favourite stamping ground – the Sandy Lane golf course in Barbados. 'I used to hold my concentration by walking down the wicket after the bowler's bowled, find something to do, pat the pitch, fiddle with my gloves, or walk away somewhere, until the bowler was ready to run in again. Then I'd switch on. That's where a lot of play-ers make mistakes. They stand up there waiting for the bowler to bowl and they're thinking "I wonder if he's going to bowl me an outswinger, I wonder if he's going to bowl a bouncer." That's all concentration that you don't need.

'Clyde Walcott got me to the three hundred and sixty-five. After I'd got to three hundred and one, he came to me and he said: "Listen son, you only need sixty-four more runs," and I said "What's that for, sir?" And he said: "For the world record! So put your head down, you only pass this way once." The only way I could get those sixty-four runs was to think that they weren't for me but for the team. I had to believe that West Indies really needed them [despite the fact that they were 720 for three at the time]. And that's what made me get my head down and pass the world record.'

Sobers makes reference to the 'switch off switch on' method

which a lot of batsmen use to maintain their focus during a long innings. Switching *off* was obviously very important to him. He regales the time he put on 399 with Frank Worrell against England in Barbados. The partnership spanned three days' play and a rest day in between. 'Frank and I were rooming together at the Marine hotel and I would wait at the bar till two or three o'clock in the morning until Frank got in. Then we'd have a drink and go to bed about four. If he got in before me, he'd wait for me. It never worked for me going to bed at, say, ten o'clock. On one tour of England, that's what we were told to do. The thought of Trueman and Statham bowling at me kept me awake all night. If I went to bed late I slept and I forgot all about cricket until I arrived at the ground.' Switching on and off between balls was just an extension of Sobers' natural lifestyle.

It's a technique you can learn. Graham Gooch was, by his own admission, a dasher when he started. He had, he said, no structure. His innings were a bit of a lottery. He eventually turned himself into a remorseless accumulator of runs – the most prolific batsman England had ever produced. Remember his epic 333, also lasting ten hours, against India in 1990? Well, even that wasn't enough. He made 123 in the second innings as well. It's the definition of gluttony.

The key to this evolution was disciplining himself to bat for a long time, and finding a routine that worked. 'It's important to draw a line under each ball,' Gooch says. 'It's gone, forget it, move on. I remember picking that up from Barry Richards. After every ball, he scratched his guard again with his spikes. Didn't matter what had happened. It was his way of shutting down his mind, clearing his head, switching off. He'd wait until the bowler was about to turn, then he'd get into his stance and switch on again. That way you can sustain maximum concentration on every ball.'

Gooch identifies with the way Rafael Nadal plays tennis – a sport that demands similar intermittent bursts of concentration. 'He looks fairly relaxed at the back of the court between points, he doesn't betray much emotion or beat himself up. But he plays every point as if it's his last.'

Drawing inspiration or ideas from other sports is becoming more common. After a disappointing 2013 season for Yorkshire, in which he scored two hundreds and averaged 34, the emerging English opener Adam Lyth used golf to help enhance his concentration. Encouraged by Yorkshire's sports psychologist Simon Hartley, he went to a nearby course and practised holing as many two-foot putts in a row as he could.

'Professional golfers only get to about a hundred before they miss one,' Lyth said, 'but I got two hundred and thirteen on the run. You shouldn't really miss, should you, so it's all about concentration. It took me about an hour and a half. It just shows that I wasn't concentrating on my two hundred and fourteenth one because I missed it.' The acquired discipline had a major impact on his batting. In 2014, he made seven hundreds, including two doubles, averaged 70 and was voted PCA Player of the Season. If he doesn't make it with England in the near future, he could always coach Lee Westwood.

Here's the deal. Assume that, from the start of the bowler's run-up to the time when the ball comes to rest, the ball is live for an average of only six seconds per delivery. That means there's only about 45 minutes actual play in a whole Test match day (you see, a highlights programme of 48 minutes is perfect!).

South Africa's video analyst bolted together every delivery of Daryl Cullinan's career-best score of 275 and the recording lasted just 16 minutes. In other words, for a batsman there is a lot of time to kill between balls. Conserving physical and mental energy during that time is the key to longevity at the crease.

Batsmen evolve their own ways of doing this. Rahul Dravid, who faced more balls than anyone in the history of Test cricket (31,258), preceded each with a little step away from the crease to briefly think about anything other than cricket before regaining his stance and taking 'two deep breaths' which was his cue to re-engage. Cullinan would look up at the sky, across at friends and family in the stand, wonder what they were saying, then look down at his gloves which had W for 'watch the ball' and S for 'play straight' written on them before looking up at the bowler.

Justin Langer hummed to himself at the wicket to shut out all the extraneous noise between balls and avoid getting distracted. Andrew Strauss listened to meditation tapes before a Test match and in the middle, having played the ball, stepped away and 'concentrated on my breathing, especially if there was too much going on in my mind. It's a great way to stay in your bubble, oblivious to the crowd, the opposition, the situation. Then I'd resume my stance and, after four taps of the bat on the ground I'd look up and focus again.'

When Channel 4 broadcast Test cricket and introduced fixed wicket-to-wicket cameras at each end (to adjudicate LBWs with the 'red zone'), I spent a lot of time in the VT truck (the 'caravan' as it was known) watching batsmen between deliveries. Yes, I know I needed to get out more. But

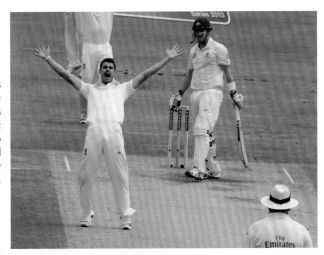

Shane Watson falls LBW for 20 in the 2013 Ashes. His failure to convert decent starts into centuries had caused him to call The Analyst.

Colin Cowdrey in action during the 1968 Ashes series, when he became the first player ever to appear in 100 Tests. As a boy I tried to emulate his effortless style.

You wouldn't have thought a whippersnapper like Malcolm Marshall could cause such damage to a big hairy brute like Mike Gatting, but Marshall was seriously fast. The ball removed a piece of Gatting's nose during a one-day international at Sabina Park in 1985-86.

Batsmen evolved many different methods at the crease to try to enhance their ability: Don Bradman's stance (*above left*) was quite unconventional – bat between the feet, blade turned inwards, head tilted to the offside, but it wasn't as unorthodox as Peter Willey's eccentric two-eyed stance (*below*), though he adjusted to a more conventional position as the bowler released. Brian Lara's extravagantly high backlift (*above right*) was the source of his amazing bat speed, but it occasionally made him vulnerable to a fast yorker.

Steve Waugh fends off just one of the 150 short-pitched deliveries that came his way during his mammoth knock of 200 against the West Indies in Kingston in 1995.

Graham Gooch allowed a rare opportunity to play off the front foot during his courageous undefeated 154 against the West Indies at Headingley in 1991. Made out of England's total of 252 all out, it has been voted as one of the greatest innings ever played.

'A guy gotta have shots' – and Viv Richards had plenty, as he demonstrated during his blistering 189 not out against England in 1984. Derek Pringle is the suffering bowler here.

Ricky Ponting was a phenomenal puller of the ball, maximising control, placement and power, making him very hard to contain.

Garry Sobers had remarkable power and flexibility and a follow through borrowed from golf that many modern T20 players seek to emulate.

Mark Ramprakash falls to the pace of Ian Bishop in the Lord's Test of 1995. One of England's most precociously talented batsmen suffered not just at the hands of an awesome West Indies attack but from his own intensity and the vagaries of selection.

Mike Atherton's famous duel with South Africa's Allan Donald at Trent Bridge in 1998. Despite Donald's furious pace, Atherton was as tough as teak.

The most prolific century-maker in history, Sachin Tendulkar looks up in relief after reaching his 100th international hundred after 33 innings stuck on 99. Notice the unusual bow in his bat. When he began his Test career bats were about half that width.

Kevin Pietersen turns left hander to deposit Scott Styris for six – one of the greatest shots ever played.

Modern helmets, supreme agility and outrageous audacity facilitate amazing shots like this one from Brendon McCullum during an IPL match. T20 has made batting a true 360 degree adventure.

Breathtaking ingenuity and astonishing hand-eye co-
ordination from A.B.de Villiers during the Cricket World
Cup in 2015. This kind of shot borrows much from de
Villiers' diverse sporting background and renders the stumps
practically irrelevant.

Laser-guided precision from the immaculate Kumar Sangakkara – notice the superb
balance and poise – during his meticulously planned century at Lord's in 2014.

An incident that sums up my batting. I pull Australia's Geoff Lawson to the boundary for four but annihilate my stumps in the process. Ian Healy is the amused keeper.

Now THAT's how to play the pull shot – Nancy Hughes, the author's daughter, striking one of her six sixes in the final of the Middlesex Under-15 girls' league in 2014.

their behaviour was revealing. Marcus Trescothick, a fairly relaxed, laconic sort of soul, leant on his bat between balls as if he was resting on a gatepost chatting to a neighbour. Andrew Strauss and Alastair Cook each went for a little routine walk to square leg and back. Michael Vaughan stood calmly at the crease and re-marked his guard. In their different ways they all looked at ease.

But a youthful Ian Bell rehearsed strokes and fussed with his equipment, and Kevin Pietersen was hyperactive, replaying shots, tapping the pitch, hitching up the short sleeves of his shirt to make his biceps bulge more or flexing his hamstrings. Neither Bell nor Pietersen looked at all at ease, and were much more likely to play a loose shot, which the commentators would often explain as 'a lapse in concentration'.

That is exactly what it was. They hadn't yet evolved a fool-proof method to ensure they didn't lose focus. They were either stressed, or tired, or overexcited and they allowed it to affect them. Bell admitted, after his Test debut, that he had 'tried to take in everything', meaning the opposition, the crowd, the state of the match, the media coverage etc. It was understandable but the wrong way to go – inevitably mentally draining.

Sports psychologists have helped him and others develop better routines to help dissipate the build-up of pressure in the middle. These include diluting their focus between balls – applying what they call the 'dimmer switch' to their concentration – briefly taking their mind off the cricket and thinking about something else – music, holidays, the credit-card roulette they lost last night – before switching on again as the bowler turned at the end of his mark.

'Focusing intently uses up lots of energy,' says Dr Jamie Barker, a sports psychologist attached to the ECB and the co-author of *The Psychology of Cricket*. 'Neuroscientists have worked out that the brain burns twenty-five per cent of the daily calories you consume. No wonder you feel tired after making your brain work so hard. You have to learn to switch on (focus) and switch off (relax). On an Indian tour I got one batsman to tune in to the sounds of the car horns to help him relax between balls.' (Not that imagining the riot of Indian roads would necessarily be relaxing.)

Wanna Be a Batsman Rule No.5 – Locate the dimmer switch.

Cracking under Pressure

I thought back to Mark Ramprakash's initial foray into Test cricket in 1991. He had had an excellent season for Middlesex in 1990, scoring five hundreds, and deserved his England selection. His promotion was a big story in the press – a 21-year-old prodigy of Guyanese extraction pitched in against the invincible West Indies. It was a baptism of fire. He was batting at No.5 against an attack of Ambrose, Marshall, Walsh and Patterson. They were seasoned assassins. He had barely started shaving.

I bowled to him a lot before his Test debut, sacrificing having a (largely pointless) net myself to give him a longer knock. I tried to replicate the actions of the men who he was going to face – especially the whippy Marshall and the slightly open-chested Walsh – though I would have needed to bowl in stilts to mimic Ambrose. It was of negligible help (and his bowling imitations were way better than mine), but

I passed on everything I knew about the way they bowled: how Walsh pinned you on the back foot before pitching one up; Marshall's preference to try to nip the ball *up* the Lord's slope from the Nursery End looking for LBWs; and Patterson's vicious bouncer and murderous stare. He seemed capable of handling anything that the bowlers could hurl at him. He had an impregnable defence, great balance and timing and every shot in the book. I believed he would be an instant success.

England were 45 for three when Ramprakash came in to play his first Test innings. I watched him as if he were my son – keenly, nervously, willing him on, cursing when his partner, Robin Smith, wasn't backing up properly for singles. I kept his score and practically counted the balls faced. He batted, almost faultlessly, for two hours 20 minutes, scoring 27 before edging Marshall to second slip. It was a solid beginning. He matched it identically in the second innings. It encapsulated his series. He stayed at the crease for more than 17 hours in the five matches, battling it out in awkward conditions and unfavourable situations. He was never dismissed for single figures, but never got out of the twenties either.

He never found the natural fluency and panache of his batting for Middlesex. That, of course, was partly due to the quality of the bowling. But he was so intense at the crease, constantly rehearsing his defence between balls and looked generally anxious, as if he didn't know what to do. His defence was immaculate, but rarely did he ever play an aggressive shot. He was ultra-committed but seemed intent only on survival. Never was there a moment of relaxation. The pressure was immense. And that was the problem. Eventually, after two hours of resistance, he would crack. He had nothing left to give.

When he reflected on that series recently, he admitted he got it wrong. 'I probably showed them too much respect,' he said. 'I wasn't proactive enough. I wasn't alone. They were a superb attack. Graeme Hick struggled and he had a lot more experience than me. An excellent player like Allan Lamb didn't last the series. He thought we should be more aggressive, get after the bowlers a bit, even just quick singles. Test cricket didn't have the run rates then that it does now and I didn't feel able to do that. There was so much going on in my mind, I wasn't playing the game.'

He was of course only 21, in his first Test series. You felt for him. He would have benefited hugely from someone helping him with his demeanour at the crease, and introducing some techniques to relax more and clear his mind between balls. But there was no one to turn to. England's support staff consisted only of the manager, Mickey Stewart, and the physio, Laurie Brown, rather than the legions of coaches and analysts and psychologists it does now. There was no one to confide in and, as he was the quiet type who didn't drink or socialise much, he just bottled it all up.

Batting in a club match in north London recently, I tried some of the methods Dr Barker recommends to sustain concentration for long periods. I focused intently on the ball in the bowler's hand as he was running in and tried to watch it onto the bat. Then, I walked away from the crease, and looked at an old bloke hunched over his radishes in the neighbouring allotments, or watched the buses trundling along Park Road, remembering the time I had parked my fiancée's car outside a nearby flat, accidentally leaving the keys in the car door. When I came out ten minutes later, the car had been nicked. (No, the marriage didn't last long.)

I concentrated on my breathing, ignoring the wicketkeeper's attempts to engage me in conversation, and the captain's Urdu instructions to his bowler, though I was aware of a young lad at cover saying: 'Come on Saj, knock this old guy over!' I didn't worry about looking a bit at sea early on (I hadn't batted for about three years), or failing to connect with a ball down the leg side or the fact that one of the bowlers was almost certainly a chucker. Each time as the bowler was about to turn, I looked down at the crease, placed my bat in position and tapped it three times, then looked up, saying 'Watch the ball' to myself.

It worked. I played each ball on its merits and didn't fret about nearly dragging one on or mistiming a drive or playing out a maiden. I didn't attempt to play strokes that I knew I couldn't. I stuck to the ones I knew I could (a block-drive). I took my time between deliveries, and tried to inhabit my 'bubble' (ie shutting out all the peripherals). Before I knew it, I had hit eight boundaries, all straight or through the off side, and I was on 45. I was feeling good.

Then guess what I did? At the beginning of a new over, I eyed up the short, mainly unprotected boundary on the leg side. I decided I was going to make a bit of a statement and hit one into that allotment at not-very-deep mid-wicket. That would be an excellent way to go to fifty. It would impress my team-mates (including my elder son) and finally silence the lad who'd been calling me old. A tall youth was bowling modest medium pace. As he was about to let go of the ball, I stepped across my stumps A.B.de Villiers-style, planted my front leg down the pitch and swung hard in the direction of mid-wicket. With the big modern bats, I only had to make reasonable contact to send the ball into orbit.

Bowled middle stump.

Some people just never learn, do they?

CHAPTER 7

Relax, and *Do* It

To Walk or Not to Walk

Aged 29 I did eventually get to raise my bat to the assembled masses, having compiled a first-class fifty. *Wisden* even commented on it: 'Either side of tea, Hughes flayed a tiring attack.' You won't have heard of many of the bowlers. There was N.C.W. Fenton and A.M.G. Scott and R.A. 'Pumper' Pyman – hardly household names – though you might know the (occasional) leg-spinner M.A. Atherton. The 'assembled masses' was a handful of students skiving off lectures and the odd whiskery professor lamenting the days when counties took their trips to Fenner's seriously. It was a fifty against Cambridge University. Not one to be jumping up ecstatically punching the air about. The next time I went to the wicket I was clanged twice on the head in successive balls by Imran Khan as a sober reminder of what being a batsman was really all about.

An incident in a one-day match at Lord's put my (lack of)

batting prowess into better perspective. It was Middlesex against Hampshire. There are two overs to go and we need ten to win. I have just come in and am on strike. Malcolm Marshall is brought on for the penultimate over. 'Finish this off, Macco!' they call from behind the wicket. 'Two balls will do it!' He probably can't hear as he's at least 70 yards away at the end of his curving run.

The field is set – two slips and a gully, third man, long leg and four saving one in the ring. He comes galloping in to bowl, this small but athletic figure, arms pumping, eyes fixed on the target. I am thinking watch the ball, back and across, low backlift, look to glide a single to third man. Paul Downton, a decent batsman, despite what Kevin Pietersen believes from Googling him, is at the other end.

The ball is shortish and around off stump. I am in a perfect position to glide it wide of the slips. But it flies off the surface rib high, past the edge and soars into the keeper's gloves head high. Smack. 'Bowled Macco, get him next ball!' they call out. I'm thinking it's OK, still 11 balls to go, ten to win, two wickets in hand. 'Keep going, Yoz!' Downton calls out supportively. (Back in the day we didn't meet in the middle every ball for glove punches.)

'Cappy, Cappy gimme Dougal finer, Judgey behind square.' Marshall moves his offside fielders a fraction. I know it is going to be another short one and it is. Again I try and deflect it to third man. Again it flashes past the edge and through to the keeper 20 yards back. 'Ahhhhhhhhh!!!!' Marshall shrieks with a mixture of disappointment and annoyance. 'It's coming, lads,' Dougal in the gully says. 'They're bottling it!'

Ten to win, ten balls to go. I really need to get a single

this time. I'm confident that I can. I've got the measure of him now. It's just the Lord's slope that's making me play and miss. The third ball is a shade fuller, but still shortish. I get across a bit further to counter the movement, and fence hard at the ball slightly away from my body. It lifts and jags away off the surface, a brilliant ball, completely unplayable. It flies past my flailing bat. But there is a faint but audible click as it passes the edge and slaps into keeper Bobby Parks's gloves.

'Yesssssssss!' cries Marshall continuing his follow-through up the pitch towards the close fielders who are chorusing 'Howzzzayyyyyy!!!' in acknowledgement of the wicket. But the umpire is unmoved and I don't think I've touched it. I didn't feel anything. (Isn't that what all batsmen say?)

Marshall stops in his tracks, a yard from me. He is breathing hard and sweat is running down his brow. He wheels round to face the umpire. 'How's that, ump?!' he demands, his tone agitated and insistent. The umpire shakes his head. He turns back to me. He purses his lips and sucks air through his teeth – a Caribbean sound known as 'Steupse' indicating serious irritation. 'Well, *fuck* me!' he says incredulous.

I am standing there still convinced I haven't got a touch. Ten runs to win, nine balls to go, I say to myself. Still easily gettable. And then I stare at the panting, perspiring individual in front of me, eyes blazing, nostrils flaring, veins protruding from his temples, and I hear the Hampshire fielders, some of whom I had a beer with last night, exclaim, 'What a fucking cheat!' and 'He must be deaf as well as blind!' And I think: 'Three of those nine balls are going to be bowled by Malcolm Marshall.'

And I walk off.

I just felt my feet heading towards the pavilion and I couldn't stop them.

'Well – did you hit it?' Gatting asked when I got back to the Middlesex dressing room.

'I . . .er . . .I'm not sure,' I stammered.

There was a stunned silence as the players considered this appalling dereliction of duty. Then the 12th man Jamie Sykes said: 'I fink his arsehole fell out.'

He was sort of right. But it wasn't so much a lack of bravery as a lack of self-belief. I didn't really feel I *belonged* out there, attempting to make runs against a man who had 350 Test wickets at one of the lowest averages (20.94) of modern times. He deserved to get me out, given who he and I were. I didn't have the courage of my convictions to stick it out, and risk alienating my 'mates' in the Hampshire team. So I gave myself up.

The most successful batsmen don't care about getting up the noses of the opposition. They are impervious to the gripes and moans of bowlers and fielders. Often they sub-consciously thrive on it. They are immersed in their world, retaining the belief that it's their divine right to be out there. That's why they don't 'walk'. It doesn't matter how blatant the edge. They will stand their ground until officially told to do otherwise.

'Did you ever walk?' I asked Geoff Boycott once.

'When the umpire gave me out I did!' he replied.

Their self-preservation instincts are so strong, they will actually convince themselves they didn't touch the ball, even if it was palpably obvious that they did. 'I didn't nick that!'

they will say defiantly, and won't be swayed from that line. They are bullet-proof. Have you ever had an argument with a top batsman? It's a waste of time, they never give in. Boycott, Vaughan, Strauss, Atherton, Hussain, Stewart, Pietersen to name but a few. They rarely see anyone else's point of view. Particularly not the bowler's. It was what made them all so prolific.

Their success came from a deep reservoir of self-confidence. They believed the middle was their stage for however long they wanted, or needed, to be on it. It was the place where they were the most comfortable, where they could express themselves best. They didn't worry about how they looked. They were defined by the runs they made. They walked tall, carrying themselves with conviction, re-inforcing their confident demeanour, sending a strong message to the bowlers.

It's a chicken-and-egg situation, of course. Their self-confidence was largely derived from their success. A good start was a massive help. Atherton made 151 in his third Test, Boycott 113 in his fourth, Strauss 112 (and 83) on debut. Vaughan and Hussain both got several reputable scores in their first ten innings. Pietersen made two fifties on debut. In fact, early success is a common denominator among all the leading Test batsmen. Each of the 11 men who have made over 10,000 Test runs had made a Test fifty inside eight innings. Most were a good deal quicker than that (see table). All except two (Steve Waugh and Shiv Chanderpaul) had at least three fifties and a hundred by their tenth Test. They quickly knew they had the ability to perform at that level.

LEADING TEST RUNSCORERS*

	Test inns before first 50	Inns before first 100
S.R.Tendulkar	2	14
R.T.Ponting	1	11
J.H.Kallis	8	10
R.S.Dravid	1	15
K.C.Sangakkara	6	17
B.C.Lara	4	9
S.Chanderpaul	1	30
D.P.M.D.Jayawardene	1	6
A.R.Border	3	8
S.R.Waugh	6	42
S.M.Gavaskar	1	3
A.N.Cook	1	2
G.C.Smith	2	5
Younis Khan	2	2
G.A.Gooch	5	36
Javed Miandad	1	1
Inzamam-ul-Haq	8	13
V.V.S.Laxman	2	30
M.J.Clarke	1	1
M.L.Hayden	5	5
V.Sehwag	1	1
I.V.A.Richards	3	3

* As at 1 April 2016

The Power and the Glory

Mark Ramprakash did not enjoy early Test match success. He stayed in, yes, but did not score runs. He did manage a fifty in his 17th innings, but after three years in Test cricket, that 64

RELAX, AND *DO* IT

against Australia at The Oval was the only time he had got past 29. England had just finished a tough series in the Caribbean during which he had been thrust in to bat at No.3. He didn't look happy there (few do when you're coming in at 8 for one to face Ambrose and Walsh). His batting looked tentative and uncertain. A struggling beginning to his Test career had left him plagued with self-doubt.

I watched the 1994 series and spent some time with him in Trinidad, trying, in an avuncular way, to encourage him to free his spirit. He admitted that he couldn't, often coming to the crease early, and wondered why someone more experienced wasn't batting at No.3 (Smith, Hick and Thorpe were next in the order). 'Deep down I didn't believe I should have been batting at three,' he said, reflecting on that series recently. 'Viv Richards attended the Antigua Test. He came up to me afterwards and he said: "I like watching you bat. You've got it all. But there's something missing. And I feel it's belief." And he was spot on.'

He had made that 63 not out on his Middlesex debut and proceeded to plunder county attacks. He was brimming with self-belief at that level. But with only one decent score in his first 24 Test innings, he was addled with insecurity on the international stage.

He received a serious lesson in assertiveness during that fifth Test in Antigua. The whole of the England team did. Brian Lara, who had himself played only two more Test innings than Ramprakash at that point, and was the same age (24), had announced before the series that he would make a triple hundred during it. (He had already made 277 against Australia, in his fifth Test.) In Antigua, Lara came in at 11 for one that shortly became 12 for two. Adeptly, he negotiated the new-ball spells of Fraser and Caddick, and moved carefully to fifty by early afternoon.

On a perfect pitch, he eased smoothly to his third Test hundred and beyond, finishing the first day on 164 not out and, on the second, played at the same relentless tempo as the Iron band boisterously trooping round the boundary. Whichever shots he selected – sizzling off drives, cuts, clips, pulls, deft paddles, featherlight glides wide of slip – they were exquisitely controlled and laser guided all along the ground into space. Batting mostly in a cap, he seemed to score runs at will. He was never hurried or flustered. There was both a beautiful purity and a complete certainty in his play as he progressed to 320 not out at the close of day two.

There was feeling of total inevitability as we cricket writers arrived for the third day. It must have been awful to have been an England bowler confronted by the same thing. In fact, Lara's batting was a little sketchy at the start, and there was even a play and miss to Angus Fraser. But the bowlers were powerless to intervene and a sumptuous off-drive took him equal with Garfield Sobers' Test record of 365. A swivel pull off an attempted bouncer from Chris Lewis saw him past the record that had stood for 36 years. The fact that, in playing that shot, he had tipped the stumps and dislodged a bail but it had remained precariously balanced on the edge of its groove, was vivid evidence that this was meant to be.

Ramprakash remembers being struck by Lara's calmness and composure during that 12-hour innings. 'He scored at the same relentless pace but he never even broke sweat,' he said. 'He seemed so relaxed all the time, as if he was having fun batting in a club match.' That sort of relaxed *joie de vivre* is what he, now as England's batting coach, is trying to instil in the current crop of young players like Moeen Ali and Gary Ballance, to reconnect them with the fun they had playing the game as kids. He regrets not rediscovering the youthful joy of batting himself until much later in his career.

A Tenth of a Second

Better late than never. I completely failed to ever locate the apparent enjoyment and beauty of batting. In the good players, batting improves with age. Mine deteriorated. Having joined Durham in the 1990s, I still took my batting equipment enthusiastically to the nets, the coach Geoff Cook noted. 'But when I saw you bat I wasn't quite sure why.'

I did feature in one significant partnership with the Australian star Dean Jones, Durham's overseas player. It was against Northants. I got 20 (of course!), Jones made 157. The bowling of Curtly Ambrose in that match exposed the stark discrepancy, in batting terms, between the Slick and the Slack. Ambrose was in a foul mood. He didn't like Jones. Not many opponents did. They were riled by his strut and his matador antics. He was a red rag to fast bowlers (especially when he made them take their sweat bands off, which he asked Ambrose to do in a one-day international in Sydney. Ambrose responded with five for 32).

Here, in the unprepossessing surroundings of Stockton on Tees, the 6ft 7in Ambrose was summoned by his county captain Allan Lamb to see off Jones and wrap up the innings. He tore in to bowl and sent down an awkward short ball that Jones fended expertly to backward square leg for a single. I was now on strike. The field closed in. Gliding to the crease, Ambrose pinged down a shortish ball around off stump. I sparred at it hopefully as it climbed past my edge and soared into the wicketkeeper's gloves. This happened twice more. The deliveries were not that short or exceptionally fast, but the bounce was excessive, rising past the shoulder of the bat. I kept telling myself to leave those deliveries as they were lifting chest high, not even vaguely threatening the stumps. But like a magnet my bat was drawn towards them.

When he pitched the last ball fuller I eased forward, trying to stay tall, looking to push it through the vacant mid-off position. Again the bounce was too much and the ball rose past my gloves and into the keeper's mitts. It wasn't a major problem seeing the ball. Ambrose's speed was probably only 84mph. There was no late swing. But with the amount of lift he generated, I could not see how it was possible to score off such bowling. The only runs I managed off him were two parries off the gloves just out of short leg's reach. It was like facing someone letting the ball go from an upstairs window.

When Jones was on strike to Ambrose, he dealt comfortably with the lifting ball into his ribs – which I habitually flinched at – getting his hands high and with quick footwork turning it nimbly for a single. Once he flip-pulled him for four, and another time he picked up a fuller leg-stump ball, flicking it nonchalantly over mid-wicket with a shot he liked to call the drop-kick. To the shorter, searing deliveries around the off stump he got up onto his toes and defended or, given a hint of width, got on top of the bounce and flashed them hard past deepish cover, feet off the ground with a flourish and a sly smile.

Ambrose's speed – say 88mph at the despised Jones – gave

the batsman only 0.46sec to see and play the ball. Jones may have picked up the length only 0.1sec quicker than me, but it made all the difference. After his eighth fruitless over, Ambrose was visibly deflated and skulked off to long leg. Jones farmed the strike brilliantly and was so dominant, Allan Lamb gave up trying to outwit him with crafty field settings, and kept summoning the twelfth man to see how the horses he'd backed were doing instead.

An Eye for an Eye

So do better batsmen have superior eyesight? Science suggests not necessarily. Don Bradman, as already mentioned, had slightly inferior vision to random students at the University of Adelaide. Geoff Boycott and, latterly, Virender Sehwag batted in glasses (or lenses). One of Australia's most prolific batsmen in state cricket, the Test opener Chris Rogers, is short sighted and colour blind.

What the really good players are able to do is pick up earlier cues as to where the ball is going to be than lesser batsmen. Sunil Gavaskar saw signs in various West Indian fast bowlers' approach to the crease that gave him a clue when the bouncer was coming. Both Viv Richards and Ricky Ponting seemed to be in position to play their shots a touch earlier than their partners. The same was true of Barry Richards and David Gower and Martin Crowe, and more recently Jonathan Trott. That, I suppose, is what we mean by a batsman 'having time' to play the ball.

'Time' is an illusion, of course. Seeing exactly where a fast ball is going takes an estimated 0.2sec which gives the batsman just another 0.2sec to move to (or away) from the ball and hit it. Not long, in other words. Top players are aided by ESP – a sixth sense – enabling them to do this. Andrew Strauss is typical. He talks about subconsciously picking up little signals like the position of the bowler's leading shoulder or his head in delivery that can indicate what length the ball will be. Graham Gooch could do that too. ('Well, I knew where yours were going to be anyway, Yozzer – in my *arc*!!') Keeping wicket, Kumar Sangakkara said he could tell when Murali was going to bowl a *doosra*, even though the bowler himself didn't feel he was doing anything different in his approach. The best batsmen have a sort of visual early-warning system that helps them anticipate the ball.

You can see that in other brilliant sportsmen, too. Scientists did some experiments recently with Cristiano Ronaldo and a decent amateur footballer. In an indoor arena, they were fed crosses from near the touchline to shoot into an open goal. As the ball was about halfway to the player, the lights were turned off. It was instantly pitch dark. Still, Ronaldo volleyed one and headed the other into the net. The amateur player completely missed both crosses. Ronaldo was able to subconsciously calculate exactly where the ball would be, even though he couldn't see it for part of its journey, and time his movements perfectly. That's why he gets paid the big bucks.

That is not to say that you can't improve your responses to a fast-moving object. Part of this is through repetition. I could barely see an 80mph delivery when I first played county cricket. After a few years, I could definitely follow the path of a 90mph ball and, sometimes, jerk out of its way. I had (slightly) speeded up my reactions through practice and experience (and self-preservation).

There is more scientific help available to the modern athlete. Bertrand Théraulaz, a Swiss biologist, has, with his partner Ralph Hippolyte, worked with hundreds of top sportsmen – celebrated tennis players, international footballers and volley-ballers, Olympians and cricketers – to analyse and improve their fine-motor skills.

They categorise everyone within four 'ActionTypes' based on how they walk and move and which eye they use to track moving objects, called the Motor Eye (and not always the same as the dominant eye). Kevin Pietersen, for instance, belongs to the 'Distal' ActionType because his movements are led by his feet (rather than his head) with the weight on his heels, and he likes to hit the ball out in front of him with his head up and a very tight focus.

Ian Bell's movements, however, are led by his head, with his weight on his toes, and he likes to hit the ball close to him with his head down. He is a 'Conceptual' ActionType. Watch how people catch and you'll get the idea – some take the ball out in front looking up (KP), others catch close to their body watching the ball right into their hands (Bell). Neither is wrong or right. It's just their preference.

There is a method in this mumbo jumbo. Once you under-stand what ActionType you are naturally, you can function more effectively. Pietersen's momentum comes from below (his heels/calves) with his head up. He can utilise that best with a wide, squat stance, using the power of his thighs to drive him forwards. Bell is better off standing more upright with his feet closer together and moving rhythmically as one. If your motor eye is your right one, and you're a right-handed batter, you'll need a slightly more front-on stance to allow that eye a fuller view of the ball. Adam Gilchrist, a left-hander with a right motor eye, has to stand very side on.

OK, look, I don't totally understand all this either, but, especially as Théraulaz and Hippolyte have worked with the likes of Roger Federer and helped Barcelona manager Pep Guardiola get his players into their best positions for their triumphant Champions League campaign in 2009, I thought I'd give it a try. I travelled to Millfield School in Somerset where the former England analyst Mark Garaway (part of the coaching team during the 2005 Ashes) coaches budding young players.

He conducted a series of simple tests, mainly me pushing against him with my shoulder and following his various hand movements from close range. We might have resembled those weirdos you see prancing about doing martial arts in a park, but they enabled him to work out that I was a 'Global' ActionType – I walked on my heels with my head up but had low-frequency vision, ie 'no focus' (that sounds about right). He recommended a slightly wider stance, engaging my thighs and making a proper stride to the ball (or back from it) rather than the vague movements I used to do, and making sure that I wasn't too side on and that my motor eye (the right one) was looking straight down the wicket. Then he gave me a few throwdowns.

Whether it was clairvoyance or coincidence or just his excellent throwing I don't know, but I hit the ball for half an hour better than I've ever hit it before. It even drew some oohs and wows from Garaway, though of course it is the primary job of the coach to make the player feel good. (I wonder if Don Bennett realised that.) It was as well we stopped when we did, though, as it would have all started to go horribly wrong. Half an hour was always about my limit as a batsman.

This ActionType approach is gaining increasing prominence in many sports, and is being used to enhance the skills of both the current and next generation of cricketers. Would it have helped me? Well, it wouldn't have made me any worse. When I came up against Curtly Ambrose again the following season, I could only fend my first ball into gully's hands to complete the first pair of my career. I had achieved perfect symmetry. Nought in my first match, nought in my last, and, you might say, not a lot in between. It's enough to make a man retire, and I did. I'm just glad that my father wasn't there to see my ignominious end.

'Pressure is a Messerschmitt up your Arse'

Cricket-wise from then on, I lived vicariously through Ramprakash's exploits. I was married but with no kids at that point, so he was my surrogate son. I wanted to pass on anything I could to help him avoid the pitfalls I'd seen or experienced. I monitored his progress, watching him bat whenever possible, writing positive columns about him, phoned him to offer encouragement and occasionally popped into the Middlesex dressing room for a chat, ignoring the inevitable asides of 'Ssssh . . . Press! . . . Watch your back!' from former colleagues.

He was omitted from the England team after the 1994 West Indies tour, but still averaged over 50 for Middlesex that summer, which earned him the vice-captaincy on the England A tour of India the following winter. I covered the tour for the *Daily Telegraph*, videoed parts of matches and helped out at practice, though I ended up bowling more at two young

Indian hopefuls, called Rahul Dravid and Sourav Ganguly, than any of the Englishmen. Even then Dravid had a phenomenal work ethic, frequently batting on in the nets after the day's play until it was too dark to find the balls he had drilled across the outfield.

In practically deserted stadiums against India A, Ramprakash scored runs effortlessly, topping the averages in a side that also included Michael Vaughan and Nick Knight. Halfway through the tour he was summoned to Perth to replace the injured Graeme Hick and Alec Stewart for the fifth Ashes Test. Pitched straight into the match without time to think or get nervous, he slotted in at No.6 compiling a calm 72 in the first innings and 42 in the second, coping excellently with the twin demons of Glenn McGrath and Shane Warne. We watched some of it from a dingy hotel bar in Chandigarh. He looked like the assured Ramps we all knew and admired. In his 15th Test, it seemed as if he had turned the corner.

But no. This, remember, was the era of indecision. In just over a year, 31 different players were selected by England. Having already been dropped five times in his career, Ramprakash was more anxious than ever. His batting for England became totally constipated. He only once reached double figures in his next eight Test innings and after a second successive failure at Headingley sat with his head in his hands, distraught, for nearly an hour. I visited him in the Lord's dressing room to offer encouragement before the Test on his home patch. He didn't seem excited, more apprehensive. He admitted he was worried about the cracks in the pitch. I didn't think it was a great mindset to adopt. In the end the pitch played fine, but he didn't. He was dismissed for a pair.

This was the same summer he made ten hundreds for Middlesex and topped the national averages. For England he was so consumed with negative thoughts he could barely move at the crease. In one innings, he was dismissed for a duck by the innocuous off-spin of Carl Hooper. He seemed frozen to the spot, completely inhibited by a fear of failure. Psychologists call this 'Ironic Processes of Mental Control'. Normal people call it 'choking'. What happens is you are so intent on *not* doing something – playing a loose shot, missing a penalty, slicing a five iron into the jungle – that you end up doing exactly as you feared.

Choking happens to individuals (Gareth Southgate, Greg Norman, Jean van der Velde) and it happens to teams (England v Australia, Adelaide 2007; South Africa v Australia World Cup 1999 – and at every World Cup since; AC Milan v Liverpool, Champions League final 2005). Put under extreme pressure, you *overthink* your situation and become so tense and taut that your body cannot function naturally.

Scientists also talk about sportsmen suffering from 'musta-bation', an amusing term for the unfunny condition of a player ultimately being constricted by telling himself that he 'must' do this or 'must not' do that. It only increases the pressure on him. Alastair Cook appeared to suffer from it during the one-day series in Sri Lanka at the end of 2014. Here was a fine player and normally relaxed bloke furiously chewing gum while flailing at the ball, saying to himself, 'I *must* get my strike rate up!', compulsively trying to demonstrate his suitability for opening in one-day cricket. He was so desperate to prove his detractors wrong, he ended up proving them right. You can try *too* hard.

In my first season playing for Durham against Middlesex in the NatWest Trophy, I had been super-keen to impress my former colleagues in front of my new one, Ian Botham. It was a knockout match so the atmosphere was heavy with adrenaline. Coming on first change, I charged in to bowl, rushing everything, and sent down two overs of dross that a salivating Mike Gatting and Desmond Haynes gleefully dispatched. I was immediately justifying Middlesex's decision not to re-engage me.

At least by then I'd had numerous experiences of this inadequacy, so I knew what to do. To take a deep breath and slow everything down and imagine I'm bowling to Phil Tufnell rather than Desmond Haynes. I took my time walking back to my mark and paused before each delivery rather than just turning round and running in again. I made sure my approach to the crease was measured. I visualised Tufnell standing jitterily up the other end. My natural rhythm took over, I dismissed Haynes soon afterwards, gave Gatting an awkward time and finished with four for 41. It was about the last time I bowled a decent spell before my body gave up on me. Why is it so often the case that by the time the penny drops you're too old to pick it up?

The great sportsmen handle pressure better than anyone else. Look at Tiger Woods, for instance. During his run of 14 major title wins, Woods never lost a tournament when he was leading at the start of the final round. Justin Rose offered a fascinating insight into Woods's mentality, having played with him on the last day of the 2007 BMW Championship in Chicago. Rose and Woods were joint leaders at the start of the day.

'Tiger was chatty and relaxed at first and we both got off to a good start,' Rose explained. 'He let the round come to him, with a come-what-may attitude. He wasn't taking too long over club selection or practice swings. But as he began to realise it was going to be his tournament, he went to another level, focus-wise. He was still polite but he stopped the chit-chat and he slowed everything down, and got inside himself. There were lots of practice swings, one hundred per cent concentration and focus on every shot, whereas I and many others would have a tendency to speed up at that stage. He shot a sixty-three and won the tournament.'

This first-hand experience had a profound effect on Rose, who has achieved almost all his tour wins – including the US Open, his first major – since that day. Woods's career has, of course, gone in the opposite direction. But that's another story.

Golf, as already suggested, is comparable to batting. The preparation – hitting thousands of balls – the forensic detail, the isolation are all similar. The one important difference is that if you make a mistake in batting, you're probably a gonner. If you make a mistake in golf, you might not be. There is scope for error and fragility in golf, for wayward geniuses such as Seve Ballesteros, for instance. There is often a way back from a terrible shot on the course. There rarely is at the crease. As a result, the real champions of batting are men with the hide of a rhinoceros, tough nuts aware of the precariousness of their existence but also impervious to it.

Michael Atherton was one such. He was a natural concentrator (he thinks being at quite an academic school helped) but was also relaxed at the crease. 'I wasn't particularly uptight or intense, I was happy to have a chat with my partner or look around between balls.' This helped him deal with pressure better than most, absorbing it like a sponge, especially during his remarkable 185 not out at the Wanderers in 1995 when he defied the hostile South African attack for 10½ hours to earn England a draw.

His discipline was so strong, his confidence high and his demeanour so impassive between balls, that he eventually attained a Zen-like state of complete invincibility. 'It was like a trance,' he says. 'Everything seemed to be happening in slow motion and I just knew I wasn't going to get out.' No one could get under his skin, and no one wanted to in this case as, out of superstition, he had been wearing the same clothes for two days in 33°C heat.

What was particularly impressive about Atherton was the way he recognised responsibility yet did not appear to be burdened by it. In the 1990s, when England's batting was often as brittle as a Carr's water biscuit, he knew when his team unequivocally needed him. At the start of his classic duel with Allan Donald on the fourth evening of the 1998 Trent Bridge Test, he understood his task. 'I tell myself "this is now the critical period; the game will be won and lost here; the responsibility is mine, and mine alone, to win this little battle and to get through tonight unscathed."' (from *Opening Up,* by Mike Atherton). It took a huge dose of self-belief to accept this responsibility against one of the most ferocious bowlers who ever lived, but Atherton was as tough as old boots. He survived (just) and England won the Test and ultimately levelled the series.

I Have a Dream . . .

Atherton was fortified by that being his 83rd Test with a batting average of 40 and approaching 6000 Test runs. It imbues you with a certain level of confidence. His former England Under-19 opening partner Ramprakash who, at the beginning of 1998, had played 20 Tests and averaged just 17, was bereft of it at that level. He had 39 first-class hundreds for Middlesex. But after six years as a Test player, his best score for England was 72. Nothing could be clearer. There was something wrong in his head.

Still recognising his potential, the selectors sent him on the 1998 tour to the West Indies, but he didn't get a game for the first month. He was languishing on the sidelines frustrated and forlorn. His first opportunity for a knock was against Guyana before the fourth Test in Georgetown. He top scored with 77 and was selected for the Test. His supporters braced themselves for more disappointment.

The England coach David Lloyd had had the foresight to recruit the sports psychologist Dr Steve Bull for the tour. He had an informal chat with Ramprakash by the swimming pool at the Pegasus hotel.

'He offered me a simple framework to fall back on when I felt nervous and had self-doubt,' Ramprakash says. 'He suggested I spent some time imagining a wicket falling and visualising the process of walking out to bat in the Test match. He encouraged me to rehearse the whole experience of being out in the middle. Also he suggested some key words to remember – like "look to score" and "assert yourself".'

'I did the rehearsals the day before the Test – I took the walk out on to the pitch. In the match I went in at sixty-five for four. I remembered the importance of scoring. When I was on ten I was facing Jimmy Adams' occasional left-arm spin. I recognised that was a time to be positive. I tried a slog sweep and got a bottom edge and was caught behind. But it was a no ball. I thought – OK, that's a sign that this is the right mentality.' He made 64 not out as England subsided to 170 all out and top scored in the second innings as well.

The next Test was in Barbados. He followed his new pre-match routine. It was the same scenario when he went in – England were 53 for four. Soon afterwards his friend and partner Graham Thorpe temporarily retired hurt. 'Jack Russell came in and his energy and positivity helped me during the early stages of my innings. I was still able to play myself in. We put on seventy. Then Thorpey came back in. I always bat well with him, we have a great understanding and run well together.' Ramprakash got to the close 80 not out. 'He just hasn't looked in any bother from the very beginning,' said Tony Cozier on commentary.

He had a restless night. 'I never sleep well when I'm not out overnight,' he says. 'I tend to have that dream that I'm next in to bat when a wicket falls and I haven't got any gear on.' He should count himself lucky that he hasn't actually experienced that for real. About once a season.

I also had a restless night, mainly attending to our newborn son rather than contemplating the imminence of Ramprakash's milestone, but I was desperate for him to succeed. I watched the whole of the following morning session on telly trying to burp two-week-old Callum over my shoulder. I was hoping he would witness the great moment.

It was very tense, as Ramprakash progressed in singles and I tried to prevent Callum being sick on a new sofa. Ramprakash was anxious, too. You could see it in his rigid body language. But he was determined to hang in there.

'Courtney Walsh bowled practically all the next morning,' he remembers. 'Of all the bowlers I had to face, Walsh was the most bloody awkward. He gave me absolutely nothing, making me really work for the runs. I inched my way into the nineties.'

After playing out successive maidens on 93, he had a wild hack at a widish ball. Luckily he sliced it over cover for four. But then he eased into the perfect position to force a shortish delivery through the covers and he was finally the proud owner of a Test hundred in his 38th innings. He thrust his arms to the sky and reclined his head in triumph and exulta- tion and wore a smile as wide as the time, eight years later, when Craig Revel Horwood gave him a 10 for his Salsa in the final of *Strictly*. I was so pleased for him I absent-mindedly squeezed baby Callum rather hard, resulting in projectile vomit across the sitting room.

'Oh the joy and the relief of achieving something I'd waited and worked so long for,' Ramprakash said when I bought him a congratulatory coke three weeks later. 'I've dreamt about it so many times and doubted whether I could ever get there. When I did I was smiling for ages thinking to myself: "Here I am in Barbados, I've made a Test century and no one can take it away from me." There were about fourteen thousand people in the ground and I think ten thousand were English so there was a huge ovation, and when I got to the other end Lara came over and shook my hand which was really nice. It was a very special moment.'

With his perception and practical advice, Steve Bull seemed to have unlocked Ramprakash's gifts. That year against oppo- nents of the highest calibre – the still-challenging West Indies,

the ultra-competitive South Africans, the oppressively dominant Australians, and Muralitharan . . . er . . . Sri Lanka – he
scored 961 runs at an average of 48. The key was helping him
to feel at ease in the Test match environment.

'I tried to listen to a bit of music before I went in to bat that
would relax me and take the tension out of me. Early on in
Test cricket I forgot to look to score. There was so much going
on in my mind, but if you look to score you forget about a lot
of things and start to play the game. All these elements came
together to create a different Test career than the one that had
gone on before. It's a shame in a way because so many years
were wasted.'

Imposters

They weren't 'wasted', of course, though it's scant consolation
to him. They were very instructive. The first part of Mark
Ramprakash's career illustrated very clearly how *not* to manage
a young batsman. It was all our faults. People mistook his seri-
ousness and reluctance to come out drinking as aloofness and
arrogance. We were a bit intolerant. Judging from his flam-
boyant ability with the bat, and occasional flare-ups in the
dressing room, we assumed he was not exactly short of confidence. But as time elapsed, it emerged he was actually shy
and introverted. We realised too late that he needed reassurance and encouragement, and stability too. What he didn't
need was being slagged off for an ill-judged shot and being
constantly unsure of his place in the England team.

As a result of Ramprakash's experiences, we learnt to
watch a batsman more carefully through his innings, and how
he reacted when he was out, and draw conclusions. Was he

ranting and raving, his face taut with emotion as he walked off, apt to hurl his kit everywhere as soon as he got into the dressing room and attack furniture? Then he was a volatile type who put intense pressure on himself and needed persuading not to be so hard on himself.

Did he stare in aggrieved manner at the big-screen replays of his dismissal and complain about the umpiring/the pitch/the light/a fly on the sightscreen? Then he was an escapist who needed to be helped to see things – including his own mistakes – more clearly, and try to minimise them.

Did he come off smiling in a self-satisfied way and say he couldn't do anything about that stupid shot? – 'It's the way I play!' Then he could be encouraged to be a little more responsible and flexible in his thinking and try to set the bar a bit higher.

Graham Gooch got it right. He would invariably plod off the field after being out in exactly the same manner as he had trudged on to it. You couldn't tell from the way he gratefully accepted a drink from the twelfth man when he arrived back in the dressing room and then methodically packed away his kit whether he'd got nought or 180. He managed to adhere perfectly to Kipling's advice – '... if you can meet with Triumph and Disaster, and treat those imposters just the same ...' (although Gooch most likely associated Kipling with exceedingly good cakes). His approach was what the modern players like to call 'taking the emotion out of it'.

That, unfortunately, was what Ramprakash was rarely able to do. He was a very public advert for our national inability to manage a talented but tortured soul. Gazza was another high-profile victim (as in a way was Kevin Pietersen). But whereas, post-Gazza, English football plumbed the depths, Ramprakash's struggles inadvertently improved English cricket's lot. They hastened the arrival of central contracts and the ECB Academy and proper pastoral care. They led to a better understanding of how to prepare a young player for the international stage, how to make him feel comfortable in such a pressurised environment. A sports psychologist now accompanies the team everywhere.

As a result, in the last decade or so, the record of England's newcomers has been outstanding. A sequence of players – Trescothick, Strauss, Bell, Pietersen, Prior, Cook, Shah, Trott, Root and Buttler – all made at least a fifty on Test debut. Four of them made a hundred. Gary Ballance made three Test hundreds in his first ten innings. *That's* how to make an entrance. (Looking at some of England's recent performances, it's the senior players that seem more in need of the psychologist.)

Ian Bell would be a major beneficiary of Ramprakash's fallow years. They are remarkably similar. Both classical players – beautifully balanced and stylish with exquisite timing and a deft touch – they can make batting look ridiculously easy. Perhaps that's where the problems start. They are earmarked for success at a young age and we expect so much from them, and they do from themselves. When I first met the 19-year-old Bell at the inauguration of the ECB Academy in 2001, he said all he wanted to do was play for England.

Yet he has no ego. He is the same sort of relatively quiet, unobtrusive character as Ramprakash (and equally prone to the odd outburst), who also fidgets and frets at the crease and is significantly affected by what's around him (remember, he said on his Test debut that he 'wanted to take everything in'). He is equally fragile and uncertain at times and can be dictated to by situations. He needed help to be more assertive. He lacked self-belief. That's why he often got out for a pretty 30.

Like Ramprakash he needed constant reassurance.

The difference is Bell received it. He has always had plenty of encouragement and support from various members of England's entourage. He is made to feel an integral part of the family. Even through unproductive periods, he has rarely been dropped. This sensitivity and stability has enabled him to convert his obvious potential into outstanding performance: more than 7000 Test runs, average 45 with 22 Test hundreds. So far.

Perhaps it won't surprise you to know that when recently I asked Ramprakash, now England batting coach, who he felt closest to in the England team, his answer was: 'Ian Bell.' By rights he should hate him, begrudge him every run, claim half his Test centuries really belong to him. But he is far too polite to ever think that. And that was ultimately his problem. Batting isn't for nice guys.

CHAPTER 8

The Agony and the Ecstasy

Stormin' the Defences

The 1980s and 1990s were the nose and toes years. That's where the ball seemed to be a lot of the time. If Marshall, Ambrose, Donald and Co. weren't making you 'smell the leather', then Waqar and Wasim were looking for the 'sand-shoe crusher'. It was a severe test of a batsman's courage and reflexes. Few players emerged unscathed. It was remarkable that no one was seriously hurt. The worst injury during that era – a shattered leg – was sustained by New Zealand opener Trevor Franklin when he was run over by a baggage trailer at Gatwick airport.

For the first decade of the 21st century, the world's batsmen were taken on a mystery tour. As the West Indies fast bowling conveyer belt ground to a halt, the spinners took over. Not just any spinners. These guys were clever, deceptive, spun the ball both ways, and they were aggressive, too.

They had a fast bowler's mien. Pakistan had Saqlain Mushtaq and Mushtaq Ahmed, for India there was Anil Kumble, Muttiah Muralitharan wheeled away unstintingly for Sri Lanka, and of course Australia had the irrepressible Shane Warne.

After the batsmen-shelling of the previous decades, this was a more subtle kind of warfare. With variety and sleight of hand, they were playing a sort of hide and seek with the ball. They weren't targeting your body, they were toying with your mind.

'Which way is this one going? ... You're not sure are you?! ... Watch it more carefully!'

'Here, I'll show you another ... Go on see you if can hit it! ... Come on, you know you want to ...'

This was exactly the sort of ongoing dialogue you got from Warne over after over, day after day, as he attempted to hood-wink another victim. It was brilliant theatre. Warne was cricket's greatest con-man.

He was smart and perceptive, too, instantly spotting bats-men's inclinations and weaknesses. He bowled a tighter leg-stump line than most previous leg-spinners (who aimed more at off stump), forcing right handers to play across the line. After he had bowled Atherton behind his legs with his famous pickpocket delivery, Atherton readjusted his stance, batting on leg stump instead of middle in the next Test, to guard against that (outside leg stump) angle of attack. Warne noticed immediately and changed his line to a more pre-dominantly off-stump approach. Unable to adequately cover the leg-spin from his new position, Atherton was soon caught behind. Warne teased out his prey with beautifully conceived variations, accompanied by a cheeky wink and a cheesy smile. Sometimes it was a slow death, but there was rarely any escape. Australia won 92 of the 146 Tests in which Warne played. No bowler in Test history has ever been on the winning side so often.

And yet if you asked any top batsman which bowler they would least like to face, it would be Murali. Once his double-jointedness had enabled him to bowl the *doosra* (the back-of-the-hand delivery that spins the other way that Saqlain popularised) as well as his big-spinning off break, he had become virtually unfathomable. The best players confessed they would rather have been confronted by any of the world's great pace bowlers than him. They were more fearful of slow torture than fast fracture. And while Warne might steal your wicket, Murali made you look a complete imbecile.

With flight and guile, these men, bowling barely faster than a tractor, tormented batsmen who had been camped on the back foot for ten years, exploiting their lack of exposure to quality spin. Batsmen struggled to read them, and some were completely mesmerised. The new England coach, Duncan Fletcher, countered with the 'forward press'. A great student of the game, he had got the idea from watching destroyers of spin like Sachin Tendulkar and Mohammed Azharuddin. It involved a half stride forward as the spinner released, enough to get your feet moving but not enough to make the body overcommitted. From there the batsman could ease further forward to block or drive, but could also push back if the ball was short.

Fletcher's impassioned beliefs, conveyed to various batsmen in a darkened room on a whiteboard, convinced the likes of

Atherton, Trescothick, Thorpe and Hussain. They all introduced the forward press against spin and it was partly responsible for England winning a Test series in Pakistan for the first time for 40 years in 2000-01. At least we were told that was what had happened. At the climax of the series in Karachi, it was so dark only the England batsmen could see the ball (with the aid of sightscreens). Once it was hit, it completely disappeared. The fielders, and cameramen, hunting for it in the outfield, were largely clueless until it thwacked into a boundary board.

I got up at 6am to watch the series on TV while giving our baby son Callum his bottle, and bought him his first cricket jumper and a swingy fur-ball suspended over his cot to get his hand-eye co-ordination going. I positioned his reclining chair near the TV hoping by osmosis he'd pick up the essence of batting. You've got to start 'em early these days. Tiger Woods was playing golf before he was two.

There was more trouble brewing for batsmen, though, and the advantage of the forward press was short-lived. The threat came from an unlikely source. A bespectacled former sports cameraman, Simon Normington – answering to the name of 'Stormin'' – had been hired by the cricket producers Sunset+Vine to work on the creative side of Channel 4's cricket coverage. Using something called a 'half mix' which sounds more like DJ-speak, he had invented a way of making the batsman partly transparent on screen. You could see the stumps behind him as the ball hit his pad (done using a 'grab' of the stumps from a fixed camera before the ball was bowled and then mixing the 'grab' with the actual ball from the same camera). This was ground-breaking. For some batsmen it was ruinous. No longer could they march off claiming that 'that wouldn't have hit another set!' when they were shown on the replay being struck on the shin slap-bang in front of middle stump.

As the precursor to Hawk-Eye and the Decision Review System, its initial impact was subliminal. Only the TV viewers had access to these 'half-mix' images. But some of those viewers were bowlers and umpires. Reviewing their day's performance, they would watch the Channel 4 highlights, and see for the first time how close an LBW they hadn't given (or hadn't been given) actually was.

Before Stormin', all adjudication of LBWs was pure guesswork. An umpire would see a batsman hit on the pad on the front foot and say 'Not out, too far forward' or 'Hit outside the line' or 'Going down' and no one could argue, despite bowlers' plaintiff assertions that 'It was knocking all three out!' It was all just inherited interpretation, handed down from one generation of men-in-white-coats to the next. Now there was evidence. A batsman propping forward to a spinner, bat alongside pad, would assume he was perfectly safe when hit on the pad – well down the pitch, presumably outside the line – until the stumps were revealed directly behind his front leg as he was struck.

My old Middlesex colleague John Emburey, one of the straightest off-spinners around – which is partly to say he didn't turn too many – was one of the first to see these revolutionary images when he popped into the Channel 4 truck. 'Well, I'm fackin' facked!' he said, typically. 'I should have had so many more fackin' LBWs instead of fackin' appealing and wasting my fackin' breath!' He had a point.

The West Indian umpire Steve Bucknor was one of the first to understand the implications of the see-through batsman. From watching recordings of the 2001 Ashes series in which he officiated, he realised that more LBW appeals were legitimate and began giving more batsmen out. (Remember the slow death – his implacable face, then, after considering all the angles a little nod and finally a raised finger?)

Hawk-Eye, the ball-tracking system developed by the minor-county player and missile-guidance expert Paul Hawkins in conjunction with Sunset+Vine, made its debut in 2001. It reiterated what the bowlers and many umpires (usually ex-bowlers) had begun to think. The six special cameras mounted around the ground that fed into a sophisticated computer showed that more balls were hitting the stumps, line-wise, than was previously believed. (Although one surprising revelation was that more balls were bouncing over the top of the stumps than we had expected, especially from the pacemen.)

One of the first bowlers to capitalise on this development was, you may not be surprised to know, Shane Warne. He began bowling more 'sliders' – the straight-on delivery that looks like a leg break. (To add to his 'mystery', he also said he had a 'zooter' but it was actually the same ball.) Batsmen playing to allow for the leg-spin would be hit on the front pad and Warne would holler to the heavens. In the past he'd have got a stubborn shake of the head. But in a two-Test series between Australia and Pakistan on low, slow pitches in Sharjah, Warne took 16 wickets. Nine were LBW. One of the umpires was ... you've guessed it ... Steve Bucknor.

This was, of course, long before Hawk-Eye was used in

decision-making, and the increasing number of LBWs caused inevitable complaints from a legion of batsmen claiming that they shouldn't be given out on the front foot. The myths of them being hit 'outside the line' (and therefore not out) had not been properly exposed. When shown the computer-animated evidence on the TV replay, they merely denounced the technology as flawed. 'How can a computer know what the ball was doing?' they'd rant. 'Well, you obviously didn't!' was a bowler's usual retort.

Much depended on the umpires' interpretation. It was ever thus. When the smiling assassin Kenny Palmer was in charge, you always knew that one strike on the pad could be enough to send you packing, especially if you were a tail-ender. 'Oi'm afraid that's 'ittin' middle 'n leg, my soorrn!' he would say, trying to sound sympathetic. Whereas if Dickie Bird was the umpire you had to be a midget hit on the ankle standing right in front of middle, with leg and off stumps visible either side and the bails above your head to get the finger of doom. It was the same now. Some umpires had become enlightened by the new technology and were firing more batsmen out. Others were sceptical of the increasing influence of television and worried about their jobs. 'Soon we will just be out there to count to six,' said Peter Willey, ruefully.

'Sometimes you don't even get that right!' I replied, after there'd been two five-ball overs in a Test.

Paralysis by Analysis

The growing number of cameras exposing every flaw, and the microscopic analysis of those flaws by irritating people like me using the super-slow-mos and all the other gadgets, plus look-ing at their mannerisms between balls, made it a tricky time to be an England batsman. Not only were their techniques and mentalities examined by a litany of fine bowlers still knocking around, but by the commentators and the media, too. The tiniest error was amplified out of all proportion and pontifi-cated about endlessly.

I'm so lucky that such gizmos were not around when I was attempting to bat. I can see them now in the studio shaking their heads, or worse, laughing, at a slow-motion sequence of me playing a hurried hook shot with my eyes closed and then overbalancing and splattering my stumps with the bat. Or being hopelessly bowled through the gate, with Boycott declaring: 'I could have driven a boos through that!' In this era of microscopic analysis relayed at 75 frames a second on giant plasma screens, you have to be tough to survive.

The double misfortune for Mark Ramprakash at the time was England's dearth of openers. Just when he had had his most successful year as an England player – batting mostly at No.5 – he was thrust up the order by Duncan Fletcher to become Michael Atherton's 12th opening partner. I thought it was the right move, as the previous incumbent was Darren Maddy, and Ramprakash had the aptitude to handle the new ball.

The change looked good to start with. In their second Test together, he made 56 and he and Atherton put on 121 for the first wicket. I drew lines on the screen to show his perfect head position and used some stills of his method in a photographic book I was putting together on technique. I spoke to him in the middle and told him this would be the making of him. But that innings was against Zimbabwe. As soon as those West Indian demons Ambrose and Walsh came to town, four failures ensued. I was as sympathetic as I could be in my Analyst 'caravan', trying to show how the ball kept low or seamed back unexpectedly.

In fact he was in turmoil. He was a reluctant opener yet too unsure of himself to protest, so had accepted the job despite having not gone in first since he was at school. Added to that, he was disillusioned with Middlesex, who were now in Division 2 of the County Championship and going nowhere, and he wanted to leave. But it was his benefit year, and the club, having invested 14 years in him, were refusing to let him go.

It was not a mindset conducive to making runs at Test level, and you could see it in his demeanour at the wicket. He was tense and rigid again, and wrestling with his conscience between balls. Atherton was relaxed at the crease, doing a bit of gardening or imagining the salmon run on the River Tay or having a chat to umpire Kitchen – 'Getting a long way forward today, aren't I, Merv?!' But Ramprakash seemed constantly uptight. I felt guilty for having illuminated his dismissals on TV and causing him extra stress. But he says: 'It was my fault. I didn't really believe I should have been opening. But when you get picked for England you should just get on with it. I wish I had embraced it in a more positive way.'

Soon he was dropped (again) and Marcus Trescothick was promptly installed as Atherton's 13th opening partner. A rosy-cheeked, bucolic type, he wasn't freaked out by expectation or the calibre of the opposition and he was used to opening. Despite a relatively modest county record, averaging a shade over 30 for Somerset with just seven first-class hundreds when he was picked, Fletcher had seen something in his manner – a calm, unruffled presence at the crease – that impressed him. It was an inspired choice. He was an instant success (making 66 and 38 not out on debut) and was a superb England opener for six years, never straying far from his simple, unfussy, forthright approach. Nothing seemed to faze him.

'I actually found Test cricket easier,' Trescothick reflects. 'The pitches were better than in county cricket and the bowling was quicker, meaning I didn't have to move my feet as much.' That will be a revelation to all those who believe that making a big stride back or forward is the only way to bat.

Ramprakash, meanwhile, was ultimately allowed to leave Middlesex and joined Surrey. He scored a hundred on his Surrey debut at The Oval and, among familiar England tour mates such as Mark Butcher, Graham Thorpe and Alec Stewart, immediately felt at home. He got another recall to the England team midway through the 2001 Ashes – back at No.5 this time – and his Surrey pals were all around him in the batting order. He played a sequence of solid, but unspectacular innings. In the final Test at The Oval, with the Ashes already lost and Australia's batsmen having filled their boots on a flat pitch, he delivered at last on his promise and made an assured 100. It was his second century in his 81st Test innings.

There was relief all round. At last I could do an appreciation of his style and panache and technical polish, rather than highlighting the way he had got an inside edge because his bat had come down crookedly. I put the compilation on a DVD and showed it to our two kids, hoping they'd glean something about pure batsmanship, although admittedly they were only three and one and were not happy about me interrupting *Teletubbies*.

And at last he could luxuriate in six hours initially defying but eventually dominating McGrath, Gillespie, Lee and Warne, one of the best attacks Australia had ever fielded. 'I really enjoyed that innings,' he reflects. 'Hot weather, good pitch, familiar surroundings – I always liked batting at The Oval – and I felt I handled McGrath and Warne really well. I played myself in, but then I managed to go on. When I got in I started to put the ball away when I had the opportunity. I feel I played really well. I am very proud of that innings.'

This is said in a dignified tone laced with regret. He knows that on that occasion the batsman that he wanted to be showed up. He knows that, aged 31, that should have been the start of a rich vein of run-making for England. He also knows that it wasn't. It was anything but. The retirement of Atherton in that Oval Test match, after a distinguished 115-Test career, created a genuine vacancy in the England batting order. It was a passing on of England's sturdy, reliable baton. Ramprakash was not able to pick it up. He made only one more decent score (58 v India) before his Test career fizzled out with a few dismal failures in New Zealand. He finished with an average after 52 Tests of just 27.32.

Why?

'I wasn't ruthless enough. My best batting for England was in 1998, in Australia. Then I felt like a Test batsman. Everything was in sync, the pitches were good, the Kookaburra ball is easier to face. I got sixty-nine not out in Brisbane, two fifties in Adelaide and then I was sixty-three not out at the MCG when I got caught in two minds against Steve Waugh's phantoms and got out caught mid-on. I didn't make the most of those opportunities and, though I topped the averages on that tour, two Tests after we came home I was going to be dropped. *Two Tests!!* But then Nasser broke his finger and I played.

'The winter after my Ashes hundred in 2001 we went to India and I was still batting at five and six and I felt if things went wrong I would be the one to go. I never felt sure of my place. I knew I had to get three-figure scores. And I didn't do that enough.' The obvious conclusion is that he always put himself under such severe pressure at Test level, it suffocated his natural talent. One statistic illustrates that above all else. At Lord's, the ground he knew best but where, like many, he coveted a century most of all, he played eight Tests and averaged 10.38. Even James Anderson averages more. The spotlight was too intense. What's that phrase – Blinding Ambition? It can be a hazard not a help.

In the end he just thought too much, about everything other than simply watching the ball and responding. His mind was generally too cluttered with extraneous matter to see a clear way forward. (I know the feeling.) The final word on this comes from the greatest international hundred-maker of all time, Sachin Tendulkar. Apart from revealing a passion for Harry Ramsden's giant fish portions, the other killer line in his otherwise bland autobiography is this: 'I've always felt that I've batted best when my mind has been at the bowler's end of the pitch, not at my end.' Nicely put. But easier said than done, eh?

Wanna Be a Batsman Rule No.6 – When you get in, *stay* in.

Exceeding the Speed Limit Is Fun

One of the things I learned from close video examination of the game was the fascinating variety of batting styles. There was Brian Lara with his extravagant, up-periscope backlift, and whiplash assault on the ball, and there was Paul Collingwood who barely lifted his bat off the floor and shovelled the ball through the leg side with hardly any follow-through. There was a big front-foot bully like Matthew Hayden, and a little crab-like manipulator of the ball like Shivnarine Chanderpaul. There was the elegance of Jacques Kallis and the ugliness of Graeme Smith. There was Sachin Tendulkar's classic orthodoxy and Sanath Jayasuriya's outrageous audacity. There was Ricky Ponting's savage pulling and Michael Vaughan's sumptuous driving. There was the carefree Virender Sehwag and the often careworn Rahul Dravid. The conclusion you can draw, I suppose, is that in a batting sense, there was no one right, or necessarily wrong, way.

In the Noughties there was one obvious trend. Through diet and training, batsmen were getting bigger and more aggressive. The old, nimble 5ft 10in prototype was being superseded by some strapping individuals who strode up the pitch and assaulted the bowling. The proliferation of one-day cricket – which properly began after the 1996 World Cup in India – was the catalyst, as well as the development of bats like trampolines and boundary ropes brought in from the fence to allow officious security guards to sit on the grass all day confiscating inflatable toys being harmlessly tossed around in the crowd.

As a result, Test match scoring rates were rising rapidly. The

Australians led the way, regularly rattling up more than four an over, and the South Africans were no slouches either. Hayden, a man-mountain with the physique and mentality of a second-row forward, heralded an era of intimidatory batting, which continued right down the order, with someone like Adam Gilchrist coming in at No.7 and scything the bowling to shreds, wielding his bat like a samurai sword. It wasn't just the power and bat-speed of these players that had been enhanced, but their attitude, too.

This was amply borne out in a batting masterclass conducted on Channel 4 by Geoff Boycott and Michael Slater. Boycott, immaculately turned out in his old cricket flannels, talked about 'soft hands' and the intricacies of defence on uncovered pitches. After a while, Slater grabbed the bat off him and demonstrated the attacking mentalities of modern players like himself whose main inclination was to dominate. It illustrated how the game had moved on.

There was a greater premeditated element to batting now, too. Not just in deciding which ball to attack, but how. The advent of the reverse sweep, pioneered in the 1990s and gradually expanded, had given batsmen a new range of options, but the decision to play it had to be made before the ball was delivered. It had made batting more complicated, and yet clearly more fun.

A batsman was definitely the thing to be. I bought my kids (now two boys and a girl) their first miniature bats (autographed by Tendulkar) and rolled them underarm deliveries in the kitchen. It all went well until there was a disputed catch and they started using the bats as weapons. Tanya, their mother, was tall and fit and, perhaps even more invaluably, confident, which allied to my sporting background, gave them a good head start in a sporting context. They were all lively and none of them had any problems expressing themselves. I did a fair bit of the daily childcare and fed them the rib-eye steak that Matthew Hayden had recommended, and lots of spinach to build up their strength, and carrots to enhance eye-sight (though no raw eggs at 2am).

The Twenty20 format, launched in 2003, was the perfect showcase for batting's increasing range and diversity, especially for kids. At the expense, perhaps, of subtlety, it cut out the boring bits of cricket – the shouldering of arms, the bowling of maiden overs, the fiddling about moving a fielder a step to the left, which undoubtedly have their place in the longer game – and boiled batting down to its core essence: making runs. It deterred any 'fannying about at the wicket', as Mike Gatting used to describe my batting efforts.

The newest version of the game helped some of the more introverted batsmen, too. I went to the first ever Twenty20 match staged at Lord's. Just shy of 28,000 people – City blokes, office workers, pretty PAs, students, young couples sipping Chardonnay, mums, dads, kids and extended Asian families as well as more traditional supporters – had turned up to Middlesex v Surrey, an encounter that, when I had last played in it might have attracted a quarter of that (on a Sunday) if you were lucky.

Coming in at No.3 for Surrey against his old county, Mark Ramprakash looked visibly invigorated by the atmosphere and the music. He treated the Lord's crowd to a stunning cameo of clips and flicks and saunters up the pitch and flam-boyant drives over cover for six, each boundary marked by a noisy rendering of MC Hammer's 'U Can't Touch This' over the PA. This was the brilliant self-expression of his youth that had rarely been seen since. The new platform, and the new environment, had given him second wind. He began piling up runs for his new county in all forms of the game. There were 31 Ramprakash centuries in the next four seasons. The prisoner of his own conscience had been set free.

Brick by Brick

Cricket is obsessed with hundreds. It is funny in a game that is essentially governed by imperial measurements – a pitch of 22 yards, a bat 4¼ inches wide, a ball weighing 5½ ounces – that it could be so metric. Yet a hundred is regarded as the benchmark of success. Not four-score or six-dozen but a century of runs. It is the ultimate goal of (most) batsmen. A hundred tends to give them status and credibility and their name in gold lettering. It indicates total supremacy. It is common to judge a batsman's ability and worth by how many hundreds he has made.

Actually this is wrong. The yardstick (there I am, using imperial terms again) *should* be how many games a batsman has won (or saved) for his team. That is harder to ascertain, perhaps. Who is to say that, for instance, Alastair Cook's sturdy, nerve-settling 95 against India at Southampton in 2014 wasn't more valuable than Ian Bell's 167 (coming in at 213 for two)? Yes, Bell's innings was definitely more attractive, a purer exhibition of the art. But Cook blunted not just the new ball but also India's optimism after they had seized an unexpected victory at Lord's.

Or what about Michael Slater's brilliant 77 for Australia v England in the first Test at Edgbaston in 2001? It seized the initiative and crucified the England bowling (he took 16 off the first over of the innings, bowled by Darren Gough). Adam Gilchrist (152) came in much later and picked off the remains of the carcass. But was it a more important innings than Slater's? Probably not.

Was Sachin Tendulkar absolutely a better batsman than Ricky Ponting because he scored 51 Test hundreds to Ponting's 41? Of Tendulkar's 51 centuries, only 20 (39 per cent) culminated in an Indian victory (and only three of those were scored in the decisive third or fourth innings of the match). Brian Lara, one of the most dominant batsmen who ever lived, fares worse. Only eight (23 per cent) of his 34 Test centuries resulted in West Indian victory. Whereas Ponting was on the winning side in 27 of the games in which he made a hundred (71 per cent).

This is equally a reflection of the relative strengths or weaknesses of the sides they played in, rather than purely of the batsmen themselves. Ponting's Australia was one of the strongest teams in history. Lara's West Indies veered from outstanding at the start, to abysmal at the end. For much of Tendulkar's career, the Indian bowling attack was hardly terrifying. But the stats probably do indicate that some players' hundreds have more of an impact on match outcomes than others. (Incidentally, ten of Geoffrey Boycott's 22 hundreds resulted in England victory, and none in defeat. And that's *not* according to his mum.)

Hundreds are, by definition, a selfish pursuit, however. Especially the end bit. Throughout, they require huge dedication and perseverance, but as a player nears the 'milestone' (imperial again!) they often take precedence over a team's concerns (all that pottering nervously through the nineties). Teams have lost wickets, momentum and even matches seeing someone to a hundred. Sometimes it gets silly, such as in 2011 at Cardiff when England were 491 for five at the end of the fourth day against Sri Lanka, with Ian Bell 98 not out.

They batted on for seven balls on the last day so he could get his hundred. England argued that it was really important for team unity and Bell's own feeling of self-worth to do so (you see, I told you they look after him!). But it wasted 20 minutes of the final day that could have been crucial as England sought to bowl Sri Lanka out to win the match. (As it happened, they rolled over for 82 so it wasn't a problem in the end.)

As England captain, Michael Atherton famously went to the other extreme in 1995 in Sydney when he declared on 255 for two in mid-afternoon on the fourth day with Graeme Hick 98 not out. Atherton had become frustrated with the dawdling run-rate and wanted half an hour at the Australians before tea. The alienating effect it had on Hick, and the ripples it created in the team, caused him to regret the decision afterwards, but he believes strongly that a hundred should be the by-product of the match situation, not the focus of it.

Everyone is agreed, however, that a hundred is a major achievement. It's a triumph of will and concentration and self-control. So you've done the preparation and the practice and the visualisation and you've got your trigger movements sorted and you're happy with your basic technique, and your method for switching on and switching off at the crease. You've got your earplugs ready for when the Aussie leg-spinner comes on.

You've looked at the videos of the opposition bowlers and a few of yourself hitting runs and you're feeling confident. Great. How do you convert that into a century?

'Take it one ball at a time,' is the old mantra. Sounds boring, but over years and years of trial and error, it seems to work. In fact it's the same with anything that takes a long time – writing books, running marathons, bringing up kids. If you thought at the outset how hard it was going to be, or how much you would question your sanity along the way, or what state you're going to be in by the end (not that there ever is an 'end' to bringing up kids), you probably wouldn't bother. It sounds more like torture. You've got to break it down into little hurdles to steadily, systematically overcome – one ball/page/mile/feed at a time.

Chris Broad, Stuart's father, states it simply. 'Making a Test hundred is likely to take about five hours. I couldn't possibly imagine batting for five hours! So I broke it down into ten-minute chunks. Ten minutes batting – that's easy. It's incredible how quickly that time passes and then you set a target for another ten minutes. Suddenly you've been batting for an hour and you're almost a third of the way there.' That's if you're any good. (He was.)

As one of the most organised and consistent of England batsmen, Jonathan Trott is worth listening to on this one. You might call his approach to an innings pitter-patter: lots of small but significant steps. 'When I batted with either Strauss or Cook, I batted in fives. So if we're on sixty I'll say come on let's get to sixty-five. Let's not look too far ahead. You can get to sixty-five in two balls, so you don't think about overs. It's more thinking positively about runs, not time. If you look at batting time, you're putting pressure on yourself. Batting in fives is limitless and positive.'

Wanna Be a Batsman Rule No.7 – Don't think too far ahead.

'If a guy's swinging it away quite a bit, I'm not thinking "I need to be careful here and see him off", I'm thinking "I won't have to play too much and he'll get fed up eventually and he'll come straighter and then I can work it through mid-wicket." It's vital to have a stable base to work from and to find a rhythm to your batting, keep drawing on the same thing and believe in your game.' It was this rhythm and belief that had deserted him when he attempted a return to the England fold in the Caribbean in 2015.

During his most productive period (an average of 50 in his first 30 Tests with seven hundreds), he felt that improving his fitness and preparing scrupulously were the secrets. 'I'm very disciplined in what I eat and how I prepare. It's also important to do a little bit extra. Gary Kirsten was at the same school as me and he gave a speech once at an old boys' match. He said: "It's about going the extra mile" and I do that. I'll go for a run and then I could turn left and go for home or go a bit longer, and I go a bit longer and test myself. It's almost more benefi-cial than nets. Because I know when it gets to a difficult spell out there at the wicket I can overcome it.'

The best players get into what they call the 'zone'. They talk about inhabiting their 'bubble'. It all sounds a bit sci-fi, but they have conditioned themselves to do it. It is what Sachin Tendulkar calls 'surrendering yourself to your subconscious mind'. It goes back to that analogy of driving a car on a long journey: focusing in a relaxed way, letting your mind wander when the road is relatively clear (ie between overs) while still being alert, concentrating a bit harder in busy traffic (when the bowler is running in), but not too hard that you are taut and rigid and can't fluidly react to something in your path. And it's best not thinking too much about how far away the destination is (hard when your kids in the back are saying 'Are we there yet?' every ten minutes).

There are periods during a long journey/innings when things get tougher. The kids/bowlers are squabbling/irritated and you are the culprit. They start getting fractious and say things like 'Why can't I have some more Haribos?!' or 'It must be boring being you' (delete where appropriate). It's a skill staying calm and clear-headed, especially if you are getting tired and fed up yourself.

This is when Andrew Strauss resorted to his meditation techniques. 'At such times you can feel anxiety building up in your chest. You have to control your emotions. I'd try and listen to my breathing in the middle, let my mind settle. I watched how players like Tendulkar and Kallis handled stressful situations or build-ups of pressure. They always seemed so serene, I can never remember them playing a wild shot.'

Maybe it came naturally, or perhaps they were just good actors. Crucially, it's vital not to betray what you may or not be feeling to the bowlers. They can detect an anxious batsman like a rottweiler senses a nervous postman. Body language is very important. Alastair Cook maintains an extraordinary equability throughout an innings. You can't tell what he is thinking. There is no curse or kick at the ground when he is out or plays a loose shot. Equally, he does not do the manic celebration and jump about like a terrier on steroids when he reaches a landmark. Like his mentor Graham Gooch, he manages to treat those 'twin imposters' just the same. It is the secret of their prolificacy.

Nnnnnninety ...

Most batsmen's anxieties are heightened in the nineties.

Interestingly, Gooch was out only twice in the nineties in 215 Test innings and Bradman, get this – *not once*, and he made 29 hundreds. It's fascinating evidence of his sangfroid. As he said to an interviewer once: 'I don't get nervous.' By contrast one of the edgiest batsmen, Michael Slater, who bristles with hyperactivity even in the commentary box, was dismissed nine times in the nineties. He had no chance of inhabiting his 'bubble': he kept bursting it.

History is littered with batsmen losing their cool at this point. Four short of his first hundred for Gloucestershire, Chris Broad drilled a half-volley uppishly and was caught at extra cover. The great South African all-rounder Mike Procter, who holds the world record for scoring six hundreds in successive innings, was captain. Procter told Broad: 'You don't need to get there in one hit, nudge it in ones and twos.' Broad remembered the advice and in the next match on 96 pushed a couple of singles, then worked a delivery from Peter Willey off the inside edge for two to get his century.

'Getting close to a hundred does put extra pressure on you,' Broad says. 'It's ridiculous but the first thing selectors do is look down the columns and see how many hundreds you've made. Nineties don't really register.'

Desmond Haynes speaks for many when he talks about

something messing with your head when you're a couple of shots away from a century. 'I suffered!' he says. 'I was on ninety-two against India in Barbados, and there's a little man in your head that tells you a lot of nonsense when you're in the nineties. He gets very loud and he was telling me: "Come on man, you've got to slog that Shastri! Put him into the scoreboard! Don't get it in singles!" And I go down the wicket and try a slog sweep and I get caught.

'And I tell myself, next time I get into the nineties I don't care how long it takes. I am just going to bat and whenever it comes, it comes. And when that little man came into my head again and was telling me to slog it, I'd tell him: "SHUT UP! You're not going to trick me again."'

The 'little man' eventually vacated Haynes's head and went and resided inside Kevin Pietersen's instead, though he was renamed the 'inner chimp'. That's the term the self-styled 'mind-mechanic' Steve Peters gave to the emotive, irrational side of your brain that can make snap decisions and get you into trouble. Peters helped Olympians such as Sir Chris Hoy manage their 'inner chimp' and was invited by Roy Hodgson to work with the England football team before the World Cup in Brazil. Hodgson no doubt wished he'd sent a family of chimps out against Costa Rica instead. Pietersen's 'inner chimp' is the voice telling him to go for the big hit over deep mid-wicket on 94, even though there's a man back there. One of the reasons the chimp hasn't been so loud recently is because it's almost two years since he's scored anything like that many in top-level cricket until his extraordinary 355 not out for Surrey in May 2015.

Marcus Trescothick suffered from a nineties problem (which is not a bad problem to have if you think about it). Before his

Test debut in 2000, he was tensing up getting close to three figures and trying, and often failing, to get there in one hit. He was out five times in the nineties. 'I had the yips!' he says. The sports psychologist Steve Bull came up with a solution.

'He got me to rehearse being in the nineties. Every time I had a net, I'd hit a few for a bit, and then after a while I'd bat imagining I was on eighty-five. I'd really get into the mindset, visualising the field settings and the bowlers and discipline myself to take my time and get it in singles. You're going to get the odd four-ball anyway. The main thing is not to go looking for them. It really helped, taking the pressure off me in the nineties and I converted a lot more into hundreds.'

Oddly, the strange neurosis revisited him in later years playing for Somerset in 2009 with a sequence of scores over two months in mid-summer of 98, 95, 96 and 99. He resorted to the same practice technique as before and four hundreds followed in August.

Hearing these tales made me realise why I could never be a batsman. Every time a 'little man' came into my head at the crease, he was telling me all the ways I could get out (he was usually right). A chimp could probably have done better. He would certainly have used his feet more.

Yet the presence of such gremlins in a batsman's mind also proves something. The fact that a player has to overcome such emotional torment to make a hundred illustrates that it *is* a credible estimation of a batsman's ability. It is proof that they have the skill and stamina to bat for a long time, but also that they have the mental agility to negotiate awkward phases and get through the nineties (which on Cricinfo's Stats Guru are even labelled as the 'nervous nineties').

When a batsman is on 96 he knows he is one shot away from a hundred – achieving a 'First' in batting terms – and the bowlers play on that. They know he is trying to play his ambition down and put it out of his mind. It's the cue for them to advertise it, chirping 'Eye on the ball mate, don't think about those three figures' or, if they're smart 'Don't listen to that chimp, fella!' and they bring the field up and plug the gaps through which he has been picking up easy singles. They up their pace a touch and make it as hard as they can for him. They know a 96 just doesn't look as good on the CV.

This scenario often reignites interest in an idling match. The batsmen have been dominant and the spectators have dozed off. But now the mid-afternoon crowd awake, sensing the batsman's desire and the bowlers' intent and they start getting involved, the noise rising in a crescendo as the bowler runs in. It only heightens the pressure on the batsman and galvanises the fielders. Previously apathetic mid-ons (usually knackered bowlers) are suddenly on their toes and square legs interrupt their chats with the umpire about Man United's back four to pull off brilliant diving stops. Wicketkeepers execute swift leg-side takes and whip off the bails and look challengingly at the batsman as he warily keeps his back foot planted and bowlers yell for unlikely LBWs accompanied by 20,000 voices in the crowd.

Overcoming all this is a testament to a batsman's will and focus and fortitude and his efficiency at shutting out unsettling influences. Therefore it actually is a reputable label of achievement. A hundred is perhaps the best gauge in sport of a player's character and his ability to handle adversity. Playing a faultless final round in an important golf tournament is probably the closest equivalent. But in golf you can recover from the odd mistake, and you haven't got 11 opponents in your face searching for a chink (or chimp) in your make-up and willing you to screw up. Achieving a hundred is something to be rightly celebrated, visible in the usual ecstatic punches of the air, bat waves and bear hugs with your batting partner. The relief, as well as the delight, is tangible.

Yet these are not their real feelings. In fact the batsmen themselves only properly celebrate a while later. Like any major achievement, the enormity of it is too great to absorb initially. The sense of deep satisfaction and pride takes time to sink in. Often it is only when they leave the ground and can sit somewhere for quiet reflection that they can really treasure their performance.

'I sit on my hotel bed and replay the innings in my mind,' says Sri Lanka's Mahela Jayawardene, architect of 34 Test hundreds. 'I think back to the preparation and planning of the innings, executing the plans, thinking on my feet, overcoming the difficult moments. It's the whole process that gives you the real satisfaction.

'I felt particularly good after my hundred and sixty-five against South Africa at the Sinhalese Sports Club last year. I came in at sixteen for two on the first morning and was facing Steyn, Philander and Morkel. I had thought carefully about how to play them, where to score – mainly off my legs – and what to leave. You've still got to look to be positive and I was very happy with my shot selection.

'They brought on the leg-spin of Imran Tahir after the first hour. It was a surprise, but I wasn't going to let him bowl on a flat first-day pitch with a new ball. I used my feet and hit him over the top and knocked him around and that got my score going. That wasn't in the planning, but you've got to be ready for anything. I had fifty by lunch. After that I played nicely and the pitch was flat. There was nothing in it for the bowlers. I just had to not make a mistake. The pleasure in reaching my hundred came from the way I had planned the innings, and the way I reacted well to different situations.' It might have also come from the knowledge that he had now scored the same number of Test hundreds as Sunil Gavaskar and Brian Lara.

Trescothick prefers reflecting on the impact he's had on the match. 'If I've made a hundred, especially a big one, I've dictated terms in the game. I've given the team control. That's the best feeling. The joy of getting us into a winning position. That's the true satisfaction. And the first thing I will do afterwards is speak to my family. I want to share it with them as they've lived through everything with me.'

And what's that 'feeling' like? 'Fantastic, better than anything,' says Mark Ramprakash who, of course, experienced it more than 100 times.

'Better than sex?' I ask.

'I'm not saying.'

'Go on . . . Is it better than sex?'

'Well . . .,' he pauses for thought, 'depends who with.'

And Finally . . .

OK, so you get the distinct impression that nearing a hundred – especially in a Test match – is a fraught business. Being on 99 is like being close to the end of a very long electronic buzz wire game (the one where you have to pass the loop along the undulating wire without touching it) in front of a packed stadium and a million on TV with constant interruptions and lots of people trying to put you off. One slip and you're effectively dead.

Now imagine being in the nineties *and* on 99 international hundreds. It is six months and 16 innings since your previous hundred – a fact you are reminded of about 70 times a day – and you have already twice been out within a dozen of becoming the first (and surely only) person ever to make 100 international hundreds. And you're playing in front of a packed home stadium with about a *billion* people willing you on.

'By November 2011, the pressure had really started to get to me,' Sachin Tendulkar admits. 'Every day I was getting a lot of text messages wishing me well for the century and asking me not to worry. They were sent with the best of intentions, but unfortunately they made it impossible for me not to think about the landmark all the time. At times it became quite unbearable.' The price of superstardom, eh?

So Tendulkar arrives at Mumbai's Wankhede Stadium on the fourth day of the Test against the West Indies. He is 67 not out overnight. It's always chaotic outside the Wankede during a Test. Today there are at least 20 outside broadcast vans lined up in the road outside, along with the crowds of people with tickets, the crowds of people without tickets, the cars, the taxis, the buses and the hundreds of police tripping over each other to get a glimpse of the Indian players rather than keep order. It's pandemonium.

Somehow Tendulkar controls himself and progresses to 93.

'Just then I looked at the scoreboard and started to feel distinctly strange. My feet were heavy and it was as if I had no strength left. I had never felt as nervous in my career, not even when I had been about to make my first Test hundred in 1990. I walked away towards square leg and took a few deep breaths. I kept telling myself to concentrate hard and not to lose focus.' He was promptly out caught at second slip for 94.

Four months and 17 more innings – on tour in Australia – elapse before, in the relative anonymity of Dhaka, he is into the nineties against Bangladesh. 'The pressure started to build again, but somehow I played a shot for four that calmed my nerves a little.' With four singles in the next two overs, he was two runs away. His 99th hundred had been more than a year before. 'They were the two most difficult runs of my career. I had experienced nothing like it. Determination, anxiety, relief – all of these feelings came together. I kept telling myself to stay focused and play each ball on its merit. It was time to go back to basics and rely on skills I had practised all my life.'

An inside edge for one off Shakib Al Hasan in a one-day international at the Shere Bangla Stadium was not the dream way to bring up your 100th hundred for your country – after 33 failed attempts – and India lost the match. But fairytales don't happen in sport. Look at Bradman – out for nought in his last Test innings denying him an average of 100. It is reassuring to the rest of us. These superheroes are mortal after all.

Friends told Tendulkar afterwards that his 100th hundred celebrations had been muted. 'I reminded them that I have been like that for over two decades. I have always preferred to be restrained, except on a few occasions.' You see – take the emotion out of it. It's the only route to consistent performance. Treat those twin imposters just the same. Or just think yourself lucky that your dad's not Simon Cowell.'

Alternatively you could bat like A.B.de Villiers. He has just scored a hundred against the West Indies in 31 balls. *31 balls*!! Some blokes take that many to get off the mark! He came in during the 39th over and had a century by the 46th. That shut up the little man and the inner chimp, didn't it? It's the bowlers who need psychiatry after that.

CHAPTER 9

A Test of Character

Boom Time

On the 25th anniversary of my Middlesex debut at Lord's, I took my family to a match there. The kids were seven, five and two, and cricket had just got interesting. It was 2005 and there was Twenty20, the most keenly awaited Ashes series ever and Freddie Flintoff had just come back from injury to play for Lancashire against Middlesex.

I pointed out the dressing room where we used to change and the pavilion balcony from where we'd train our binoculars on any well-endowed females in the Tavern and the gate that we'd walk out of and the Nursery End that I used to bowl from and the Mound Stand in front of which I enjoyed doing diving stops off Phil Tufnell.

It was an all-day match and I was worried they would get bored, but well, so what, a bit of boredom is good for over-stimulated kids, so I was determined to stick it out for a session. They might glean something. Hopefully in time they'd inherit my love of the game. As luck would have it, in the space of seven overs we saw three wickets, including one in which two stumps were uprooted, five fours, a six and several brilliant diving stops – in front of the Mound Stand. Still, the general comment was: 'When can we go?' And, after the Hula-Hoops and Wotsits had run out, I conceded defeat.

I was confident that the trip had been a positive first experience of cricket, and before reading them their bedtime story – *Mortimer Also*, the tale of the cricket-obsessed mouse who befriends an aging umpire and attends matches in his hat – I asked them what they thought of the day. Do you remember the name of the ground we went to, I asked seven-year-old Callum. He hesitated for a bit. Then he said: 'Was it Mould or something?'

It was a great summer of cricket, not just because of the Ashes, but also because of a still-ebullient Darren Gough charging in on a hat-trick at the Rose Bowl in the first-ever Twenty20 international and hitting Andrew Symonds on the shoulder, and the dead-mongoose-headed Pietersen's demolition of the Australian attack in a one-dayer at Bristol, and Michael Atherton who had (justifiably) dissed my bowling in a charity match for cystic fibrosis, being then dismissed by a clubbie for 8.

It was a wonderful Ashes series, every match keeping the increasingly captivated nation on tenterhooks. After the huge build-up, the Lord's Test was like two heavyweight boxers unleashed from their corner to try to obliterate their opponent in four rounds. England, after scoring the first blows, were comprehensively knocked out. But at Lord's the emergence of Kevin Pietersen, the 114th player England had tried since last winning the Ashes in 1986-87, was the catalyst for the rejuvenation of English batsmanship.

You could boil his impact down to three shots. England are 101 for eight in the first innings, and sliding into oblivion. Glenn McGrath is on his usual metronomic length, waiting for the pitch to do its work and the batsmen to succumb, as most of them already have. Pietersen has quietly played himself in, despite the wreckage occurring 22 yards away. To the first ball of McGrath's next over, he puts his foot up the pitch and bludgeons the ball back past him head high for four. It was an audacious stroke that took even the ogre McGrath by surprise.

Next ball, Pietersen takes a step or two up the pitch. Subconsciously, McGrath bangs the ball in a touch shorter. Pietersen brings his bat back, opens his shoulders and BOOM! The ball, still rising, is met with a colossal swing of the blade and it soars skywards, flying 80 yards, higher than the great pavilion, clearing the rails and landing in the eighth row of the members' seating. There was some astonished chuntering among the bacon-and-egg tie brigade, roused from their discussions about lumbago..

Pietersen turns his attention to Warne. He's been defending him cautiously, picking up the odd single. Warne teases away on and just outside off stump, perfect length, hint of turn, subtle variations of pace and trajectory. Come on then, what you gonna do, his bowling was saying. OK, says Pietersen. He puts his big front dog down the pitch and using his massive reach, slog-sweeps a good-length ball off the stumps. BIFF! He makes clean contact. The ball flies flat into the hospitality boxes in the Grand Stand, lobster thermidor and all. Incredible shot! You just don't do that to the great Warne on your Test debut.

England lost the Test, but Pietersen had single-handledly tamed Australia's two-headed dragon. He had showed the way forward, not to be cowed or intimidated, but to impose yourself on the oppressors. The other England batsmen took the lead. At Edgbaston, Marcus Trescothick bunted Brett Lee through the covers and thumped Jason Gillespie past mid-on. Andrew Strauss, benefiting from the advent of Merlin – the spin-bowling machine – shimmied up the wicket to Warne and planted him over long on. Michael Vaughan pulled and drove, Pietersen spanked them through cover and unveiled his one-legged 'flamingo' shot, and Andrew Flintoff, who had battled like a mouse at Lord's, clubbed sixes off his nose and wellied Michael Kasprowicz onto the roof of the commentary box to squeals of sadistic joy from Geoff Boycott. Batting was undergoing a seismic shift.

It was a series of tailend heroics: Lee and Kasprowicz nearly seizing a remarkable one-wicket win at Edgbaston, McGrath and Lee valiantly holding out for a draw at Old Trafford, Hoggard and Giles nudging England to knuckle-chewing victory at Trent Bridge. Through proper practice and application, they were making the most of their limited batting ability, making every match compelling viewing.

Déjà Vu

The nation had cricket fever for the first time for a generation and we staged our own mini Test in my parents' back garden –

the same place I'd first imagined being an Ashes hero aged ten. There were our three kids – Callum, Nancy and Billy, my sister Bettany's two girls and Michael Atherton's son Josh. Despite Callum's inswingers, Nancy's whippy arm and Billy doing a passable impression of Murali (a half-chuck that turned a bit), we couldn't get Josh (three) out, even with the help of my father's umpiring. Atherton (jnr) had obviously inherited good genes.

Aged 83, my father still ran the Ealing Under-17s colts team. He'd been coaching and fetching and carrying and phoning and cajoling almost every day for 30 years. He'd be up at the club every other day, taking nets or collecting the kit-bag or repairing fraying pads or pinning up his carefully written-out team lists, only to be rung up at 11 o'clock the night before the match by a father to say Salim and Arshad have to stay in and study for their design technology exam next week. So he spends an eternity on the phone the next morning trying to rustle up substitutes.

Ever since I was nine, he'd packed his car with players and bags and spare kit and negotiated the rush hour to get them to the venue. He'd sorted out the batting order and outlined the strategy and offered encouraging tips to the batsmen or whispered that square leg's a bit deep when he's umpiring. The players nod and smile and the bright ones listen and the stupid ones don't. (I didn't, mostly, but then that's sons for you.)

He'd be late for lunch most Sundays because Under-17 fielding practice overran and he'd eat his roast in his whites still sweating from the exertion, his bad knee (the result of me failing to help him over a stile) swelling up like a pomegranate.

He'd be back on the phone that afternoon, rustling up a team for Wednesday and placating fathers who can't understand why little Oscar isn't opening the batting and bowling and keeping wicket.

My father's enthusiasm, his commitment, his love of the game was total. And yet, that year, because of a new government directive on the handling of minors, he had been asked to sign a lengthy form from the Criminal Records Bureau detailing almost his entire life history and agreeing he would have no physical contact with juveniles. Essentially, it was seeking an assurance that he was not a paedophile. It even suggested he was not allowed to go into the dressing room.

He was so insulted he considered packing it all in, to become another innocent victim of the bureaucracy hampering sport.

He didn't though. He swallowed his indignation and carried on, determined not to dump the responsibility on others, reminding me that I owed all the opportunity, enjoyment, fascination and occasional frustration I've had from cricket to him. I only wish I could have repaid his devotion to me with some good innings. I vowed to give my kids as much support, encouragement, direction (and lifts) in their sporting endeavours as he gave to me. I felt sure that one of my sons would listen more to me than I did to him. Hope springs eternal.

In the lead-up to the final Ashes Test at The Oval, there was a PR opportunity with Pietersen organised by his sponsors Red Bull, whose product he'd often be seen swigging in the dressing room. (Such was the frenetic nature of the early part of his innings, I always thought he'd be better off being sponsored by Night Nurse.) In a moment of madness, I suggested I bowl an over at him.

He came to the club, Ealing, strapped on his pads and I set him a target of 24. I had never conceded more than 16 off an over in my entire career (I luckily retired before the carnage of T20 had been unleashed). He failed, mainly because the pitch was a bit dodgy and his bat lousy and he probably wasn't trying all that hard, but he impressed our kids with his huge stature and mad hair and the way he assaulted the ball and his promise that 'I'll score off every ball against Warne. He thrives on building up pressure and I won't let him do that to me.'

'Go for it, Kev!' we all said in unison.

Seven sixes and 158 breathtaking runs later, the Ashes were England's for the first time in 16 years. He had refreshed the parts other Boers could not reach.

Indian Takeaway

Pietersen repeated that score in Adelaide 15 months later in the famous match in which England declared with 551 on the board ... and lost by six wickets. I stood outside the ground, by a statue of Bradman playing an off drive, demonstrating to a TV crew how Pietersen, with his height and long levers and big forward stride, had probably the longest reach of any batsman in history.

Few tall batsmen had ever moved their feet much and none had regularly slapped a fast, short-of-a-length ball still rising through mid-wicket off the front foot quite like him. Sometimes he added some top-spin, too. It was like a Roger Federer forehand passing shot. He was using his 'Distal' ActionType (see page 153) to exceptional effect (like Federer). He had continued the trend of intimidatory batting started by the Australians, and most teams were now following Michael Vaughan's lead and posting sweepers on the boundary at square leg and cover for most of a Test Match day to reduce the boundary count.

The T20 phenomenon was already having an influence on all cricket. South Africa successfully chased 435 to win in a 50-over match against Australia at a run-rate of 8.7 an over. We chuckled at the memory of the incomparable Richie Benaud saying, 'Now, let me tell you, you don't want to let that required rate get above six!' during umpteen NatWest Trophy matches in previous decades.

Holding the bat right at the top of the handle to maximise leverage, Adam Gilchrist missed by two balls scoring the fastest Test hundred of all time, a record remarkably still held by Viv Richards (56 balls v England in 1986), until the incredible Brendon McCullum overtook it with his 54-ball assault on Australia in February 2016. Yuvraj Singh hit an over from Stuart Broad for six sixes, and Pietersen hit two sixes off the New Zealand medium pacer Scott Styris *left handed*. One soared over wide long off like a Phil Mickelson five iron.

Pietersen had switched his hands and feet, reversing his body completely, as the ball was on its way down. No bother about which was *his* 'motor eye'. It was the most amazing shot ever played. David Gower admitted he couldn't have hit it that far 'and I *am* left handed'. Wisely, the MCC, the game's law guardians, did not condemn the switch hit, saying instead that it was 'exciting for the game of cricket'.

They also did not legislate against the huge bats players were now wielding, with edges as thick as floor joists. I experimented with a broad selection in a net recently. It is slightly alarming how easy it is to thunder the ball back from where it came. Even the mishits fly off at unprecedented speed. Bowlers (and umpires) are increasingly in mortal danger. Not many old trundlers on that law-making MCC committee, I might add.

Batting styles had already been elevated so far beyond the old idea of getting your foot to the pitch, left elbow up to keep the ball on the ground. The launch of the Indian Premier League in 2008 took it into the stratosphere. The firestarter Brendon McCullum strode to the wicket in Bangalore after a spectacular and innovative opening ceremony to give an extraordinary display of pyrotechnics.

With the weeks of pre-tournament hype, the TV bombardment of dramatic, Bollywood-styled ads, the 50ft advertising hoardings from which star players glared down with Tarantino expressions proclaiming 'Be scared, be shit scared', the thumping dance music in the stadium whipping the crowd into a frenzy, the live acts and laser shows and fireworks and the preening Bollywood stars, there was a danger that the actual event (the cricket) might be an anti-climax.

No chance. Inspired by Michael Jackson's 'Beat It' resonating round the stadium just before the off, McCullum, bought by the Kolkata Knight Riders for $700,000, pulled, drove, clubbed, swatted, carved and sliced 13 sixes and 10 fours on his way to an extraordinary 158 not out from just 73 balls. The highly respected Indian pace bowler Zaheer Khan's opening over was pummelled for 18, sometimes from two steps down the pitch, and the fifty was posted after four overs. With hands faster than a Chinese chef, McCullum diced the other muscular bowlers into mince. The Washington Redskin cheerleaders, hired for the night to jig about every time there was a boundary, were soon wearily waving their pom-poms sitting down.

I sat in the stand in Bangalore, my senses assaulted by the crazy shots and the deafening music and the wild cheering and the smell of burning sulphur and contemplated what my boyhood batting hero Colin Cowdrey – he of the elegant off-drive – whose birthplace this was, would have made of it. When the heavily tattooed McCullum finished the innings by jabbing a low full toss for his 13th six, Kolkata had posted 222 from their 20 overs. That's more runs than I often made in a season.

The rest of the new competition continued in the same vein. There were 622 sixes (rebranded 'DLF Maximums') struck in the 59 matches, and a new vocabulary of strokes created, many of which had more connection to a kitchen than a cricket field. As well as the 'slice' and the 'carve', there was also the 'scoop' (the flick over the batsman's own head pioneered by the Sri Lankan Tillakaratne Dilshan and therefore renamed the Dilscoop) and the 'flip' or 'frying pan' – the batsman getting low down and using his wrists as if he was tossing a pancake to lift a fast ball over the close-in field.

Helmets were originally introduced to protect batsmen from serious injury as they tried to avoid a fast, short ball. It still hurt when you got one on the bonce. Now they were *encouraging* batsmen to get their head as near as possible to the trajectory of an 85mph delivery so that they could deflect it over their shoulder with the 'ramp' shot. They usually laughed it off if they got hit.

The conventional idea of playing yourself in had completely gone out of the window. There was no time. You had to get on with it immediately. A dot ball was sacrilege. Maiden overs? They were as rare as a virgin in Soho. You had to bat adventurously, fearlessly. You took guard visualising you were 20 not out even though you hadn't faced a ball. It required a totally different mentality.

In a way T20 took the selfish individualism away from batting. You had to forget about building an innings and feeling comfortable at the crease and your average to the second decimal point. Personal 'form' was irrelevant. You were taking risks on behalf of the team, and if it didn't come off and you were caught on the boundary you got a pat on the back for the effort rather than a rollicking for a stupid shot. Thirties were celebrated like fifties. No committee man would eye up your stats and mutter darkly, 'That Hughes only averages 16.13.' I think I would rather like to have been able to bat under those conditions, especially with bats like railway sleepers. Nobody in their right mind would want to be a bowler.

Stick or Twist?

And yet, T20 was/is light relief for batsmen. It was tough elsewhere. With the increasing intrusion of TV, the greater analysis and the global spotlight – cricket matches shown all over the world (the 2005 Ashes were even apparently followed in the Malaysian jungle by a bloke on his laptop) – the pressure on batsmen was more intense than ever. Technique and dismissals forensically dissected, character unravelled, statistics scrutinised, batting at international level was like a daily interrogation.

Some leading Test batsmen reached breaking point – like Marcus Trescothick and later Jonathan Trott, who both exited England tours suffering from severe mental fatigue (the official term was 'stress-related illness'). The endless pressure and responsibility were crushing. There was no down time or fun (Trescothick had barely played for Somerset for five years). The relentlessness of their job had turned them into nervous wrecks.

They might have had the slogan 'Form is temporary, class is permanent' stuck on their kitbags or embedded in their mind, but after a few failures, magnified and pontificated on by the unscrupulous media, self-doubt began to creep in. Once you show any sign of uncertainty to the bowler, you're toast. A batsman who's out of nick and betrays it is a dead man walking. He's back in the hutch before he's had time to iron out his flaws, and then facing an agonising wait for his next opportunity. It's a lonely business. At least an out-of-sync bowler has a few overs to find some rhythm and confidence.

'You could never have been a batsman,' Andrew Strauss said to me.

'Why?'

'No discipline, no organisation. You have to have a structure of practice and method and stick to it religiously whatever happens. You're the wrong sort of character. A batsman can't just make it up as he goes along.'

The wrong sort of character? Hmmm. Maybe. Well, what sort of character am I? I decided to find out. (I've only been on this earth half a century.) Knowing that sports psychologists and coaches pin a lot of faith on the Myers-Briggs psychometric questionnaire, I did one. I answered 92 multiple-choice questions examining my preferences and attitudes as faithfully as I could.

I pressed the 'evaluate' button and held my breath. I was terrified it would tell me I was a psycho that should be locked up or something (my ex has been telling me that for years). It declared that I was **ESFP** – Extrovert (89 per cent), Sensing (1 per cent), Feeling (50 per cent), Perceiving (78 per cent). 'ESFPs,' it said, 'love people, excitement, telling stories and having fun.' (Right so far.) 'They are spontaneous and impulsive and love to entertain – on stage, at work, and/or at home.' (Must be my actor father's fault.) 'ESFPs are attracted to new ideas, new fashions, new gadgets. Perhaps it's the newness of life that attracts ESFPs to elementary education, especially kindergarten.' So I should have been a Nursery school teacher!

I had been labelled with the scientific version of FOMO (Fear Of Missing Out). Strauss was right. Batsmen in general need to have a more ordered, regimented, less freewheeling approach to life. Their whole game is based on structure and organisation and repetition. They don't like surprise or spontaneity. They are creatures of habit who like to stick to a tried and trusted routine.

This starts in the morning with a particular breakfast (you see, I tend to vary mine). Then their preparation continues, as we have seen, with a certain number and type of throwdowns to groove their footwork and timing and a visualisation of their innings standing in the middle. They retreat to a preferred corner of the dressing room to prepare their bats and equipment and change into their lucky shirt and maintain a superstitious order in which they put on their kit – usually left pad first. (I always thought superstitions were the first stage of insanity, and, as previously admitted, put my kit on in a random order often on the way out to the middle.)

Batsmen who have been successful over a long period of time are loath to change any of this detail, even in the midst of a poor run. They are convinced that the method that enabled them to scale the heights will do so again. (This is when they repeat the 'form is temporary, class is permanent' line.) As long as they are patient the rewards will return. They would always rather 'stick' than 'twist'. In particular their 'trigger movements' are built into their DNA. Changing that is almost like trying to learn to walk again.

Some batsmen have a tipping point, however, a day when their carefully honed method, grooved over years and years and previously producing buckets of runs, lets them down once too often. After a lot of soul-searching and consultation and hair pulling (most seasoned batsmen are bald or have had hair transplants), they try something different. Though virtually imperceptible to outsiders, it's a big step to the person involved, like finally accepting you're ugly (or bald), and it has to be taken gradually. Sometimes it works. Sometimes it doesn't.

Graham Gooch, captain of England at the time, famously had difficulty with Terry Alderman in the 1989 Ashes, moving across his stumps and missing wickedly straight balls. In fact the problem was so notorious it even appeared on a piece of political graffiti daubed on a prominent London wall. Underneath 'Thatcher Out!!' someone had painted 'LBW Alderman'.

'I was walking across the crease too early, and when I took guard outside leg stump to counter it, I found I was moving even more across to compensate. I went to Boycott and he remembered how I used to bat, and he suggested I take leg stump guard again and take a step back slightly as the bowler bowled. Everything clicked back into place.' The following summer he made his 333 against India.

Strauss, naturally a back-foot cutter and puller, found as his Test career progressed that bowlers were denying him those shots and bowling fuller. He went through a phase of getting out driving or playing forward without transferring his weight properly or hitting through the line. He tried to counter it. 'I did loads of driving practice, getting further forward and trying to hit straighter down the ground more. I actually became more rigid and less effective as a player and missed out on a lot of cuts and pulls.' If, by attending to your weaknesses, you sacrifice your strengths, it's counter-productive.

It's a delicate balance. You have to understand your assets, but realise over time that the bowler understands them, too. A bit of 'tinkering' (a Strauss word) is sometimes required. But not too much. The classic mistake is a batsman who has been getting out LBW a lot by getting too far over and playing across a straight ball (eg Gooch v Alderman), trying to adapt by standing more on leg stump and delaying his movements. They then find they are getting out caught at slip because they are not moving over *enough* to cover the ball on off stump.

Or vice versa. The bloke fed up being constantly caught at slip because he is not getting over far enough, then introducing a big lunge across his stumps. He finds he is now overbalancing, missing straight ones and departing LBW. Alastair Cook has been experiencing this, so then went back to delaying his movements and was caught slip again. As yet he still has a full head of hair. 'When you're in form you're thinking about nothing,' says Michael Vaughan. 'When you're out of form you're thinking about everything.' Batting can be a head-fuck. You can't put it any other way.

Dancing with the Stars

Strauss came round to our house with his young family for Sunday lunch and we played a bit of cricket in the garden. His son Sam (two) already looked useful. After they'd gone I tried to work out which one of my kids had the best character for batting. Callum, now nine, definitely liked routine, eating the same food religiously and being extremely risk averse ('Be careful on that ladder, Dad!'), but he wasn't very competitive. Billy, four, was the opposite. He was very adventurous and always falling over or getting hurt ('Get down off that ladder, Billy!') He didn't have enough discipline. Nancy, seven, seemed to have the best balance between competitiveness and order and the best hand-eye co-ordination of the three. A right hander, she had even successfully copied Strauss's left-handed method. But what future did a girl have as a cricketer? Anyway she was mainly obsessed with Mark Ramprakash on *Strictly Come Dancing*.

It was an understandable fascination. He was brilliant! No nerves, no apprehensions, great rhythm and balance and plenty of flamboyance. Still very fit, he looked fantastic. All the women I knew fancied him. I went to watch him train. The rehearsal studios were a converted warehouse by Dalston Junction, London's version of the Bronx, the opposite of *Strictly*'s glittering, glam setting.

He eased stylishly around the dance studio floor with his partner, Karen Hardy, waltzing through his steps as he would were he ritually dispatching a mediocre spin bowler. I realised that dancing was the perfect vehicle for Ramprakash, allowing self-expression without the constraints of convention or statistics. His natural batting ability had been inhibited by expectation and obligation and uncertainty. Here, there was no expectation. Essentially he was a novice and everyone knew that. And he didn't have to think too hard or worry about the future or his place in the team. Just follow a sequence of steps.

Also, his outstanding ability as a mimic was handy. His superb imitations of players' mannerisms – Viv Richards's swagger, Geoff Boycott's poise, Gooch's funny wobbling head in his stance, the oriental swirl of Abdul Qadir's bowling action, the manic charging of Malcolm Marshall – marked him out as an excellent observer of bodily movement and rhythms. It enabled him to almost perfectly copy a dance routine, a special skill now on display to nine million viewers.

He loved the training with Karen. 'Every session she is so enthusiastic and she makes it varied and fun, and it's an attitude that could really make a crossover to cricket. Cricket practice can be so technical and stereotyped. Everyone's so worried about the left elbow – is it in the right place? Cricket's a game! Something to be enjoyed. That would be one massive thing I've got from this.'

He won *Strictly*, you'll recall. He and Karen were awarded the perfect 40 score for their Salsa. It was quite an achievement. Securing a ten from Craig Revel Horwood is as hard as getting a 'better than my moom's battin'!' from Geoff Boycott (unless you're a Yorkshireman). To be fair, their compliments mean more because they are so hard-won.

Ramprakash transferred his new-found enlightenment and confidence into his batting. He scored over 2000 runs in consecutive seasons in 2006 and 2007 for Surrey and averaged 100 in both. And on 2 August 2008 he became the 25th, and probably last-ever, batsman in cricket history to make 100 first-class hundreds. He had attained batting nirvana, although he was still usually depicted in the papers doing the Rumba in a sequinned shirt.

'It was the culmination of a lot of factors. Physically I was in good condition, technically I knew my game. I had motivation – I said to myself I want to play the innings of the day, not the best shot of the day. I was disappointed in my Test record and for Surrey I wanted to play innings that allowed my team the chance to control the match. I got great satisfaction from that.

'I was comfortable in the environment at Surrey and felt very relaxed at the crease. I handled batting for long periods much better. I learnt to switch down between balls or at the non-striker's end. I liked it when someone like Gunner [Ian Gould] was umpire because I could have a laugh and talk about football. If I played and missed a couple of times, or went through a tough period, I didn't get fazed by it, I just carried on. Of course, I had a lot of experience to call upon. I got better at knowing when to soak up pressure during a good bowling spell and hang in there, and when to counterattack and break free of it.'

'The hundredth hundred was very, very special.'

I guess that means it *was* better than sex (irrespective of who with).

'It was at Headingley, so there was a nice symmetry [it was where he scored his first]. Darren Gough was captain of Yorkshire. When I was on about ninety-seven, this young left-arm spinner David Wainwright was bowling. Goughy brought all the men in saving the one. And there's that little man in my head saying "Run down run down!" Being a bit wiser now, I thought: "OK, fake." He'll be expecting me to run down.

'So he bowled me five very good balls and then, I pretended to come down the wicket, and he saw me and gave me a fraction of width and I managed to cut it for four for the hundred. So experience won out. I don't see many players do that now, disrupting the bowler like that. I often throw it into our England practice sessions, talking to young batsmen, saying how do you think you can get him to bowl the ball that you want.'

Now that *is* the secret of batting – making the bowler bowl to your strength. Aged 37, Ramprakash had uncovered it and when added to his supreme skill, innate desire and composure at the crease, he was now the complete batsman. He was an unstoppable run machine, and had become the fifth Surrey player, after Tom Hayward, Andy Sandham, Jack Hobbs and John Edrich to make 100 hundreds. No other county can boast as many to have reached the landmark.

Wanna Be a Batsman Rule No.8 – Play at The Oval.

Don't Get Your Leg Over Too Soon

I took my family to The Oval for the fourth day of the final 2009 Ashes Test. The series had built to a climax – not quite as exciting as 2005, but still beautifully poised (Australia needed an improbable 546 to retain the Ashes and were 80 for nought overnight). It was the kids' first experience of a Test match and I wanted them to absorb the rhythms of the ultimate form of the game and savour the atmosphere of the Ashes as England homed in on victory.

In fact, only three Australian wickets fell in the first two sessions and the boys were mostly immersed in playing Super Mario on their Nintendo DS's, except when they met Daniel Radcliffe in the *TMS* box. Nancy followed the action more carefully, however, pointing out Strauss's field changes and cheering his catch in the deep and remarking on Ricky Ponting's cuts and sweeps. But by 5pm England were looking as fed up and weary as the kids. 'The game will definitely go to a fifth day,' I said confidently, and sent them all home in a taxi while I finished work. Half an hour later, the match was over. England had regained the Ashes. They missed their 'friend' Strauss being presented with the urn.

It had whetted their appetite, though, and after that garden Test matches attained higher levels of intensity, enhanced by the artificial grass we had just laid which was bouncy and playable in any weather. The garden wasn't very long so run-ups started in the kitchen, past the dining table, through the double doors and onto the patio. With a slip and a silly point and a deck chair at short leg, keeping the ball down was vital.

Sometimes we used an Incrediball which spun prodigiously and I threw in a few *doosras*. Other times we used a tennis ball with tape on one side to make it swing dramatically and I produced a few Waqar Younis-style inswinging yorkers. I was really trying to give them the full gamut of bowling styles. Despite the boys' greater strength and stubbornness (in other words, they never admitted they were out), it was again Nancy who seemed to be the best at handling the movement – when we could drag her away from DVD reruns of *Strictly*.

(She had also some inner steel too, obvious when she nervelessly slotted home two penalties in a sudden-death shoot-out in the Under-11 Mayor's Cup final in front of about 150 crooning parents. The only serious penalty I had ever taken was in the commentators' 'World Cup 2004 challenge' on Channel 4's *Cricket Roadshow*. I blasted the ball onto the roof of the VT truck and damaged an aerial.)

Making sure my kids were well versed in modern batting philosophy, I stressed the growing importance of *using your bat*. It sounds obvious. But batsmen are reared on the idea of getting their foot to the pitch with bat and pad close together. That's how we were always told to play. Sometimes that means you are playing the line of the ball with your pad more than your bat. If the bowler was moving or spinning the ball away, you tended to play outside the line and allow for the movement, using your pad as a first line of defence. Once the Decision Review System was introduced into international cricket in late 2009, playing that old way – lining up the ball with your pad – was fatal.

It was a boon to spinners in particular. Graeme Swann had just emerged on the Test scene. Almost half (25) of his first 60 Test wickets were dismissed LBW. A typical wicket was his dismissal of the South African Mark Boucher, who stretched well forward to Swann, bowling around the wicket. The ball turned into him slightly and hit him on the pad. Appeal. 'Not out,' said the umpire. Previously that would have been that. The batsman would have believed he was too far down the pitch to be given out, the bowler would have shrugged disconsolately. Instead, Swann asked for a review. Hawk-Eye said that the ball had turned enough to hit the stumps and the batsman had been struck in line. Decision reversed. Swann had arrived at the right place at the right time.

A lot of batsmen weren't so happy. Kevin Pietersen in

particular. He already had a problem with left-arm spinners, plunging his big front dog down the pitch and trying to work their straight balls to leg and sometimes missing. Before the DRS, he had usually got away with it because of his long stride. Now batsmen who believed they had a divine right to be given not out because they were 'so far forward' were getting their come-uppance, even if the umpires did, initially, sympathise.

Batsmen were, for once, entitled to gripe. LBW decisions were now upheld if the ball was shown on Hawk-Eye to be just shaving the stump by 2mm. These deliveries would have been assumed to be missing five years before and therefore the batsman would have been given not out. But now umpires were more wary of being shown up by technology and more inclined to award marginal decisions in favour of the bowler.

The wicket (in the umpire's interpretation and Hawk-Eye's evaluation) had become higher and wider – almost a ball's width on either side and above. I did the maths. It had increased the bowler's potential target area by a whopping 70 per cent (much to the chagrin of many a retired bowler – God only knows how many 'well, fack mes!' John Emburey would have uttered when he heard that).

This 'virtual' expansion of the wicket was the biggest change in any of the game's fundamental properties since the third stump was introduced in 1775. And with Pietersen playing across his front pad against left-arm spin, he was dicing with death.

There was, of course, the bravado aspect with Pietersen, too. He appeared to be thinking: 'How can this little left-arm nonentity bowl at me?' His inner chimp was yelling: 'He's got to go! Take him downtown!' The wily sub-continent spinners were playing on that, teasing and tantalising him with simple straight-on deliveries, aiming to hit him on the pad with him playing for the turn. He was all at sea and, worse, *denying* he was all at sea. Denying it publicly, anyway.

Rahul Dravid came to his aid. This is one of the hidden benefits of participation in the IPL. You meet, talk, eat, drink, train and play with the superstars of the game. There's a whole day to kill in the hotel before you go to the ground. You forge strong friendships with great players from other parts of the world, exchanging thoughts and ideas. The IPL is a cricketing brainstorm. It's a fast track to success. English players' (and coaches') regular absence from the IPL is the main reason England lags so far behind in one-day cricket. (England's one limited-overs triumph – winning the World T20 in 2010 – was after five of their team and one coach had participated in the IPL.)

Pietersen and Dravid had played together for Royal Challengers Bangalore. With silky movements and delicate touch (and no ego), Dravid was a master of playing spin. He suggested Pietersen practise without pads against left-arm spin to stop him planting his foot at the ball. 'My coach would tell me you should never need pads to play spin!' he added. He recommended *looking* to go forward but not committing, and seizing any opportunity to score off the back foot.

To Pietersen's credit, he took the advice on and adjusted. He stood up straighter and stayed more leg side of the ball against left-arm spin, and tried not to plant his front foot. He also looked to open the bat face and hit more through the off side, with the direction of the spin rather than against it. He appeared a more balanced, rounded player. He scored big runs, and was rarely out to left-arm spin. Problem solved, for a while, culminating in England getting to number one in the world.

It was all fine until those dastardly left armers started going closer to the stumps, bowling wicket to wicket and aiming to go past the *inside* of the right handers' bat rather than the outside. They preyed on batsmen now so nervous about getting their leg in the way that they were lunging outside leg stump. As a result they were leaving a massive gap between bat and pad and being bowled through the gate. England were thumped 3-0 by Pakistan in the UAE. The orthodox left-arm spinner Abdur Rehman took 19 wickets in the series, 14 of which were LBW or bowled. The dynamic, cat-and-mouse relationship between batsman and bowlers is what makes the game – especially the Test match version – so endlessly fascinating.

This Wall's Got Legs

Rahul Dravid is the ultimate student of the game (he has even read my book *Jargonbusting – Mastering the Art of Cricket*. God knows why.). Having negotiated more balls in Test cricket than any batsman ever, he was unfairly dubbed The Wall, and he didn't like it much either. He was usually described as 'obdurate' or 'adhesive', but he could be a very fluent player able to play at different tempos and he unravelled many batting issues.

Dravid solved the spin conundrum. He made an exquisite hundred against England at The Oval when all the Indians around him (including Tendulkar) were floundering. On a dry pitch, he soon recognised Graeme Swann was the main threat. He never let him settle, picking him off repetitively for runs, destabilising England's four-man attack, which rotated around Swann.

The platform for Dravid's batting against spin – this will be music to Geoff Boycott's ears – was his footwork. It was balletic in its nimble springiness, dancing back onto his stumps at the first hint of a short ball – bearing out his advice to Pietersen that you should look for back-foot scoring opportunities against spin. Swann countered by bowling fuller, trying to catch him back on his stumps. Dravid stretched out far in front of his body to stun the ball and nullify the spin or reach forward to work it to leg with a wristy flick. He used his bat – never his pad, of course, given his practice against spinners without wearing them – and the full depth of the crease brilliantly.

What was especially compelling about this innings was that Dravid confounded the accepted norm of 'playing with the spin'. He looked to score primarily *against* the spin's direction. He explained that one morning on The Oval outfield after practice.

'There are more scoring options against the spin [ie on the off side when facing an off-spinner], because there are less fielders on that side,' he said. It was such a simple observation, yet no one had really commented on it before. Swann, for instance, bowled typically to five men on the leg side, and only four on the off (and two of them were close catchers). That left only two men in defensive positions on the off side. Therefore Dravid looked to force the ball on that side – off back or front foot – whenever possible.

Theoretically this is playing into the off-spinners' hands. Swann wants the right hander to try and hit through the off side (against the direction of spin) hoping to bowl him through the gate. It is a risky method because the bat is flowing across the line of the ball spinning in. Dravid's judgement of Swann's length had to be perfect. A fraction short and he could dance onto the back foot and punch the ball with a straight bat through cover (or dab it backward of point.) A tad over-pitched and he looked to step right out to steer it wide of mid-off. If he misread the length, this strategy spelt potential danger. But he never did.

He picked up runs on the leg side with dinks and deflections when Swann aimed straighter. All his strokes were played with a straight blade, using his wrists at the point of contact to steer the ball into a gap. He never attempted to sweep – very much the English escape route against spin, despite the inherent danger of being LBW – and yet he was impossible to contain. In the end, it was more effective to give him a single and bowl at the other bloke.

The secret to Dravid's success was revealed afterwards when

DRAVID STRIKE POINTS AGAINST SWANN - THE OVAL 2011
DOTS · RUNS · BOUNDARIES · WICKETS Hawk-Eye

looking at that awful, dirty, unmentionable thing – the 'data'. His 'interception points' against Swann (the point at which his bat struck the ball – see graphic) were either less than six inches or more than three feet from where the ball pitched. Never in-between.

In other words he had either got very close to the ball's pitching point if it was full – ie well forward to negate any spin – or as far away as possible from the pitching point if it was shorter – ie well back to play it after the spin had occurred. He was never caught halfway between the two – what batting experts call 'no man's land', what commentators might describe as 'done for length'. (That would be the area on the graphic in between the two clusters of balls.) Dravid made 146 of India's 300. No other senior batsman got past 23. It was an immaculate exhibition by a master craftsman. Definitely not a bricklayer.

It's a Batter's Game

Fast bowlers put six times their body weight through their knee and ankle every time they deliver the ball. It's a shocking fact. In my case, that was a force of almost 500kg per delivery. Multiply that by 40,000 (the number of balls I sent down in professional cricket, never mind amateur and nets) and it makes 20,000,000kg worth of pressure. That's the equivalent of the 22,000 ton Brittany ferry through my joints. It's the reason why my knees sounded like packets of rice crispies and I went to work with a slight limp. I'm lucky I don't need a zimmer frame. Yet.

Batting was the future. I was surrounded by successful people who had made runs for a living. There were 229 first-class hundreds in the Channel 5 commentary box: Geoff Boycott (151), Michael Vaughan (42), Mark Nicholas (36) and none of them limped (much). The talk was invariably about the 'techneek' and ability and attitude required to bat as we watched Test matches unfold.

Boycott, for all his blather about his 'moom' and sticks of rhubarb, is a fantastic observer of the game, watching it as closely as he did the ball when he was at the crease, and you learnt something new every day. His unbridled passion for batting was still evident. When he talked about a good innings he was practically salivating, reliving the joy of himself devouring the bowlers' best offerings. It was bordering on sadism.

'Which would you prefer, a Test hundred or Kim Basinger?' I asked him once.

'A Test 'undred!' he said, without hesitation ' . . . and Kim Basinger after . . .' He is the definition of insatiable.

Celebrated batsmen – Michael Atherton, Andrew Strauss – were good friends and we had dinner together and they played cricket with my kids. Ricky Ponting had even kindly bowled to them on the outfield at a charity match. On holiday in Jersey we went to the Boycotts' house for tea and he conducted an impromptu coaching session on the back lawn after. 'See the ball early, play it late!' he kept saying, taking a particular interest in Nancy's square drive. This is something Ted Dexter always emphasised to me too when I was growing up. 'Wait as long as you can to play the ball,' he used to say. My problem was I didn't see the ball early enough to play it late, if you see what I mean.

We watched the Test highlights as a family and staged our re-matches in the garden – or kitchen if it was raining – and

I dragged them away from playing Harbour Master or Angry Birds on their iPads to go to the local club nets. I spent a shed-load of money kitting them all out with bats, pads and helmets and all the other batting paraphernalia. Billy's size 4 bat was chunkier and hit the ball harder than any full-sized version I had ever played with.

When I was working on the IPL for ITV, I ferried them into the Waterloo studio after school to see on a giant plasma screen Chris Gayle boom the ball into the stands or A.B.de Villiers flip a 90mph yorker over fine leg for six or M.S.Dhoni bludgeon a challenging target to smithereens. When Chennai Super Kings needed 64 from four overs in Dharamsala to get into the play-offs, he got them there with several balls to spare. The winning hit soared into the night sky, beyond the startled Dalai Lama, way over the main stand and disappeared into the foothills of the Himalayas. Mishits were sailing for six. Run-rates were going sky-high. Bowlers had the Samaritans on speed dial.

Something of the essence and rewards of batting was hopefully percolating into the kids' subconscious. Now there was an opportunity to take their cricketing education to the next level. In April, we were invited to the Super Skills cricket camp in Forte Village, Sardinia. Run by the former England rugby player Will Greenwood, the coaches were Michael Vaughan and Alec Stewart (most top coaches are former batsmen because they are the only people who can still run).

The England analyst Mark Garaway was on hand to film, monitor and advise. He had an app on his iPad which enabled him to slow down, stop, draw coloured lines and do split-screens on video footage of the junior batsmen. To think when I was that age the only video camera we had used reel-to-reel tape which took an age to spool and then you had to erect a projector on a pile of encyclopedias and take off all the pictures on the sitting room wall to beam it on to. And batsmen were like specks in a field.

Practice in Sardinia started every morning at 9am on artificial grass and there were more drills than in a Black and Decker factory. Every conceivable shot was demonstrated and grooved with tennis balls. Despite all that, both Callum and Billy headed down the bowling route. Neither seemed to possess either the technical, or mental, ability to bat. Like father like sons. Whereas Nancy, with an increasing range of controlled strokes and a determined focus, had both.

'She's a better batter than you!' Vaughan said to me.

'Yes,' echoed Stewart, 'mind you, that wouldn't be hard.'

She had a decent bowling action too, and threw flat, like a boy. After a few solid performances for a boys' colts team, she was told about a trial for the Middlesex Under-11 girls. I hadn't realised there was county cricket for girls of that age. I was amazed to find at least 50 at the trial, many with smart kit bags and highly ambitious parents.

Nancy bowled well and scored a few runs in the trial and got chosen in the Middlesex Under-11 team to play Kent. It made me immensely proud. I had not played for the county at that age. Remembering how Mike Gatting used to prepare, I persuaded her to eat a large quantity of eggs and bacon before the match, and then gave her plenty of practice on the outfield, and advice on how to bat having inspected the (dampish) pitch. Middlesex fielded first and she opened the bowling. I immediately felt guilty about making her eat so much food.

A TEST OF CHARACTER

I did what my father used to do and sat on a deckchair conspicuously behind the bowler's arm filming and, worse, shouting out bits of advice (which he thankfully never did). I was more nervous than I ever had been as a player – even bowling the last over of a Lord's final. I needn't have worried. She bowled five overs and took four for 10. She was not required to bat.

It was a good deal better than any of my early performances for Middlesex at any level, although I knew that batting was her stronger suit. Before the next match, against Essex, I bowled to her in the nets and gave her endless throwdowns, and talked to her about taking her time and looking for singles until she was set. I helped her get padded up and wished her good luck as she went in at No.4 and sat tensely by the boundary watching. She was run out without facing. Tears were shed. Nancy wasn't too happy either. I suppose it was divine retribution for what I had done to the Middlesex coach 30 years ago.

Is there any worse feeling in sport than being run out without facing? It happens in slow motion. You try to send your partner back, then realise they have come halfway and it's too late, so you finish up straining desperately to get to the other end. You are briefly optimistic, but your legs won't move fast enough, it feels like you're running through treacle; you're willing the throw to be wide, knowing it is destined to beat you; you see the wicketkeeper in position by the stumps ready to receive it, watching his eyes track the ball as it flies towards him. Your innings is momentarily suspended in time until it is brutally ended with the bails being whipped off. Life and death – love and hate – are one second apart.

In the end that reality is what a batsman has to deal with every time he goes to the wicket.

It separates the men from the boys. Or should I say the women from the girls?

CHAPTER 10

The Science of Art

If You Wanna Be the Best

Batsmen used to be regarded as artists. There was a simple purity about their play. From K.S. Ranjitsinhji and Frank Woolley in the so-called Golden Age through Walter Hammond, Denis Compton, Ted Dexter and Tom Graveney to Viv and Barry Richards, Majid Khan, David Gower, Martin Crowe, Mark Waugh, V.V.S. Laxman and Brian Lara, the shots of the great runmakers were often, perhaps pretentiously, described as brush strokes on a canvas using a broad palette of colours.

There are still some batting artists about. The beauty of art is in its variety. The same could be said about batting. Mahela Jayawardene and Kevin Pietersen both made a hundred in the same Colombo Test in 2012. Jayawardene was Monet to Pietersen's Picasso.

The Sri Lankan's brush strokes are delicate, careful, silky. There is a beautiful evenness about his movements, he has a steady hand as he guides, steers, caresses the ball across the green canvas. He glides across the ground, never seeming to exert much energy, but with a wristy flick on the point of contact, the resultant images are vivid. You can see the class and skill even in a brief sketch.

Pietersen, by contrast, is bold, outrageous, avant garde. His batting is a juxtaposition of the brazen and the bizarre. Some of his innings are almost incomprehensible. They defy logic and geometry. They are born of experimentation. They have surreal qualities. He is a reminder that genius and madness are closely related.

Jayawardene is meticulous, precise. Every stroke has a plan, to manipulate the field and manoeuvre the ball into gaps. Like a snooker player he is always working several shots ahead, with perfect control of the cue ball. There is the early paddle sweep to shift a man from mid-wicket to short fine leg. It is exquisitely played with fluid movement and perfect timing. Then, once the fielder has been moved, he persuades the ball into the vacant legside space for easy singles. He plays the ball tantalisingly late, watching it right onto the bat, using whatever pace he is given to deflect it to the boundary.

Early on, Pietersen also looks around to note where the fielders are. But he looks at large open spaces, rather than minute gaps. His shots are not governed by the line or length of the ball, but on where he has decided to hit it. He is a child of a more demanding environment. He wants it, and he wants it now. He seeks to impose himself, to dominate. He wants to make a statement, to play the game on his own terms. It is his stage. Conformism is irrelevant. He doesn't wait for the ball to arrive, he goes out in search of it, taking it on the up, as early as possible. Such is his power that once his eye is in, it is imma-terial where the fielders are. He just strikes the ball through or over them.

So here are two men, both right handed, both batting at No.4, both artists averaging almost 50 in Test cricket. Using totally contrasting methods. What we are saying here is there isn't a right way or a wrong way, just different ways. The bottom line is: be true to yourself. It is why batting reveals character perhaps more than any other discipline in sport. And that is the real beauty of it.

Art-at-the-crease is being gradually overtaken by science. Spontaneity and elegance have been replaced by selectivity and efficiency. Or occasionally outright crudity. Sachin Tendulkar's career straddles the change (it was that long it straddled most things, including the dismantling of apartheid, the develop-ment of satellite TV, and virtually Wayne Rooney's entire life). His beginnings were fluent, stylish, charismatic, occasionally uninhibited. As time went on, he became more compact and clinical, using a scalpel rather than a sword. Where Lara might destroy a bowling attack, Tendulkar systematically dissected it.

Instead of expansive drives with a big follow-through, Tendulkar's shots were more controlled. The ball was laser-guided into spaces. He phoned his brother every day to talk batting plans and angles. He deliberately had practice pitches roughed up when Shane Warne toured India. He averaged almost 57 against Australia at home and Warne dismissed him only once in 13 innings. Slightly out of sync in Sydney in 2004, he was finding the cover drive – his favourite shot – dif-ficult to time. So he cut it out. In ten hours of batting he made 241 not out and hit 33 fours, not a single one through the covers. There was still some discernible elegance and grace in his batting, otherwise you'd say he had become a pre-programmed run machine.

He still practised assiduously morning and evening, but after more than two decades playing international cricket, Tendulkar's conveyer-belt of runs gradually slowed to a halt. He missed the odd tour and began spending his summers in England. Life was less hassle in London, he didn't need protection wherever he went. There were downsides. There was the ignominious scoreline at my old club, Ealing, that was an unmistakable sign of decline. It read:

Tendulkar b Hughes 6.

In fact the batsman was his son Arjun, and the bowler was my daughter Nancy who had developed quite a nifty yorker. But the sight of seeing his lad castled by a girl would have sent him scurrying headlong back to India.

Tendulkar (snr) retired in 2013 after his 200th Test. It had been an incredible career, during which he shouldered the daily burden to, as the Indian poet C.P.Surendran put it, 'Lift us up from the dark pit of our lives to well-lit places of the imagination with your skill-wrought perfection.' (Tendulkar is India's saviour in so many ways, but his prowess has not alleviated the country's dodgy electricity supply.)

Following his departure, there ensued a fascinating duel at the top of the world batting leader board to decide who is Number One. Sri Lanka's Kumar Sangakkara had won the bragging rights in Test cricket, but South Africa's A.B.de Villiers was breathing down his neck and topped the one-day rankings. Nancy followed this battle avidly. Most 12-year-old girls have pictures of One Direction or Zac Efron on their walls. Hers were plastered with lists of ICC Player Rankings, each name neatly written in different-coloured felt pens. In the back garden, she tried to copy the style of whoever was on top.

De Villiers is the man of the moment. That record-breaking 31-ball century in a one-day international against the West Indies was absolute carnage. Mayhem. Obliteration. You'd run out of explosives. Or expletives, if you were the bowlers. He doesn't suffer from nervous nineties syndrome. He flew from 82 to 104 in four balls. He went on to make 149 from just 44 balls with 16 sixes. Chris Gayle bowed to him theatrically as he had been officially dethroned as the king of one-day bullies.

De Villiers' batting is less science, more art – but very much of the post-modern variety. The innings featured an amazing array of strokes. There were flicks and scoops and ramp shots played from yards outside off stump – the wicket ignored and practically irrelevant – as well as switch hits and good old-fashioned slogs – that borrowed much from his diverse sporting background.

He was an incredible young athlete. He was on the fringe of national junior sides in football and hockey, captained South Africa juniors at rugby and was in the national junior tennis team – dreaming of one day winning Wimbledon – as well as excelling at badminton, sprinting and swimming. He's a scratch golfer, too. And he's a decent bloke with it. Makes you sick, doesn't it?

He only began specialising at cricket in his teens – when his two older brothers couldn't get him out, even sometimes 'bowling beamers at my head' – but he still kept up many of the other sports. You could see the tennis coming through in his outrageous sweep of a low full toss over fine leg, sometimes one handed – like a top-spin passing shot picked up on the half volley – and the two-fisted backhand morphing into a reverse flick over third man. Golf was visible in the massive follow-through of some of the big hits, getting his hips through the shot to achieve greater momentum, the bat finishing up wrapped round his back like Rory McIlroy's driver. Hockey came into play in some of his more wristy deflections. He created shots like Shane Warne invented deliveries.

There is preparation and planning in his play. He rehearses his shots and doesn't just go out there swinging and hoping. He couldn't possibly achieve the level of consistency he does otherwise. The most outrageous shots are played from a stable base – he gets into position early (though not too early) – with head resolutely still and eyes lasered onto the ball. He hits all his shots from a controlled space around him which he calls 'the box'.

He watches the game carefully before he goes in, assessing the bowlers and the conditions and the state of the match. He considers the shots he thinks are right for the situation. And whatever he does, the team is the priority. He never bats for himself – witness his four hours of defiance against the Australians in 2012 for just 33 runs and *no* boundaries to save the Test in Adelaide. And by contrast his amazing 162-run decimation (off just 66 balls) of the West Indies (again) in the 2015 World Cup. He deserves to be the highest-ranked one-day batsman in the world. He has taken destructive hitting to nuclear levels.

In this era of uber-specialisation, his varied sporting upbringing is a good antidote. Not only does it aid his hand-eye co-ordination and enhance his fitness, but such diversity allows someone to *enjoy* their main sport because it is not a job or just an extension of a series of drills but a proper expression of his dynamic skills. It banishes apprehension, promotes fun and experimentation. Batting to him is almost like exploration. 'Sport is ninety per cent about having confidence in your ability and strengths,' he says. De Villiers is fearless. His mother said: 'He has always played without fear. It is just enjoyment. He has always been like that and it is such a gift that he simply doesn't feel pressure.' I wonder if he would have been the same if he had taken up bowling instead of batting . . .

Good Morning, Dr Kumar

I walk down a quiet, jasmine-scented road in the early-morning sunshine and through the gates of a rambling villa, set in verdant hills, its pleasant, leafy garden spreading out on all sides with glimpses of the sparkling lake below. It is the sort of place a stressed-out modern bowler ought to retreat to. I could be in New Zealand or Italy or Sweden, except that, at 9am, the temperature is already a sweaty 28°C. In fact, I am in Sri Lanka, on the outskirts of the bustling city of Kandy.

I am greeted at the covered porch by a housekeeper and shown into a large, airy room with a small goldfish pond set into the stone floor. There is a familiar sound of young children clattering around in the kitchen and someone playing an out-of-tune piano. A friendly, middle-aged Sri Lankan woman offers me a cup of tea. Soon afterwards her son appears, looking a bit bleary eyed as if he has just got up. He probably has. He didn't get away from the Pallekele Stadium till after 10pm last night, having run the England bowlers and fielders ragged.

This is the house where the world's number-one-ranked Test batsman, Kumar Sangakkara, grew up and learnt to bat and still returns for a regular check-up when he's in the country. Perhaps the place should be referred to as a laboratory, because Kumar Sangakkara has got a PhD in batting. Since his Sri Lanka debut in 2000, he has turned art into science, analysing and adapting and fine-tuning his method to score more international runs in the 21st century (almost 28,000 in all formats) than anyone else. I came to find out how he'd done it.

Part of the answer was provided before we'd even sat down. His father Kshema, a retired attorney, emerged from his study brandishing a book. It was Bradman's *The Art of Cricket*. It was open at a black-and-white photo-spread of the great man demonstrating the pull shot. 'This is where you made the mistake yesterday,' Sangakkara snr declared. 'Look at the great man, Bradman, and how he played the pull shot!' He points at the sequence of pictures. 'Look, you swivel on the ball and roll your wrists to keep it down. Not like you played it!'

Using the book as a makeshift bat, Kshema played the stroke as portrayed by Bradman, pirouetting on his back leg and hitting the imaginary ball along the ground. He was overlooking the fact that his son had made a previously faultless 91 the night before and, looking to accelerate in the last ten overs, was only caught on the boundary edge when he attempted to plant Chris Woakes over deep square leg for six. Kumar smiled, accepting the criticism graciously. It was obviously a regular occurrence. (In fact there is a YouTube clip of a similar scene in the family home – https://www.youtube.com/watch?v=Sdx03cSJhHc).

Son has obviously inherited one ingredient from father: perfectionism.

'My batting starts at training, leading up to a game,' Sangakkara says. 'That's where I get my confidence from. Not only hitting a lot of balls, but ensuring that when I do hit a ball my movements are easy and comfortable and unthinking. I don't want to go into bat worrying about technique because technique is something that is a base, but when you are playing, it's got to disappear – you've got to be instinctive and reactive. You want clear-headed execution of muscle-memory that you have trained your body over and over to ...' He hovers over the word 'perfect' and then prefers '... do'.

'The moment you see technique obviously in someone who's batting, I think that's where someone's not really *flowing*. When everything's flowing you don't see technique, you see style, you see grace, you see timing. That's what I work towards. I don't want to be fiddling or worrying about where my backlift is going, or whether my foot is going to the ball or how I balanced I am. I just want that flow.

'Because timing is your body and movements being in rhythm with everything, not just hitting the ball effortlessly down the ground but in rhythm with the wicket, the bowler's run-up and the pace the ball is being bowled at. Your movements have to be synchronised. And that comes from training. Training in the days before, and on match day too, assessing conditions correctly. And if you allow your body to fall into that rhythm on the day, that is when your timing is really good. That's when you're not fighting against the wicket or the pace of the ball or yourself. Everything has to be instinctive in the match. The moment you think, it slows you down.

It restricts your body and your movements and that's when you make mistakes.'

So batting is about rhythm, and flow. I have heard this often before, most recently from the former Kent and Middlesex batsman Ed Smith, who draws comparison between batting and chopping wood. He found when he tried to be short and precise with the swing of the axe and focus on a specific point on the log, he was quite clumsy. When he looked more vaguely at the log and just let the axe swing back languidly and brought it down fluently in one smooth motion, he was much more accurate. He equates it with batting. When you bat in a relaxed manner – intuitively – you are liable to be much more successful than if you're anxious and intense and *too* conscious of everything.

This is also true of other precise sporting disciplines, like shooting. Kevin Gill, the former world champion in double trap, is GB's head shotgun coach. He suggests that, when focusing on a target moving at 90mph (similar to a fast ball in cricket) 'you can over-stare and focus too hard. Then you don't react as fast and your movements become jerky. Your natural, relaxed, peripheral vision works very well.'

Sangakkara's reliance on the body's natural rhythms is obviously invaluable. Where did get his understanding from, I wondered?

'Much of it is from my father – I think he has a great philosophy on cricket and a very intuitive knowledge of sport in general – and Sunil Fernando [the Trinity College coach who also taught Murali]. He's coached me since I was thirteen. Even today when I'm in Kandy I go and see him for a couple of hours for a few throwdowns, because he knows exactly what my batting motions have been over the years. Both he and my father are quite old school in terms of actual technique, but where they are also really good is in believing in that flow and rhythm to your batting. Technique is important as a foundation, but you have to expand from there.

'It comes from trial and error, too. You watch other players, like Aravinda de Silva, Mahela Jayawardene, Brian Lara, Rahul Dravid, Ricky Ponting – you watch everything about them and you understand that when they do play at their best there is no stalling, no stuttering, it all flows. I tried to work out why that was and what they think about. Every player is different – the shots may be different, but when they score runs there are a lot of similarities in the way those runs come.' You could say he's been as much a biologist as a batsman, microscopically examining every top player, dissecting their skills and adjusting his accordingly.

Sangakkara deserves to be bracketed with any of the great players from cricket history. Never mind his mountain of runs, his Test average (58.66) is the highest of any batsman from the last five decades, including Tendulkar, Lara, Ponting and Sobers. It is equally outstanding abroad as it is at home. And he has just become the first player ever to score four one-day hundreds in successive innings.

Yet, unlike the others, he was no teenage prodigy. He actually wanted to be a pilot, and by his own admission, he was certainly not an exceptional player even in his early twenties. His phenomenal ability has been acquired through assiduous observation and painstaking practice. He is a great batsman who was *made*, not born.

He started with one slight advantage. He was left handed.

WHO WANTS TO BE A BATSMAN?

Left-handers have more fun. Facing predominantly right-arm bowlers, they get more balls to hit – either pitching outside leg or offering width outside off – than right handers. Watching Australia's Allan Border bat, ten-year-old Michael Hussey obviously realised this and turned himself from right- to left-hander. Sangakkara was always a left-hander, but as a teenager not a particularly good one.

'I wasn't the best school cricketer and I wasn't the best first-class player [averaging only 26 after four seasons]. When I did get some runs at club level, I was suddenly put into the Sri Lanka one-day side [as a keeper/batsman]. I had a good first series in the one-day side, but when I got into the Test side I played three Test matches where my highest score was twenty-five. In the last Test, they put me in at number three and I was out for six. It was an eye-opener. I thought: "This is a bit tough."

'Then I went to South Africa and batted number three again and got a half century in my first innings and a ninety-eight in my last and I thought maybe I could do this! And I had a few decent series. But gradually the opposition sussed me out and were bowling at me in a particular way and blocking off certain areas, and I struggled and my confidence took a huge dip.' He had more than two years without a Test century.

'But at twenty-five I had this epiphany where I suddenly realised a lot about myself. I realised the way I thought. I had a really good idea what my motions were like when I played well and when I played badly, I really took stock of what I could do and what I couldn't (and there was a lot that I couldn't do!). What I could do was quite limited. So I thought I've got to be able to improve what I can do, or hide my weaknesses for as long as I am able to, to score the runs I need.

'I realised I had to change my approach. So I worked for six to eight months to reduce my back and across movement and drive a lot straighter. I spoke to Aravinda de Silva about changing the grip of my bottom hand slightly. He taught me how to watch the ball properly, and how to keep your eyes level when you're moving, how to relax at the crease.

'When you speak to the best players in the world, you're not there to become them. You're there to take whatever can be applied to your game from them and discard everything else. Because a lot of things that work for Tendulkar or Lara, or Dravid or Ponting or Bradman won't work for me. You've got to know what your game is, how you're going to expand and improve, what your limitations are. Take little bits of them, but you're not trying to be a copy of them. Build a game that works for you. It's very important to know yourself.

'Once I had that circularisation about myself, and I wasn't thinking about the opposition bowler or other players, that's when my cricket started improving. Then I knew how to train, what to train, how to control my emotions in the middle, how to let my instincts take over and be a reactive batsman. That's the best way to do it. How to not worry too much about technique. In training I get my rhythm and my confidence and everything is in sync, so when I go into a match I'm just playing.

'You can't control everything about your game or what's going to happen on the day. You'll have your ups, you'll have your downs. The important thing is to have a really good solid working plan, and strategy about how to practise, and then when you go into a match your anxiety is taken away. I also understood that at certain times change is absolutely necessary.

You shouldn't be afraid of change. As long as you have a solid base you can always go back to it.'

Aha, a solid base. Where's that when you need it?

Immaculate Conception

P reparation
R hythm
A daptability
C oncentration
T iming
I nstinct
C omposure
E ffort

The qualities you need to be a successful batsman (bit cheesy, I know, but how else do you get people to remember stuff?). OK, a bit of skill comes in handy, too. Sangakkara's systematic acquisition of these ingredients culminated in a sequence of events in 2014 that he hoped would produce the ultimate outcome for a batsman – a Test century at Lord's.

It was scrupulously planned. Sri Lanka were playing two Tests against England in early June before the Indians arrived. Sangakkara had a relatively modest record in England – just one hundred in 18 innings, average 30 – and he wanted to put that right – for himself and the team. He arranged to play for Durham in the County Championship, purely to get accustomed to English conditions before the Tests.

He arrived in early May. The pitch at Headingley was tricky for his first county game, and he failed twice. In the second match, at Hove against Sussex, he batted for six hours and made 159, gradually grooving his method against a decent county attack. There followed a couple of warm-up matches for Sri Lanka and then a series of one-day internationals against England during which his scores gradually increased. He made a polished hundred in the fourth one-day international.

He had been in England a month, had had a thousand throwdowns and net sessions aplenty. He had played 12 innings in a variety of conditions and situations and averaged 60. His preparation was complete. He was ready for Lord's, the Home of Cricket, where, like many other greats – Tendulkar, Kallis, Ponting, Lara among them – he had never made a Test hundred. For any batsman it is the ultimate validation: an inscription on the famous honours board. This was his ambition, and he had made quite a sacrifice to achieve it.

Sangakkara sits in an armchair at his parents' home in Kandy, daughter Syree on his knee. He looks incredibly content, like someone who has found the clue to eternal life. He reflects on his performance at Lord's. Adaptability was the key.

'In England I had closed up my stance a lot,' he says. 'I didn't tap the bat too much in the crease, because it drives my hands away from my body and you need to be a bit more restricted in England because of the swinging ball. I changed my back-and-across movement to almost nothing. That allowed me to see the line of the ball a lot quicker and a lot better, especially when I was facing a guy like Jimmy Anderson who swung it both ways. I needed to stay side-on to allow for him trying to open me up with the one that goes across me.

'In England you don't need to play straight like people say. Because of the swing, you're more likely to be playing between mid-off and cover. A lot squarer of the wicket, going with the swing of the ball.' He knew exactly how he was going to play, and what to look out for, but he wasn't uptight about that or the occasion.

'Before I go into bat it's a case of trying to be as relaxed as possible. I do keep an eye on what's happening in the middle, whether there's a bit of swing, what the bowler is doing. I want to know exactly what the conditions are. The main thing I'm thinking about is whether the bowler is going to swing it into me. That's the danger ball. Anything going away I can leave or score off. Before I go in, I am watching for all that but I am still trying to be relaxed, chatting about this or that. You can't bat while you are in the dressing room. It makes you mentally tired.'

He had done his homework on the England bowlers and had a strategy for each of them. His preparation was so good he even knew what his first ball was going to be when he came to the wicket in the 13th over.

'Lord's has a special, quite intense atmosphere, and I was a little nervous when I walked out, but as soon as I took guard I was relaxed. And for some reason I just knew that Chris Jordan was going to bowl that first ball on my legs [so the great players *do* have ESP!]. It was exactly where I was expecting.' He flicked it effortlessly to square leg for four.

I told Sangakkara I had watched every ball of that innings. His batting was exactly how he had wanted and planned it to be. There was a beautiful compactness to it. A hint of movement back and across the crease as the bowler bowled, bat raised in readiness about stump high. There was nothing excessive or elaborate, little for the bowler to focus on.

His positioning was superb. He played back when the ball

was short, and forward – properly forward – when it was full. His defence was impregnable, the ball repelled right under his eyes, played as late as possible, the bat exactly perpendicular and perfectly aligned with his body.

His judgement was faultless. He left anything four inches wide, would not be tempted into an indiscretion. He played shots: either the push or the drive with a vertical bat or the pull and the cut with a horizontal bat. There was nothing half-hearted and in between with a diagonal bat. He hit the ball on both sides of the wicket, in front of square and behind, with care and deliberation. The ball was placed in the gap with a mathematician's precision.

A couple of easy clips through mid-wicket, a swivel pull or two, carefully rolling his wrists on the shot to keep the ball down (I wonder if his father noted that), a guide wide of the slips – all along the ground – and Sangakkara had fifty. He is one of those batsmen who seems to make runs unobtrusively, imperceptibly. There is an efficiency about his batting. Yet it is far from boring. It is like watching a sculptor elaborately creating his exhibit. He was unbeaten at the close of play.

I remarked that he never looks tired when he's batting.

'It's very important to clear my mind between balls. Forget what happened. It's impossible to keep your focus one hundred per cent all the time. I tried that when I started and it's exhausting. Take your mind off the game, think about some-thing, *anything*, so that you can refocus on that next ball and let your body do what the ball tells you to do. It's just as important at the end of the day.'

'After the day's play at Lord's, I went out for dinner with my wife and my manager and a couple of friends. We went to Le

Petit Maison and had roast chicken. It was a fantastic night – we talked about anything other than cricket. It completely took my mind off what I had been doing and I forgot about my innings. I went back to the hotel, slept well, woke up and did my preparation in the morning.'

The closest England got to dismissing him was to the second ball of the next day. He jabbed down on it a touch late as it angled in and thick-edged it past leg stump for a couple of runs. If there was a hint of hesitation initially, there was none two balls later as he strode onto the front foot and punched Anderson through the covers for four.

England felt obliged to immediately post a deep cover to Sangakkara, despite being 400 ahead, which to me seemed to remove one possible dismissal option by tempting him into an airy drive. Not that he does 'airy'. In fact, all he did was then exploit the gap he had created by dropping a good-length ball into that space and running an easy single.

He was now batting with his close friend and perennial batting partner Mahela Jayawardene. During their liaison they racked up their 6000th Test run in partnership together (the fourth most as a pairing after Tendulkar and Dravid, Greenidge and Haynes, and Hayden and Langer). Like all those other pairs, they are complete opposites. Perhaps that's why they're such successful combinations.

England's fastest bowler, Liam Plunkett, came on and subjected them to a hostile spell from round the wicket, targeting both batsmen's ribs. Jayawardene looked uncomfortable, and was struck on the gloves and around the body, unsure whether to duck, fend or hook. There was total certainty about Sangakkara's response. If it was short and high he ducked. If it was homing in on his chest he got smoothly inside the line and let the ball pass under his armpit. If the ball didn't get up much he pulled it resoundingly to the boundary. He was completely unruffled.

Sangakkara explained how he maintains his concentration.

'It doesn't matter what has happened – after the ball I clear my mind. I think about anything other than the ball. I look around for a bit. Then I put my foot precisely in the batting crease, tap, tap, look up and I re-focus again. I watch how the bowler puts the ball in his hand, exactly how his fingers are placed on it. I watch it all the way. I am looking for tell-tale signs about what he is going to bowl. Being a wicketkeeper, I trained myself to pick up little nuances as he is running in. I could see things when Murali was approaching the wicket, and I'd say to myself: "That's a *doosra*." [Many batsmen around the world would have killed for that precious insight.] Because I watch the ball closely in their hand, I know a lot of times what they'll bowl.' (I wondered what he would have made of my efforts: quite often when I ran in *I* didn't even know what I was going to bowl.)

On that third day at Lord's, the England bowlers were treated to a masterclass of footwork and shot selection and an exhibition of how to demoralise an attack. He did not give them a sniff of a chance. When he drove Joe Root's amiable off-spin through the covers, he had realised the ambition he had not just coveted but dedicated himself to: a Test hundred at Lord's. He celebrated appropriately, sinking half to his knees and punching the air with both fists like a man who has scored a last-gasp winner in a cup final, while being simultaneously enveloped by Jayawardene.

When he was finally and unexpectedly out – edging a long hop from Moeen Ali – he received a standing ovation. His achievement was promptly entered in gold letters on the honours board:

K.C.Sangakkara c Prior b Ali 147
(449 mins 258 balls 16 x 4)

The mere facts do it no real justice. This was a century immaculately conceived and impeccably constructed. It led to Sri Lanka winning their first-ever Test series in England. That's what you might call a perfect end to a perfect plan. It's not something we English know much about.

Things They Don't Teach You at School

After we'd finished chatting, Sangakkara took me to the spot in his parents' Kandy garden where his father used to bowl to him for hours. His first lab. It was between the back of the house and a large rock behind. It was a perfect square. That figures. He is a true all-round player, equally good on both sides of the wicket or off back foot or front. (Many other batsmen, confined to a narrower space as kids, have an obvious preference for one side of the wicket or the other.)

I left him to his family and headed to the stadium at Pallekele for another one-day international. It wasn't any old one-day game. This was special. Sangakkara had announced his impending retirement from the shorter form, and this would be his last appearance in his home town. His previous scores in the series had been 63, 86 and 91 in that order. How many do you think he made? Yep, you guessed it. Inevitable.

His 112 was another flawless performance. It was fascinating watching him manoeuvre the ball into spaces, adjusting his body alignment to angle or place the ball where the fielders weren't. When one was moved to a vulnerable spot, he hit the next ball where they'd just been. It was almost as if he was a mathematician doing trigonometry with a bat and a protractor.

But the pitch was quite spicy early on and one shot, a mishit along the ground to mid-on off Steve Finn, revealed Sangakkara's other vital ingredient. It demonstrated that his mission in life – his raison d'être – is not merely to be a 'batsman'. It is to make runs. There is a difference.

Many players, after such a miscue to mid-on early in their innings, would fret and faff at the crease and rehearse the shot they think they should have played, annoyed at the imperfection of their execution. Mark Ramprakash might be one. Ian Bell could be another. It might be still in their mind as the bowler ran in again. (I, of course, would have been lolling on my bat proudly *admiring* having hit a bowler of Finn's height and pace as far as mid-on.)

But as soon as the ball made contact with Sangakkara's inside edge and the ball travelled wide of the bowler he was off up the wicket stealing a quick single, to the intense irritation of the bowler.

After all the adulation of his last hometown hundred had died down and he'd finished the interviews and posed for a hundred selfies, I spoke to him. I asked him about that ball. In among all the nurdled twos and deftly placed fours and imperiously driven sixes, he remembered it.

'Yes, it was from Steven Finn,' he said, 'I got a bit of a thick edge. If I have not connected with a shot properly I'd rather be down the other end than face the next ball worrying about it! It's a bonus if you get a run off a miscue and then you can relax down the other end. I am out to there to score runs. I am not out there for anything else. Not to look good or to even feel good at times. I am looking for any opportunity to score runs. That's all that matters.'

This was the kind of thing Don Bradman used to say. 'Style?' he said quizzically during his orgy of run-making against England in 1930. 'I know nothing about style. All I'm after is runs.' And he made 974 of them in seven innings, still a record for a Test series. Another time he said: 'Too many players fail because their thoughts are concentrated on where their left elbow is or where something is instead of hitting the ball.' And: 'Coaching should deal with *what* to do with the ball rather than *how* to do it.' The modern translation of that is something I first heard from another remorseless Australian batsman, Dean Jones: 'Mate, it's not how, it's how *many*.'

Wanna Be a Batsman Rule No.9 – It's not how, it's how many.

No one can touch Bradman's phenomenal feats of run-making. At the risk of alienating a few of you, let's look at the data. His Test batting average (99.94) is 60 percent greater than the next man on the list (Graeme Pollock 60.97.) He played 80 Test innings and scored 29 hundreds – that's a century every 2.75 innings. Incredibly, he maintained a similar rate throughout his first-class career (117 hundreds in 338 innings – 2.88 innings per hundred). No other prolific batsman, in history, managed a century in fewer than every *six* innings, [see table].

NUMBER OF INNINGS PER TEST HUNDRED* (Qual: 24 hundreds)

		Inns	Hundreds	Inns per 100
1.	D.G.Bradman	80	29	2.75
2.	Younis Khan	186	31	6.00
3.	K.C.Sangakkara	233	38	6.13
4.	M.L.Hayden	184	30	6.13
5.	G.St A.Sobers	160	26	6.15
6.	J.H.Kallis	280	45	6.22
7.	H.M.Amla	156	25	6.24
8.	S.M.Gavaskar	214	34	6.29
9.	G.S.Chappell	151	24	6.29
10.	S.R.Tendulkar	329	51	6.45
11.	Mohammad Yousuf	154	24	6.50
12.	B.C.Lara	232	34	6.82
13.	R.T.Ponting	287	41	7.00
14.	M.J.Clarke	198	28	7.07
15.	D.P.M.D.Jayawardene	252	34	7.41
16.	I.V.A.Richards	182	24	7.58
17.	G.C.Smith	205	27	7.59
18.	R.S.Dravid	286	36	7.94
19.	Inzamam-ul-Haq	200	25	8.00
20.	A.N.Cook	226	28	8.07
21.	S.R.Waugh	260	32	8.12
22.	S.Chanderpaul	280	30	9.33
23.	A.R.Border	265	27	9.81

* As at 1 April 2016

Here we are again, using hundreds as a benchmark of ability. (Although it might be worth pointing out here that 22 of Bradman's 29 hundreds led to an Australian victory.) Basically,

Bradman was twice as good as anyone else who has ever lived. So what were his secrets and can we use any of them to enhance the human species?

Bradman was an entirely natural, un-coached batsman. He famously reared his batting ability round the back of his parents' house, using a stump to hit a golf ball that he bounced off the brick stand of their water tank. The 'wicket' was the laundry door. The ball rebounded off the brick at strange and unpredictable angles. 'The golf ball came back at great speed,' he wrote, 'and to hit it at all with this round stump was no easy task. This extraordinary and primitive idea was purely a matter of amusement, but looking back over the years, I can see how it must have developed the co-ordination of brain, eye and muscle which was to serve me so well in important matches later on.'

It must have also influenced his batting method, which was regarded as unconventional at the time. He stood with his bat between his feet rather than resting on his right toe 'because it was a comfortable and natural position'. Instead of standing motionless as the ball was delivered, he began to move fractionally before it was released. 'It saves a precious fraction of a second and appears to serve the same purpose as a preliminary waggle before your golf swing. It is not part of the swing but gets you started.' This supports the idea of *flow* and *rhythm* that characterises the best players' batting. (And nervous stutters that characterise the worst.)

His backlift was not straight towards the stumps as your coach might recommend, but out at an angle in the direction of the slips. It came back round in a loop. It became known as the 'rotation' method. Bradman argued that although this wasn't ideal for defence, it was best for attacking strokeplay as the movement got you onto your toes and gave your body momentum. He felt that taking the bat straight back was more unnatural and 'virtually eliminates pull shots and cut shots' – his two signature strokes.

In fact, if you look really closely, most top batsmen use a version of the rotation method – taking their bat back towards second slip and looping it back round to play the ball. It all happens in one smooth, fluid motion. Hashim Amla's bat, for instance, swooshes through the air in a semi-circle like Hermione Grainger's wand. Where does all this straight back-lift nonsense come from, then? Probably from previously ill-informed people like me, I guess.

Bradman's natural grip on the bat was also unusual. It caused the blade to face in towards his legs – a slightly closed face. It helped him score on the leg side and play the pull stroke and keep his shots on the deck. He accepted this sometimes hand-icapped him playing through the off side, but he wasn't worried about that. He didn't do worry. He used his flexible wrists to drive the ball through the covers when it was full enough to do so. But he stayed mainly back with his feet unusually pointing down the pitch rather than at right angles to it.

He knew he could use his pads as a second line of defence (through much of his career you couldn't be out LBW if the ball *pitched* outside off stump). So he stepped back towards his stumps and played a lot of deliveries from there. That was his masterstroke. He played 52 Test innings before they changed the LBW law (in 1937). He was only out LBW three times in that period, once for 167 and another time for 224.

The hand-eye co-ordination Bradman developed from his golf-ball games – his 'rotation' method – was fundamental to his success. He learnt how to place the ball with his bat, how to keep his shots on the ground by turning his wrists over (he rarely hit in the air), how to move both towards and back from where the ball bounced to have better control of the shot. It taught him the essentials of watching the ball carefully and concentrating hard – lack of precision playing a fast-moving golf ball with a stump could give you bruised fingers or missing front teeth. Or broken windows. He was lucky that he had tolerant parents. The incessant clunk of golf ball ricocheting off a water-tank or a laundry door would have driven most mothers nuts.

He also played tennis and football against the garage door – more irritation potential for the parents. All these pastimes were undoubtedly the foundation of his prowess. Bradman wrote later: 'I would counsel every boy who is interested in batting, to play with a ball at every opportunity. Whether it be a golf ball, baseball or any other kind doesn't matter. It will help train the eye and co-ordinate the brain, eye and muscle. The formative years of a boy's career can have a tremendous bearing on his technique.'

I am a paid-up subscriber to this theory. I made sure that my two boys, and girl, had plenty of exposure to different ball sports from an early age (though no access to golf balls anywhere near the house): cricket and football obviously, rugby, tennis, badminton and basketball. I bought them a table-tennis table and played against them regularly, as my father had with me. Added to a set of stumps for our garden matches, we had a small net to bounce catches off and one of those plastic orange ramps to skim the ball across that you see professional teams using in their fielding practices. We also did catching practice diving onto a trampoline. Whether or not all those games improve your kids' sporting ability, you get to know your neighbours quickly. You're always knocking on their door asking for your ball back.

Thinking of indoor sports and Sangakkara and Jayawardene's skill at manipulating the ball – almost like a snooker player's control of the cue ball – I purchased a small pool table. I thought that might help their focus and aim. Are you under the impression that I was trying to clone my kids, using them as a biological experiment to create the perfect batsman? You are possibly right! Actually, anything to keep them from playing Minecraft on their various devices, although I admit that learning to play pool can lead to far less healthy pursuits. Luckily none of them is into Guinness yet.

Who'd Want to Be a Bowler?

So apart from his unique method, what else was exceptional about Bradman? Where to start . . .

He had an aggressive mindset – he looked to score off every ball. 'The basic technique of the straight bat is sound for defence,' he said. 'However, there should be all possible emphasis on attack, on the aggressive outlook.' As a result he seemed, according to the England batsman Denis Compton, to 'have a marvellous way of getting into position quicker than any batsman I have ever seen, played the ball very late and was never off balance or stretching out of control'.

He was blessed with total self-belief, from sticking to his 'natural' batting method as a 20-year-old when many were doubting it – especially his cross-batted approach – to an unceasing mastery of bowlers. He believed they were just there as fodder. Defence was a last resort. 'His confidence is supreme,' wrote the legendary left-arm spinner Wilfred Rhodes, taker of over 4000 first-class wickets. 'No matter how you bowl to him, he seems to be able to place the ball just where he likes. He makes the bowling suit his batting.'

He wasn't interested in hitting sixes, as if the process of hitting the ball in the air gave the bowler hope. That produces a good quiz question. Who hit more sixes in their Test career, Bradman or Devon Malcolm? The answer of course is Big Dev (seven to the Don's six). Bradman would have been crap at T20, not least because he would have hated being able to bat for only 20 overs.

From his mid-teens, during which he made two triple hundreds, Bradman had an insatiable appetite for big scores, further fuelled by the harrowing experience of fielding as 12th man for Australia the day England's Walter Hammond made 251. It became his mission to exceed whatever Hammond achieved. He was never distracted by socialising, drink or women (Hammond was distracted by all three, which in some ways makes his 22 Test hundreds all the more remarkable). He preferred to play music in his room or write letters.

He kept himself exceptionally fit and, according to many observers, never broke sweat even while making 299 not out against South Africa in 40°C temperatures in Adelaide. He admitted to never suffering from nerves. When he was 97 not out overnight in a Test at the MCG, a vast crowd turned up after the rest day to see him score his hundred. They roared him to the wicket. Without a flicker of emotion he methodically turned his first delivery for three to complete his century. As we have seen, he was never out in the nineties in a Test match.

He was utterly ruthless. Of course he didn't walk! Even post war when he was in his late thirties. Struggling to 28 one day against England in Brisbane in 1946, he nicked a half-volley to slip and stood there. There were 30,000 people in the ground, and 29,998 thought he was out. The only two who didn't were himself and the umpire. He went on to make 187. Nursing a leg injury in the next Test he dropped himself down the order and compiled a six-hour 234 before succumbing to fatigue. 'There's runs out there if only a man had legs!' he said afterwards.

The esteemed writer R.C.Robertson-Glasgow summed Bradman up perfectly. 'His aim was for the making of runs and he made them in staggering and ceaseless profusion. He seems to have eliminated error, to have perfected the mechanism of stroke.' Bradman never seemed to suffer even a nanosecond of doubt. 'I always had confidence in my own ability,' he said. 'I am sure with a lot of players their mental attitude is terribly important. They imagine there are difficulties that are not really there.'

This supports Ian Chappell's theory that, apart from Bradman's great skill, what made him so great was 'his ability to bat with an uncluttered mind'. The result was 117 first-class hundreds – including 37 doubles, six triples and one quad-ruple. (Sounds like my Uncle Tony's drinks order.) All from mucking about with a golf ball and a stump. Not bad for a little bloke with dodgy eyesight.

CHAPTER 11

Down Your Way

Elementary, My Dear Watson

Who wants to be a batsman? Not me, after writing all this. Despite the flatter pitches and the better helmets and the bigger bats these days. There's too much to think about. Or rather, too much to think about not thinking about. The top players had been through so many processes and routines and reality checks to achieve consistency. Bradman might make batting sound simple, but he was just a freak. He had, according to the *History of Cricket,* 'a quite abnormally quick reaction commanding immediate obedience from a perfectly co-ordinated body to the message of an icily concentrated mind'. Exactly. A freak.

You do have to be a particular kind of person to be a good batsman. Disciplined – in practice and approach, resilient – enabling you to handle the inevitable difficulties and dis-appointments, open-minded – to listen to and filter ideas, composed – to conserve energy at the crease and give the opposition no stimulus, and ruthless – to capitalise on your opportunity.

I don't think I was any of these, apart from resilient to the endless exasperation – of fathers, uncles, team-mates, coaches, spectators, wives, friends and latterly children – to my lack of batting ability. Maybe in my case for 'resilient' substitute 'blind'. All these above qualities will be present to varying degrees in the modern batsman. And what a fantastic variety of players they produce.

Look at the 2015 World Cup. There are majestic stroke-players like Rohit Sharma and Mahela Jayawardene. There are savage brutes such as Chris Gayle and David Warner. There are wristy flickers like Hashim Amla and Shikhar Dhawan. There are the freewheeling dashers like Brendon McCullum and Suresh Raina. Or the short-arm jabbers like Steve Smith and Shane Watson.

There is the master of the scoop Tillakaratne Dilshan and the King of Ambidexterity A.B.de Villiers and the outrageous circus act that is Glenn Maxwell. He even calls himself 'The Big Show'. Some of his shots – like the backaway-lookaway pull that flies for four over cover – are indefinable. His wrists are incredible. There is the remorseless accumulator Kumar Sangakkara and the ruthless finisher M.S.Dhoni. The World Cup was a celebration of the diversity of batting in memory of the tragically unlucky Phil Hughes, killed a few months earlier playing the inventive brand of cricket he was renowned for.

The variety of routes these players took to get there is fascinating, too. Like Sangakkara, they weren't all teenage prodigies. De Villiers, for instance, originally wanted to be a tennis star (though he could have picked any sport and probably been a champion). The left-handed Warner was out caught so often as a 13-year-old, his coach told him to bat right-handed. He stuck with the left but was mainly just a club slugger in Sydney until being hauled into Australia's Twenty20 team at the age of 22. He hadn't even played a first-class match.

He was highly successful at the shorter form of the game and won lucrative IPL contracts, but no one thought his crude, buccaneering style could be transferred into the Test arena. Coveting serious recognition, he refined his method and is now a highly accomplished Test batsman with 12 centuries and an average of nearly 50. The only way to interrupt his career path appears to be to provoke his inner-Neanderthal by sledging him in Hindi or donning a fake beard in a nightclub.

Australia's Steve Smith is similar (not in the Neanderthal sense). An enthusiastic all-rounder, his speculative leg-spin first got him noticed at both state and subsequently international level and he batted at No.8. Test cricket looked a step too high and he was not a success. When he was recruited to salvage Australia's pride during England's triumphant 2010-11 tour, we laughed at his ungainly batting style and his buffet bowling. I think I described him as a 'village' cricketer.

The mockery was partly his own fault, as he had unwisely said beforehand his aim was 'about making sure I'm having fun and making sure everyone else is having fun, by telling a joke or something like that'. The England players certainly had fun exposing the deficiencies in his wobbly defence and tonking his bowling all about the place and he was soon discarded.

But, despite his clumsy-looking technique, bat waving about like a palm in a gale – the Jim Furyk of batting – people saw something in his unerring eye and sharp fielding and winning influence. Success in the IPL, where he seemed to revel in the pressure of tight games and took some amazing catches, suggested he had a strong self-belief. He was restored to the Australian Test team in 2013 and has not looked back. In the Australian summer of 2014-15, his 943 runs in six Tests, average 94, were positively Bradmanesque. He made four centuries in successive Tests and won a string of awards.

In the same period, our friend Shane Watson – batting higher up the order with a more conventional technique and far more experience – averaged just 29. He was a feared destroyer in shorter forms of the game. But in 105 Test innings he had only four hundreds (yet 24 fifties). In a similar way to Mark Ramprakash, he was too sensitive and not ruthless enough. I did politely suggest that to him on the phone when we spoke. It's a difficult truth to accept. Especially from a journalist with a highest score of 53 who is 12,000 miles away.

Like Bradman and unlike Watson, Steve Smith is completely unselfconscious. That is absolutely crucial. His style is unusual. He makes a large move across his stumps as the ball is delivered, bat still wafting about in ungainly fashion. He pings straight balls through mid-wicket with whippy precision. The whereabouts of the stumps is almost irrelevant. He pulls deliveries that don't look all that short with a wristy flourish. He doesn't care how he looks. He just hits the ball where he wants. He doesn't often miss. In the final analysis of batting, that's what counts.

I asked Mark Ramprakash, now after all his tribulations and triumphs England's batting coach, which of the younger English batsmen had the ideal approach.

'Joe Root,' he said. 'He has a good basic method, but he is adaptable. And very strong mentally. He doesn't get too down if he's out cheaply. He's got a good relationship with the other lads, he's very good at de-stressing – he's got humour. He practises in a focused manner. He knows what he's trying to get out of his net, he has a purpose, but he's not *too* structured – if he hits ten good balls in the middle of the bat he's quite happy. There is a good stubbornness about him – he is happy with his game – but the best players are also open to learning new ideas if you float something past them.'

The ingredient that unites all the best players is drive. They have stuck at the disciplines through thick and thin and found a way that works. Not a right way or a wrong way, but *their* way. Uncovering that is a Eureka moment. Sometimes it is fleeting – like absolutely nailing a perfect three-wood 250 metres down the fairway but thereafter constantly slicing it into the bushes again. The more astute types establish a means of replicating it repeatedly. Much progress is by trial and error. Smart people learn from others' mistakes. Idiots learn from their own. Or they don't.

A batsman has the most precarious existence in sport. Every ball, they are dicing with death. It is vital not to worry about that and try to be relaxed. Think about this. Every time you get in to a car, you don't imagine the accident you might be about to have, despite the endless potential for head-on collisions. You just get in and drive. That's the mindset to adopt in this business. The key to batting is fearlessness.

Batwoman

What I had learnt from all this observation and conversation was to let the kids be. Encourage them to play all sports, take them to practice, give them a few pointers, but allow them to experiment and find their way. They'd soon discover if they had any ability. They'd identify a hero to idolise.

Callum (now 15) wanted to be Dale Steyn. He had the swing and the floppy hair but no real pace. He was too nice (and intelligent) to be a fast bowler, and got his feet in a tangle with the bat. Billy (ten), a stroppier type, idolised Stuart Broad. He had the confrontational character – he *never* accepted he was out either – without the extra height to match.

Nancy (12) most admired Root. 'He plays all forms of the game, he can bat in an orthodox way, but he's got all the shots for T20, he can bowl, he's a really good fielder and he never seems to be out of form,' she explained. Her method was also quite similar. She was quite wristy and stylish and tended to go back to fuller balls that I thought she ought to step out to. I tried not so say anything, but I couldn't help myself.

'Get forward to that!' I said, finding her thickish outside edge in the nets. It must be a nightmare being the son or daughter of The Analyst.

She listened but kept to her own game plan, which involved looking to sweep or pull balls on the leg side, and dab or cut on the off. She drove only if the ball was really full. Her defence was straight and solid. She went to Middlesex girls' winter nets at Finchley – ironically in the same indoor school I had attended as a teenager. Except that now they do goal-setting assessments, fitness sessions, fielding drills, target practice, batting scenarios (40 to win off ten with field settings and running between the wickets) and de-briefs. A far cry from the hour and a half of random swishing and slashing we used to indulge in.

She played in her boys' school Under-13 team and batted at No.3. She was the only girl on either side and was very nervous to start with. But I said that nerves were actually excitement and her determination overcame any anxiety. She batted with a boy's skill and a girl's sense and usually held the innings together. Because of her calm competence and her short hair and the fact that she also opened the bowling and set the field, most people thought she was a boy. 'Come on, lads, let's get this guy out!' the opposition captain would shout.

A few reasonable scores followed for Middlesex Under-13 girls as well as some steady bowling, and she was made captain. The first game was washed out. The second was against Sussex on a school ground in Edgware. Nancy won the toss and decided to bat. The throwdowns I was giving her on the outfield were abruptly terminated because of an early wicket. She was at the crease in the third over.

I was very nervous but she was off the mark immediately and flicked and swept her way smoothly to 20 – normally danger time for a Hughes. But there were no rushes of blood or extravagances or stupid runs. She calmly eased the ball around, driving the half-volleys crisply through the covers, helping the long hops to the deep square-leg boundary, cutting behind point, defending the straight ones, neatly turning balls to leg for a single, always keeping the ball on the ground. A controlled square drive got her to fifty. She sheepishly acknowledged the applause.

I thought that would be the cue to try a fancy shot – a ramp or a reverse sweep – that would cause her downfall. I would have done so in that situation. But she continued her controlled progress, hitting strongly on both sides of the wicket with excellent balance and timing and determined running. She never looked like getting out. A back-foot thump past cover and a full toss bunted over mid-wicket got her to 98. A push to deep square-leg for two got her to a hundred. She paused reflectively for a moment and raised her bat high in celebration. (The nice thing about girls' cricket is that at such times the players whoop and holler with genuine excitement for each other. There is none of the boys' latent envy at a team-mate's success.)

A *hundred*! For Middlesex. The very thing I had coveted for 40 years (for anyone!) – and my father and uncle before that – and had never even got close to. Nonchalantly, nervelessly, flawlessly, modestly achieved by my 13-year-old daughter in the week of my father's 92nd birthday. She walked off 106 not out to resounding applause. It was truly the proudest moment of my life.

'What was it like, getting to a hundred?' I asked her later on the drive home after she'd taken a wicket with her first ball, two catches and led her county to an 80-run victory.

'Like laughing,' she said. 'Like the sort of happy feeling you get inside when you're laughing uncontrollably with your friends.' It sounds like the enjoyment is worth all the effort.

Now Nancy is in the England Under-15 squad. National honours, something else I never achieved. I hadn't factored in that my *daughter* would be a better cricketer than me. She deserves her recognition. She's a far more accomplished, organised batsman than I ever was and she hits it harder than I did, too. Women's cricket is really going places. The England senior players are full-time professionals. There is so much dedication and genuine talent.

Nancy attends camps at the ECB Academy at Loughborough once a month and gets specialist coaching and reaction testing and fitness enhancing and practises sweeping against the Merlin spin-bowling machine with the England captain Charlotte Edwards on hand to offer advice. She even has her fielding movements videoed and analysed. They wouldn't have needed fielder-monitoring cameras in my day – just a still-life artist.

How did she get there? Through the D/L method. Determination and Love. The determination to play predominantly male sports and show that girls can be just as good as boys, the determination to improve, the determination to succeed. 'Triumph is "Try" with a bit of "oomph",' she says.

And Love. She just loves batting. She picks up a bat – miniature, full size, old or new – and fiddles with it and plays some imaginary shots and takes up her stance and asks someone to bowl at her. She loves staying in. And she hates getting out.

You have to love batting or you'll never be very good at it. That, in fact, was Michael Vaughan's parting line on the subject. 'Batting has to come from the heart,' he says. 'That triggers the brain. You've got to absolutely love it.'

'Did you love batting?' I asked Boycott.

'I looved battin' against you!' he replied.

Wanna Be a Batsman Rule No.10 – You gotta *love* it!

The Ten Wanna Be a Batsman Rules

1. Realise your limitations
2. Keep your head still
3. Play the ball, not the man
4. Close your ears
5. Locate the dimmer switch
6. When you get in, stay in
7. Don't look too far ahead
8. Play at The Oval
9. It's not how, it's how many
10. You gotta *love* it!

Acknowledgements

Thanks to my mum and dad for their constant support, and my kids Callum, Nancy and Billy for their willingness to be my cricketing guinea pigs.

Thanks to all the players for giving up their time to be 'analysed' – especially Garfield Sobers, Desmond Haynes, Graham Gooch, Geoff Boycott, Andrew Strauss, Andy Flower, Marcus Trescothick, Michael Atherton, Rahul Dravid, Michael Vaughan, Kumar Sangakkara and particularly Mark Ramprakash.

Thanks to Shane Watson for making the effort to call.

Thanks also to Tony Shillinglaw and Brian Hale for their excellent book *Bradman Revisited*, which really helps to explain his phenomenon.

Thanks to my faithful and trusted editor Ian Marshall at Simon & Schuster, and especially to Julian Alexander of LAW whose idea this book was and to Emma for keeping me motivated.

Thanks to you for reading.

Index

INDEX

INDEX